VIET NAM

TECHNICAL AND VOCATIONAL EDUCATION AND TRAINING SECTOR ASSESSMENT

JANUARY 2020

ASIAN DEVELOPMENT BANK

ADB

Notes:
In this publication, "$" refers to United States dollars.
ADB recognizes "Laos" as the Lao People's Democratic Republic, "China" as the People's Republic of China, "Korea" as
the Republic of Korea, and "Vietnam" as Viet Nam.

About the cover: Students learning at technical and vocational education and training institutions in Viet Nam
(Photos by Sakiko Tanaka).

Contents

Tables, Figures, and Boxes

Tables

Figures

Boxes

Acknowledgments

This report provides an assessment of the trends, strengths, and issues of technical and vocational education and training (TVET) in Viet Nam. It updates the Asian Development Bank (ADB) 2014 TVET assessment report and highlights the policies, strategies, and achievements of the country toward fundamental human resources development and TVET reform, which began in 2011 and has reached the final phase toward completion by 2020.

Like its predecessor, this assessment focuses on skills development programs under the Ministry of Labour–Invalids and Social Affairs (MOLISA), specifically the Directorate of Vocational Education and Training (DVET), which was merged with the TVET subsystem governed in parallel by the Ministry of Education and Training. The DVET became the single central "state management" agency for the entire TVET sector since 1 January 2017.

Thomas Russell, a TVET lead consultant under Regional–Capacity Development Technical Assistance 8813: Information and Communication Technology for Development Initiative Facility in Asia and the Pacific, prepared this report. He conducted the assessment with the assistance of Thuy Nguyen Thi Xuan, a national TVET consultant under by the same technical assistance. Senior Social Sector Specialist Sakiko Tanaka of the Southeast Asia Department (SERD) of ADB, former Principal Social Sector Specialist Wolfgang Kubitzki of SERD, and Associate Social Sector Officer Vinh Quang Ngo of the ADB Viet Nam Resident Mission provided significant inputs and guidance to complete the report. Ayako Inagaki, Director of Human and Social Sector Development Division (SEHS) and Eric Sidgwick, Country Director, Viet Nam Resident Mission, SERD provided overall guidance and direction.

Phan Chinh Thuc, former Director General of the Directorate of Vocational Education and Training (DVET) under MOLISA, gave valuable input on all TVET-relevant topics and assisted in arranging meetings and organizing workshops involving a broad range of stakeholders, including official representatives of the DVET and the National Institute for Vocational Training.

We are grateful for the important advice of many experts and representatives of resident offices of international organizations, such as GIZ, the World Bank, and the International Labour Organization. Special appreciation to Britta van Erckelens, GIZ Deputy Programme Director, Ha Noi, Viet Nam and Lisa-Marie Kreibich, ADB Education Specialist, a former GIZ Head of Component, Ho Chi Minh City, Viet Nam, who reviewed the draft report and provided helpful advice to the team. The managers and teachers of TVET colleges and schools also participated in the assessment by contributing to interviews. This report was edited and proofread by Tuesday Soriano. Michael Cortes did the layout, cover design, and typesetting. Two consultants were supported under Regional-Policy and Advisory Technical Assistance 8977: Knowledge Development Support for Southeast Asia.

Abbreviations

ADB	–	Asian Development Bank
ASEAN	–	Association of Southeast Asian Nations
EMIS	–	education management information system
FDI	–	foreign direct investment
GIZ	–	Gesellschaft für Internationale Zusammenarbeit (German Agency for Development Cooperation)
GDP	–	gross domestic product
GDV(E)T	–	General Directorate of Vocational (Education and) Training
HRD	–	human resources development
ICT	–	information and communication technology
IT	–	information technology
LIMS	–	labor market information system
MOET	–	Ministry of Education and Training
MOLISA	–	Ministry of Labour–Invalids and Social Affairs
NIVT	–	National Institute for Vocational Training
NOSS	–	national occupational skills standard(s)
NQF	–	national qualification framework
SEDS	–	Socio-Economic Development Strategy 2011–2020
TVET	–	technical and vocational education and training
VCCI	–	Viet Nam Chamber of Commerce and Industry
VET	–	vocational education and training
VTC	–	vocational training center

Currency Equivalents

(as of 4 December 2019)

Currency Unit		dong (VND)
VND1.00	=	$0.0000431
$1.00	=	D23,177

NOTES

(i) The fiscal year (FY) of Viet Nam and its agencies ends on 31 December. "FY" before a calendar year denotes the year in which the fiscal year ends, e.g., FY2016 ends on 31 December 2016.

(ii) The school year (SY) in Viet Nam officially starts in September and ends on 31 May. "SY" before a calendar year denotes the year in which the school year ends, e.g., SY2016 ends on 31 May 2016.

Executive Summary

1. Macroeconomic Context

In 2009, Viet Nam became a lower-middle-income country. It has since doubled its gross national income per capita and continues to be one of the fastest growing economies in Southeast Asia. Despite an ongoing shift from agriculture to more value-added industry sectors and services and a buoyant foreign direct investment (FDI) capital inflow, the country's economic growth has rested mainly on its large pool of cheap but low-skilled labor and is still constrained by a huge informal business sector. Labor productivity has remained lower than other countries in the region. Relative annual productivity growth rates in some industry sectors even declined. Already, a shortage of skills is affecting Viet Nam's ability to absorb new FDI and limiting prospects for more productive employment. To become globally competitive and industrialized, Viet Nam must develop highly skilled workers who can increase industrial productivity, produce demand-oriented product quality, and provide internationally accepted service standards. The technical and vocational education and training (TVET) system needs to be improved while guaranteeing equitable access for the young poor and disadvantaged citizens in remote rural regions. Despite ambitious reform efforts during past decades, state-managed TVET and labor market support systems have remained weak, fragmented, and inadequately funded, most of them still performing poorly and lacking in ability to adapt to changing market demands.

2. Technical and Vocational Education and Training System and Coverage

Up to the end of 2016, a dual TVET governance structure offered two distinct tracks in parallel. Institutions supervised by the Ministry of Labour–Invalids and Social Affairs (MOLISA) offered formal vocational education and training at three levels for secondary school graduates: (i) elementary TVET (3–12 months) at vocational training centers (VTCs), (ii) intermediate TVET (3–4 years or 1–2 years depending on entrance qualifications of lower secondary and upper secondary graduates) at vocational secondary schools, and (iii) higher TVET at vocational colleges (3 years). Respective training certificates are awarded at elementary and intermediate TVET and a diploma for those who completed training at vocational college level. VTCs also offered nonformal skills training (up to 3 months) for unemployed youth and workers. On the other hand, the Ministry of Education and Training (MOET) institutions provided formal technical and professional training in professional secondary schools and technical colleges as well as some short-term vocational training. Resolution No. 76/NQ-CP dated 3 September 2016 (Article 14) took effect in 1 January 2017, merging both tracks into one system under MOLISA's Directorate of Vocational Education and Training (DVET), which now acts as the single central "state management" agency for TVET governance.

Since 2011, the network of TVET institutes has expanded considerably and aligned partly to particular economic sectors, regions, and localities. For 2017, MOLISA reported a total of 388 vocational and technical colleges, 22% of them private. In 2015, these institutions enrolled a total of 219,885 students. At intermediate level, secondary vocational schools and professional schools totaled 551, almost half of them privately run; altogether, a total of 303,854 students were enrolled in these schools. Yet, between 2011 and 2015, enrollments were decreasing in both TVET subsectors. VTCs, numbering 1,036, comprised the bulk of Viet Nam's TVET institutions, 240 of them private. In 2015, these VTCs offered formal TVET at elementary level and short-term courses for 1,769,095 students.

3. Main Challenges and Opportunities

System governance. The new TVET law in 2014 provides an augmented legal basis for some fundamental enhancements of Viet Nam's complex TVET system and also addresses the need for improved state management functions including detailed stipulations for public TVET institutions to achieve full autonomy after 2020. However, to perform these functions MOLISA still relies on the broad range of agencies to "directly" manage their institutions. Central ministries are responsible for almost half (41%) of public TVET institutions at the college level but only for a small share (11%) at the intermediate level. Local governments and social political organizations are responsible for the rest and administrate also 95% of the public TVET institutes that provide training at elementary level and below. MOLISA's draft project plan for TVET reform until 2020–2030 promulgates a set of propositions to improve the state management system from central to local level, develop capacity of state management staff, and apply information technology to TVET management. Unfortunately, however, these propositions still lack a clear designation of addressees and agents, rationally sequenced modes of intervention, and significant indicators that qualify tangible approaches to achieve the ambitious reform objectives.

Quality and relevance of technical and vocational education and training. Despite the government's considerable efforts during the last decade to improve the quality and relevance of Viet Nam's TVET system, industry and businesses according to the Viet Nam Chamber of Commerce and Industry and the International Labour Organization Bureau for Employers' Activities still perceive the performance of the TVET system as critical. TVET graduates do not have industry-relevant occupational skills as well as fundamental soft skills such as industry working style, teamwork, and problem solving. Prevailing reasons for this relate to the TVET system's persistent focus on school-based training delivery, hardly involving enterprises accompanied by a wide range of system-immanent problems, such as poor performance and output standards, lack of instructors with industry experience and practical skills, lack of independent assessments of graduates as well as inefficient resource management and financing structures.

After (partly) successful pilot activities over the past years, the government plans to convert gradually the enhanced legal prescriptions for quality accreditation of TVET institutions and programs into new regulations relating to mandatory procedures, criteria, and standards. These regulations will define comprehensively and stipulate essential and measurable requirements for TVET quality at different levels and in a variety of organizational aspects including school management and finances, teacher and manager qualifications, program design and training methods, materials, facilities and training equipment, learner services, and last but not least, effective and sustained internal quality assurance.

To ensure more relevant and demand-driven TVET programs, the Government of Viet Nam has acknowledged that occupational standards jointly developed and coordinated with the business sector need to serve as the basis for developing future training programs. MOLISA has started a new approach in establishing an institutionalized framework for this purpose. The approach envisages the involvement of employers as members of a "steering committee" and an "appraisal board," yet it does not include respective legal duties or responsibilities in implementation provisions. In parallel, involvement of enterprises in TVET delivery has become an important aspect in quality accreditation of TVET institutions and programs. This approach holds all TVET institutions responsible for engaging employers in the training design, delivery, and internal quality assurance. What is still missing, however, are reasonable strategies and incentives for employers to collaborate with TVET institutions that have yet to hurdle various organizational and financial constraints to perform well in their demand orientation.

Although the law regulates the minimum qualification requirements of Viet Nam's 73,612 TVET teachers and more than 10,000 school managers, the possession of an academic degree is still the qualifying requirement, which the majority largely fulfill. Of major concern is the unclear definition of "certificates of professional skills" as the only mandatory legal requirement for teaching practical lessons, since these certificates do not necessarily assert actual work experience and real industry practice. The new Law No. 74/2014/QH13 on vocational education and training mandates teachers to "participate in internships in enterprises in order to update (or) improve professional skills, and approach new technology as regulated." Respective requirements have also been integrated into new quality accreditation standards for TVET institutions and programs. Yet, MOLISA'S Circular No. 06/2017/TT-BLDTBXH on qualification standards of TVET teachers translates this prescription into the rather unclear terms of "self-study" and "participation in advanced training courses."

The same applies to managers of TVET institutes. Apart from academic qualifications, basic information technology (IT), and language skills, the law mandates that TVET managers should have been trained (and) fostered on vocational education and training management. So far, most members of TVET management staff do not have certificates for management skills and only a fraction of TVET managers participated in training on school management standards. Until 2020, MOLISA wants to extend the training scope considerably and plans to modernize IT infrastructure to apply to management and operation of TVET institutions. However, no clear propositions have been made on organizational and technical approaches showing tangible measures that address such objectives.

In addition, outdated or insufficient training facilities and poor resource management appear to constrain Viet Nam's TVET system. Reports from TVET institutions indicate that technical facilities and the means of teaching and learning do not meet the requirements for high-quality training or have insufficient scope to conduct appropriate hands-on training activities for all students enrolled in a course. In its draft plan for TVET Reform 2020/30 MOLISA intends to investigate the real situation of facilities and training equipment at TVET institutes as a basis for developing standards and norms for each training occupation and level and for implementing training courses that will enhance financing schemes and resource management processes. However, the envisaged approach narrows the focus on unilateral school autonomy issues and, hence, seems to bypass crucial elements of efficient state governance and sustained budget support schemes.

Equitable access. Statistical data constantly show large gaps by gender and geographic areas (urban/rural) in the share of the population with technical and professional training at all training levels, with no apparent trend of narrowing these gaps. TVET institutions with boarding facilities most of which are located in the provincial capital cities are generally the only option for people in remote areas. Hence, promoting access to TVET continues to play a prominent role in the policy framework of Viet Nam's human resources development (HRD) and is supported extensively by several policy propositions on TVET system development in the new TVET law and subsequent regulations. To enter into formal TVET at the elementary level, a lower secondary education remains a prerequisite qualification, but many young people among Viet Nam's disadvantaged population still have not achieved this status. Despite government incentives to channel enrollments from lower secondary schools into intermediate TVET, Viet Nam citizens' preference for general education qualifications heavily challenges TVET's attractiveness. In addition, investigations show that gender equality in TVET is still being addressed in the country's policy framework and that technical capacity needs to be enhanced to address this issue through improved policy, strategy, and implementation approaches.

4. Financing for Technical and Vocational Education and Training

The government's national budget framework aims to earmark 20% of total public expenditure for education. In 2015, the share of the education budget was only 15.9%. Over the past 6 years, MOLISA estimates suggest that the share for TVET out of the public education budget has been around 8%. Basically, state budget funds for TVET consist of three types: regular funding, capital construction investment, and national target programs, which are the main sources for financing the government's TVET reform agenda. During 2010–2014, the state budget allocated to vocational training under the responsibility of MOLISA totaled VND55,575 billion, equivalent to $2.54 billion. Funds for recurrent expenditures accounted for 37.4% of this budget, funds for capital construction investment had a share of 40.81%, and 21.79% of the TVET budget was allocated for national target programs.

Apart from state budgets, public TVET is also funded by revenues from tuition and admission fees and, to a small extent, revenues from production and business operation services. So far, these funding sources have been seen as an important means to offset the increasing gap between state budgets and actual costs of training delivery and shall successively replace the traditional opaque system of input-based state funding for those institutions achieving full autonomy status after 2020. Currently, however, there is no common perception to what extent TVET institutions are actually capable (or ready) to recover their recurrent and nonrecurrent expenditures by such revenues. There are also some indications that the strategy may lead to higher inequality in the access to high-quality TVET. Sustained private sector contributions to public TVET still play a marginal role.

5. Government Sector Strategy

The policy framework for the long-term development of TVET is defined and guided by (i) the Socio-Economic Development Strategy 2011–2020 providing direction for two socioeconomic development plans (2011–2015 and 2016–2020), (ii) the Human Resources Development Strategy and a respective Human Resources Development Master Plan for the period 2011–2020, (iii) the Vocational Training Development Strategy 2011–2020 (May 2012), and (iv) Resolutions No. 29 (November 2013) and 44 (June 2014). In November 2014, the government enacted a new TVET law which took effect in July 2015 and unleashed huge system changes in governance. Overall, the government is strongly committed to implement comprehensive and fundamental reforms to enhance the coverage and quality of HRD and TVET toward fostering TVET's relevance for the labor market and thus helping Viet Nam become more competitive regionally and globally.

Technical and vocational education and training reform agenda. The government's TVET development strategy sets out a list of ambitious objectives and specifies a broad array of respective "solutions" to be implemented under nine systemic reform components: (i) renovate state management of TVET; (ii) develop vocational teachers and managerial staff; (iii) develop occupational standards and the national vocational qualification framework; (iv) develop respective training curriculum and instructional materials; (v) strengthen standards for TVET facilities and equipment; (vi) enhance quality assurance; (vii) enhance linkage between TVET institutions, the labor market, and enterprises; (viii) improve awareness about TVET development; and (ix) promote international cooperation.

Based on a critical analysis of its performance and accomplishments by 2015, MOLISA has been drafting a comprehensive new plan for a national Project for TVET Reform and Quality Improvement until 2020 with an Orientation to 2030. The plan identifies the urgent need for a new road map to readjust perspectives, objectives, and tasks for the upcoming years. This should take into account key lessons learned and provide feasible solutions not only to overcome a range of persistent reform shortcomings and weaknesses but also to tackle a broad array of new challenges for the country's socioeconomic development. For this, the plan contains a comprehensive list of tasks and "solutions" grouped into eight major areas, which seem to concentrate more on regulative standardization rather than on solutions dealing with the concrete implementation requirements of standards: (i) renovate and improve the effectiveness and efficiency of state management of TVET; (ii) grant full autonomy to TVET institutions in association with measures that ensure enhanced accountability, independent assessment mechanisms, state control, social monitoring mechanisms, and improved administration capacity of TVET institutions; (iii) improve planning of TVET institution networks; (iv) standardize vocational training quality assurance conditions; (v) strengthen vocational training quality accreditation; (vi) link TVET with labor markets, decent work, and social security; (vii) develop the system of national occupational skills assessment and certification; and (viii) strengthen communication, scientific research, and international cooperation.

6. Conclusion and Recommendations

The Asian Development Bank (ADB) 2014 TVET assessment report for Viet Nam condensed its findings into a set of five essential problems that characterized the overall development status of Viet Nam's TVET system at that time: (i) insufficient enterprise-based training, (ii) wrong skills taught, (iii) skills not properly taught, (iv) inequitable access, and (v) less-than-effective organization and management of skills development. This report has updated those findings and provides a range of new information to show the status of the government's ambitious process to reform and improve Viet Nam's vocational education and training system. A positive aspect that has emerged and is being consolidated in policy directions is that the government (or MOLISA through its DVET) has become fully aware of these problems and is critically analyzing the limitations and weaknesses of previous solutions and trying to counterbalance them by sharpening the focus of future reform activities that address substantial quality improvements in key areas. Nevertheless, the five key problems appear to be still valid in most of their aspects and hence lead to the following recommendations:

Reform the governance structure, organization, and management of technical and vocational education and training. The lack of a comprehensive national TVET management information system (Labor Market Information System [LMIS] and education management system [EMIS]) affects all single reform propositions and potential solutions regarding TVET governance and management; hence, having a reliable LMIS and EMIS should take up a more prominent and elaborated position in the government's reform ambitions. Reliable and consistent data and analysis on enrollments, training outputs and outcomes, training capacity and quality, financial needs and performance as well as on labor market orientation of TVET institutions, challenging circumstances and respective support structures, periodically collected in a central database and professionally processed and shared among different agents and agencies through a multidirectional web portal, should urgently become an indispensable basis for the design, monitoring, and evaluation of tangible policy interventions. For only this can drive sound operative innovations and verify respective measurable improvements in system performance.

Provide the right skills and teach skills more effectively. A weakness of previous and current policy propositions regarding key input factors for TVET quality—such as teacher development, upgrade of management capacity, and investment in appropriate training facilities and equipment—is (apart from a missing reflection on budget constraints) their rather unclear and indefinite character. Largely formulated in terms of ideas or intentions, they do not clearly designate agents, modes of interventions, and indicators that qualify tangible approaches for different agents to achieve the envisaged objectives. Conceptual specifications on the change management model, its strategy and leadership aspects, as well as descriptions of the design and setup of sustained support structures are missing. As international experience has shown, attempts to change fundamental systems and processes in education are likely to fail when they are based only on high-level government visions and implemented by top-down orders that do not sufficiently integrate operational conditions and motivations of all stakeholders and clients involved. Thus, a more participatory bottom-up approach toward quality assurance is highly recommended.

Stimulate greater enterprise-based training and financial support. Greater involvement of enterprises in TVET reform and delivery has become a more prominent aspect in the new legal framework for TVET as well as in MOLISA's latest approach and undertaking toward enhancing quality assurance and quality accreditation of TVET institutions. However, MOLISA focuses still on making schools the key agents in organizing companies to commit their participation in school operations and cooperate in training delivery. Viet Nam should put a high priority on stimulating enterprise involvement in and financial support to the TVET system by making crucial systemic amendments that focus on institutionalizing sustained employer involvement in a tripartite TVET agency at national level. Such an agency should become the central institution that collaborates with stakeholders rather than a government-driven forum for directives. The private sector also needs to be involved in creating a better TVET system to attract private TVET financing, which includes playing a central role in sourcing and determining the allocation of funds to be raised as well as being involved in its governance. Lessons learned from Australia, Germany, Japan, the Republic of Korea, Malaysia, Singapore, and the United Kingdom can guide Viet Nam's government and industry associations to create more tangible attempts in this direction.

Increase equal access to high-quality training. Viet Nam's HRD policy framework highlights prominently the task of promoting access to TVET, which several propositions and regulations for TVET system development also supports. However, to improve the link between nonformal courses that address disadvantaged groups of Viet Nam's rural population (ethnic minorities) and the formal TVET system, the government needs to create pathways that facilitate the progression into higher TVET and address the widespread bias of TVET as a second option for starting a professional career. Nonformal and informal training opportunities could be made more relevant to the needs of remote rural areas by adopting community-based training methodologies that provide technical and financial services to facilitate the successful application of training in business-related activities. Better opportunities in TVET are also needed to promote decent work that is attractive for women and girls. Gender equity should be embedded in all policies, reporting tools, and regulative instruments that focus on standard compliance. To challenge social stereotypes that continue to have negative impacts on the socioeconomic status of women and girls, the government needs to make substantial investments in long-term promotion campaigns that leverage the capacity of TVET institutions.

I. Socioeconomic Development Context

1. Background

1. As widely acknowledged and substantiated in international studies such as the World Bank and the Ministry of Planning and Investment (2016), Viet Nam has made remarkable political efforts and achievement during the past 25 years. Its extraordinary success story of rapid economic development toward a market economy depicts a process accompanied by fundamental but cautiously balanced changes in its socioeconomic setting.

2. The population of Viet Nam grew from about 70 million in the early 1990s to 93.6 million in 2017, an average increase of about 1.3% per annum. The trend is expected to drop to an annual growth rate of about 1% until 2020 and then gradually decline up to 2060 when Viet Nam's population is predicted to reach its absolute peak (Figure 1.1). Although still a relatively young population, with 32.5% of total population below the age of 15 and 25% classified as "young" at 15–34 years of age (Nguyen et al. 2015), the country will face a structural demographic transition toward an aging society (Figure 1.2).

Figure 1.1: Population Growth of Viet Nam, 1990–2100

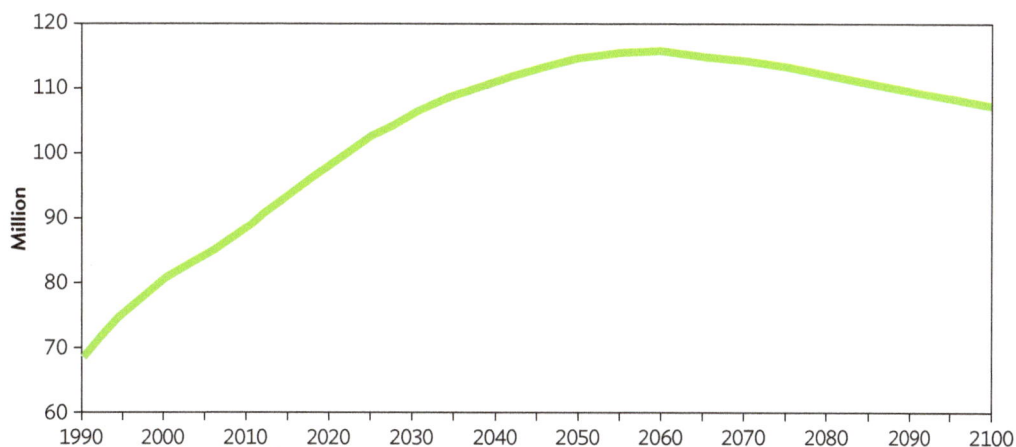

Source: United Nations, Department of Economic and Social Affairs, Population Division. World Population Prospects 2017. https://esa.un.org/unpd/wpp/.

Figure 1.2: Population Pyramid of Viet Nam, 1990–2020

	1990 (%)		2020 (%)
Age	Male / Female	Male / Female	

Left pyramid (1990 %):

Age	Male	Female
100+	0.0	0.0
95–99	0.0	0.0
90–94	0.0	0.1
85–89	0.1	0.2
80–84	0.2	0.4
75–79	0.4	0.7
70–74	0.6	0.9
65–69	0.9	1.2
60–54	1.1	1.3
55–59	1.4	1.6
50–54	1.3	1.5
45–49	1.4	1.6
40–44	1.7	1.9
35–39	2.8	2.9
30–34	3.7	3.7
25–29	4.4	4.4
20–24	4.8	4.8
15–19	5.4	5.3
10–14	5.8	5.6
5–9	6.4	6.1
0–4	6.9	6.6

Right pyramid (2020 %):

Age	Male	Female
100+	0.0	0.0
95–99	0.0	0.1
90–94	0.1	0.2
85–89	0.2	0.5
80–84	0.3	0.6
75–79	0.4	0.7
70–74	0.7	1.0
65–69	1.4	1.7
60–54	2.1	2.4
55–59	2.6	2.8
50–54	2.9	3.0
45–49	3.3	3.4
40–44	3.6	3.6
35–39	4.0	4.0
30–34	4.4	4.3
25–29	4.5	4.4
20–24	3.6	3.4
15–19	3.5	3.3
10–14	3.8	3.5
5–9	4.1	3.7
0–4	4.0	3.7

Source: PopulationPyramid.net. Viet Nam. https://www.populationpyramid.net/viet-nam.

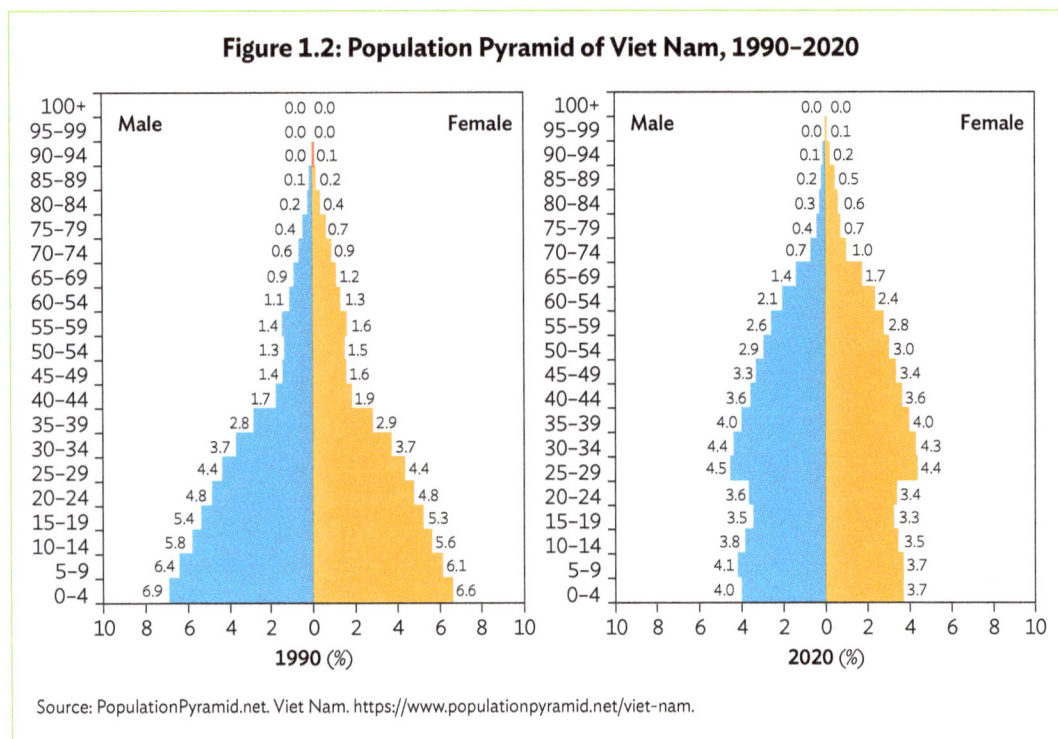

3. **Human development and per capita income.** Between 1990 and 2015, Viet Nam's Human Development Index value rose from 0.477 to 0.683, an increase of 43.2%. Viet Nam performed slightly above the average value of 0.631 for countries in the medium human development group but below the average value of 0.720 for countries in East Asia and the Pacific. In the Inequality-Adjusted Human Development Index, which measures social inequality constraints, Viet Nam outperforms the average value losses of the two respective groups (UNDP 2017). Less severely affected by regional and global economic crises than its neighbors, Viet Nam achieved the rank of a lower middle-income country in 2009 and has since doubled its gross national income per capita[1] and continues performing as one of the fastest growing economies in Southeast Asia. The proportion of the population living below the poverty line was more than halved, from about 20% in 2000 to less than 10% by the end of the decade.[2] Additionally, other dimensions of the people's welfare improved, including literacy rates among adults (over 90%) and life expectancy (over 70 years). Most of the Millennium Development Goals, particularly in health and education, have been achieved or are within reach (Nguyen et al. 2015).

4. **Gross domestic product.** In 1998, while most of the other economies experienced negative growth, Viet Nam's gross domestic product (GDP) still grew at 5.8%, the highest in the region. In 2008, the yearly GDP growth rate slowed from 8.5% in 2007 to 6.3% and to 5.3% in 2009, before recovering to 6.5% in 2010, and 6.8% in 2017. The country's vibrant economic growth has rested on a strong and dynamic structural shift from agriculture to higher productivity in more value-added

---

[1]   Calculated by the World Bank Atlas method.

[2]   According to the latest household living standards survey of the Government of Viet Nam, the poverty rate for the whole country in 2014 decreased to 8.4%. There are, however, still considerable variances between different geographic regions. In the Northern Midland and Mountain areas and in the Central Highlands, the poverty rates were 18.4% and 13.8%, respectively, although there was also a sharp decline from 29.4% and 22%, respectively, in 2010 (GSO 2016c).

industry sectors and services (Figure 1.3), with the export of manufactured goods as a main driver. A buoyant foreign direct investment (FDI) capital inflow into export-oriented manufacturing industries[3] and an increasing pool of cheap labor resources have been identified as the two main factors of overall productivity growth (World Bank and MPI 2016). Meanwhile, accounting only for 15% of national GDP, agriculture has remained a significant sector as it still employs 40% of Viet Nam's steadily growing workforce compared with the growing services and industry sectors, which currently employ 34% and 26%, respectively (Figure 1.5).[4]

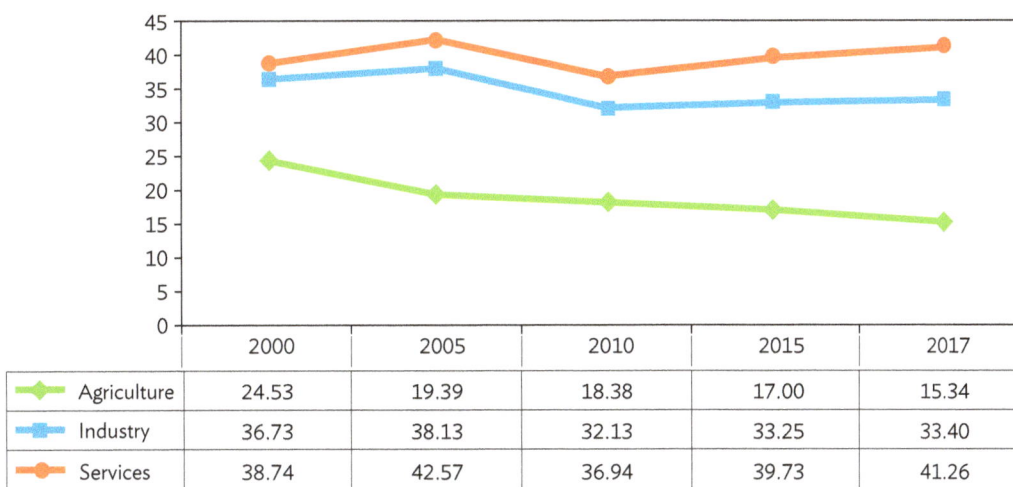

Figure 1.3: Value Added by Sector, 2000–2017
(% of GDP)

	2000	2005	2010	2015	2017
Agriculture	24.53	19.39	18.38	17.00	15.34
Industry	36.73	38.13	32.13	33.25	33.40
Services	38.74	42.57	36.94	39.73	41.26

GDP = gross domestic product.
Source: General Statistics Office of Viet Nam. www.gso.gov.vn (accessed March 2019).

5. **Labor force.** The size of the Viet Nam's labor force grew from 38 million in 2000 to almost 55 million in 2017 and is projected to increase to 56 million in 2020 (Figure 1.4). During the same period, the country's labor force participation rate has been consistently high and remains stable until present with 76.6% in the first quarter of 2017 (GSO 2017).[5] This is remarkable, since by average each year about 1 million workers shifted employment from agriculture and could be absorbed by Viet Nam's industry and service sectors (Figure 1.5), while overall unemployment remained at a low level of approximately 2.1% in 2016. Yet, unemployed youth contributed to almost half of this figure.[6]

6. The movement of workers across economic sectors has followed the trend in other Asian countries. Comparing the relative shares of labor force shifts from 2000 to 2015 for selected members of the Association of Southeast Asian Nations (ASEAN) shows that Viet Nam has almost achieved a similar

[3]   By 2015, the FDI sector was contributing over half of manufacturing output and over 70% of export turnover in Viet Nam (See World Bank and MPI [2016]).

[4]   International Labour Organization. ILOSTAT. http://www.ilo.org/ilostat/faces/ilostat-home/home?_adf.ctrl-state=1r4n0rgkm_4&_afrLoop=397160583514123#! (accessed 2016).

[5]   Labor force participation rate was 70.1% in urban areas and 80% in rural areas.

[6]   By the end of 2016, the unemployment rate of Vietnamese citizens aged 15–24 was about six times higher than that of those people aged 25 and above (11.49 % versus 1.9% in urban areas and 5.69% versus 0.88% in rural areas) (GSO 2016b).

Figure 1.4: Labor Force Growth 2000–2015 and Projections to 2020
(million)

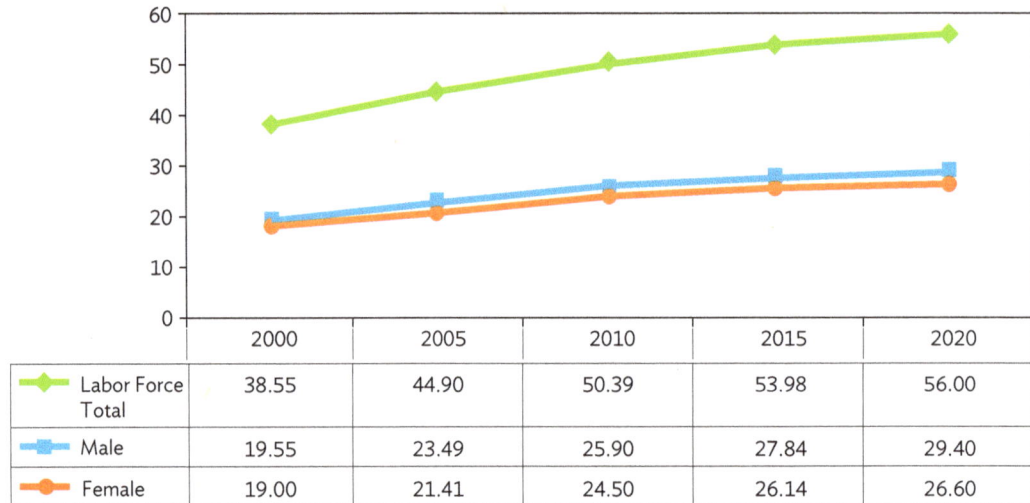

	2000	2005	2010	2015	2020
Labor Force Total	38.55	44.90	50.39	53.98	56.00
Male	19.55	23.49	25.90	27.84	29.40
Female	19.00	21.41	24.50	26.14	26.60

Sources: General Statistics Office of Viet Nam. www.gso.gov.vn (accessed June 2017); and International Labour Organization. ILOSTAT. http://www.ilo.org/ilostat/faces/ilostat-home/home?_adf.ctrl-state=1r4n0rgkm_168&_afrLoop=397701129734019#! (accessed June 2017).

Figure 1.5: Labor Force by Sector, 2000–2017
(%)

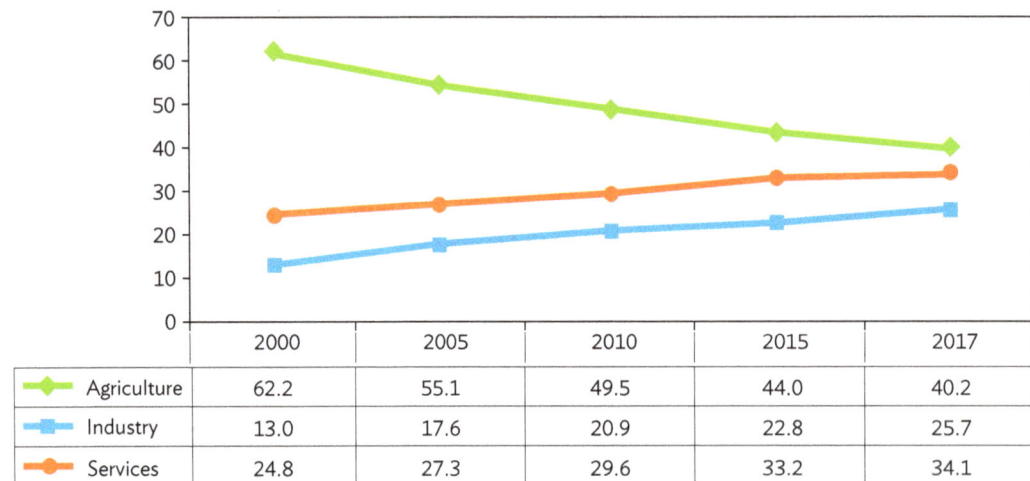

	2000	2005	2010	2015	2017
Agriculture	62.2	55.1	49.5	44.0	40.2
Industry	13.0	17.6	20.9	22.8	25.7
Services	24.8	27.3	29.6	33.2	34.1

Source: General Statistics Office of Viet Nam. *Report on Labour Force Survey 2016*. www.gso.gov.vn (accessed March 2019).

share of workers being employed in the industry sector (23.1%) as Thailand (23.7%) and Indonesia (22.2%). Meanwhile, this share is even higher than that of Singapore (16.25%) and the Philippines (16.2%), while the share of service sector employments (33.3%) is increasing but still lags behind that of more developed ASEAN countries in relative terms (Figure 1.6). Table 1.1 shows total changes in employment and annual growth rates by economic sectors from 2000 to 2016 for ASEAN countries.

Figure 1.6: Employment by Sector, 2000–2015
(%)

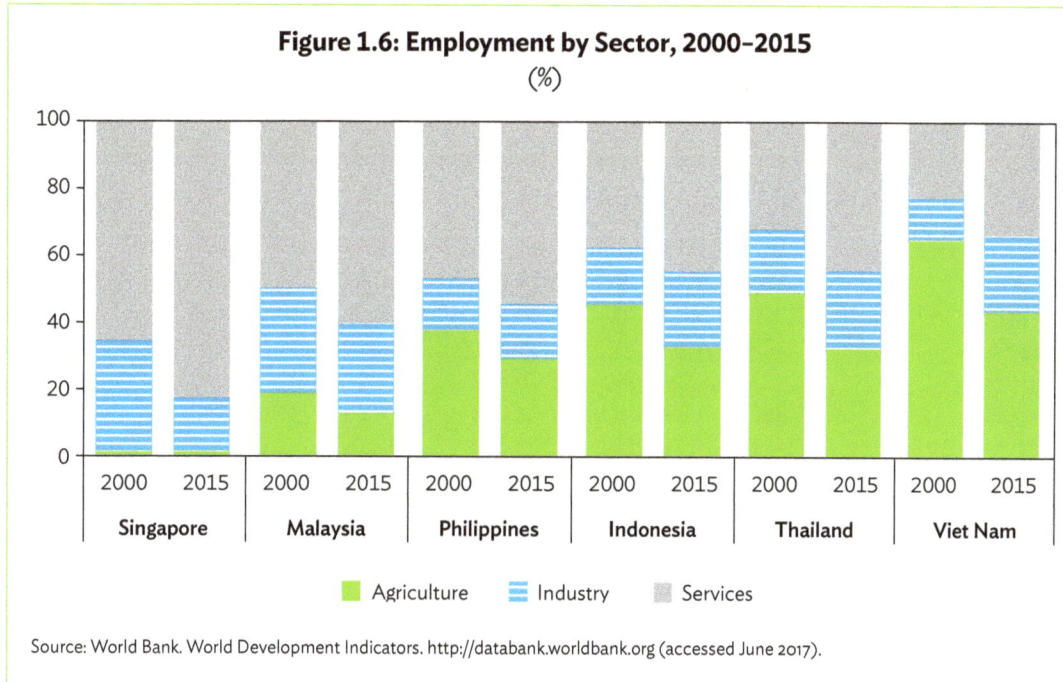

Source: World Bank. World Development Indicators. http://databank.worldbank.org (accessed June 2017).

Table 1.1: Change in Employment by Economic Sector, 2000–2016

	Total Change (thousands)			Average Annual Growth Rate (%)		
	Agriculture	Industry	Services	Agriculture	Industry	Services
ASEAN	(12,456)	27,387	63,188	(0.7)	3.4	3.5
Cambodia	(357)	1,237	2,247	(0.6)	8.3	7.6
Indonesia	(3,479)	10,597	20,037	(0.5)	3.2	2.9
Lao PDR	722	69	295	1.9	4.5	4.4
Malaysia	(12)	881	3,863	(0.0)	1.6	3.8
Myanmar	(5,249)	1,952	9,190	(3.2)	3.8	4.3
Philippines	1,809	2,443	10,524	1.0	2.8	3.8
Singapore	5	(141)	1,371	3.8	(1.4)	4.7
Thailand	(2,628)	2,863	5,655	(1.1)	2.4	2.5
Viet Nam	**(3,265)**	**7,478**	**9,959**	**(0.8)**	**5.8**	**4.7**

( ) = negative, ASEAN = Association of Southeast Asian Nations, Lao PDR = Lao People's Democratic Republic.
Source: International Labour Organization. Employment by Sector. www.ilo.org (accessed June 2017).

7. **Labor productivity.** The structural shift from agriculture to industry and services contributed to substantial increases in the overall productivity of Viet Nam's economy (Table 1.2). While the pace of structural transformation increased, labor productivity growth actually declined in a majority of economic sectors. In the four sectors dominated by state ownership—mining, construction, public utilities, as well as finance and real estate—labor productivity growth was even negative from 2000 onward (World Bank and MPI 2016). Only productivity growth in agriculture and trade increased significantly and has been projected to do so also during the next 2 decades (Table 1.3).

Table 1.2: Development of Labor Productivity 2000–2015 and Projections for 2020

	Output per Worker (GDP constant 2011 international $ in PPP)					CAGR 2000–2015 (%)
	2000	2005	2010	2015	2020 (p)	
Cambodia	2,976	3,931	4,471	5,955	7,606	4.73
PRC	6,554	10,013	16,778	23,967	32,506	9.03
India	6,852	8,252	11,944	15,521	20,421	5.60
Indonesia	13,224	16,259	18,832	22,645	27,117	3.65
Lao PDR	5,269	6,330	8,140	10,692	13,420	4.83
Malaysia	40,037	45,076	50,330	54,103	61,830	2.03
Myanmar	2,523	4,256	6,827	9,096	12,048	8.93
Philippines	11,850	12,696	14,085	16,741	21,160	2.33
Singapore	107,481	118,641	133,876	143,707	152,631	1.96
Thailand	16,972	20,122	23,293	26,449	30,378	3.00
Viet Nam	**4,948**	**6,219**	**7,715**	**9,419**	**12,191**	**4.39**

(p) = projected, CAGR = compound average growth rate, GDP = gross domestic product, Lao PDR = Lao People's Democratic Republic, PPP = purchasing power parity, PRC = People's Republic of China.
Sources: International Labour Organization (ILO). ILOSTAT. www.ilo.org/ilostat; and ILO modeled estimates (May 2017).

Table 1.3: Sectoral Gross Domestic Product, Workforce, and Labor Productivity Growth in Viet Nam, 1990–2013, and Projections toward 2035
(%)

Sector	GDP Growth			Labor Force Growth			Productivity Growth		
	1990–2000	2000–2013	2013–2035 (p)	1990–2000	2000–2013	2013–2035 (p)	1990–2000	2000–2013	2013–2035 (p)
Agriculture	3.9	3.5	2.9	1.5	0.1	(2.6)	2.7	3.4	5.6
Manufacturing	10.3	9.9	7.9	3.4	6.9	2.9	7.1	2.8	4.9
Wholesale and retail trade	7.4	7.8	7.0	6.7	5.5	2.1	0.1	2.1	4.8
Mining	7.6	2.3	2.7	(1.9)	2.7	0.5	17.1	(0.4)	2.3
Construction	8.9	8.1	6.8	3.4	10.4	3.0	6.3	(2.1)	3.7
Public utilities	11.1	10.6	3.0	0.6	15.9	(1.1)	11.0	(4.6)	4.1
Finances and real estate	6.8	5.7	6.4	3.9	10.0	2.2	4.1	(4.0)	4.3

( ) = negative, (p) = projected, GDP = gross domestic product.
Sources: World Bank and the Ministry of Planning and Investment of Viet Nam. 2016. *Vietnam 2035: Toward Prosperity, Creativity, Equity, and Democracy*. Washington, DC: World Bank; and author calculations based on General Statistics Office data.

8. **Structure of workforce.** While the number of wageworkers in Viet Nam more than doubled from 1997 to 2007, this trend has notably slackened between 2010 and 2017. Nevertheless, in 2017, this group represented more than 40% of the total labor force (Figure 1.7). Substantial increases in the proportion of "own-account" workers (those who get their pay directly from their customers) during the earlier period seem to have shifted into an opposite trend, and the percentage of unpaid family workers has slightly decreased. The entrepreneurial group, i.e., employers who employ at least one paid worker in their business or trade, decreased significantly. Although already comprising a few employers, the group numbers have shrunk from over 1.6 million in 2010 to only about 1.1 million in 2017, a figure that was already reported for 2007.[7]

---

[7] According to the ADB (2014) TVET Assessment Report, the number of employers had grown from over 50,000 in 1997 to almost 1.5 million in 2007.

Figure 1.7: Distribution of Employed Population by Status, 2010–2017

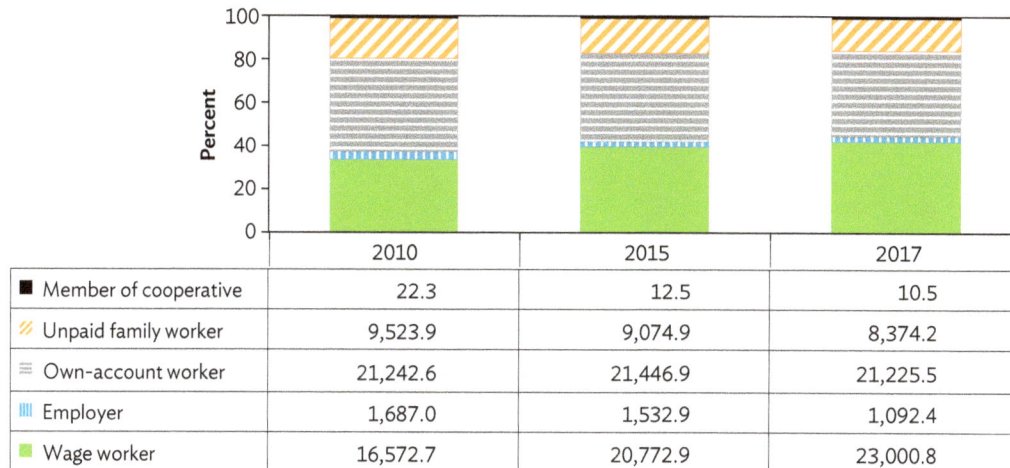

	2010	2015	2017
■ Member of cooperative	22.3	12.5	10.5
▨ Unpaid family worker	9,523.9	9,074.9	8,374.2
≡ Own-account worker	21,242.6	21,446.9	21,225.5
⦀ Employer	1,687.0	1,532.9	1,092.4
▩ Wage worker	16,572.7	20,772.9	23,000.8

Source: General Statistics Office of Viet Nam. Statistical Yearbook of Viet Nam 2017. Ha Noi.

9. In the last 15 years, only marginal changes in the employment structure of Viet Nam's workforce can be observed regarding the quality of employment. The majority of workers (almost 75%) are still categorized as self-employed, which means that they work in their households or conduct their own small businesses and, hence, belong to Viet Nam's huge informal economic sector, having limited access to secure work, low qualifications, no welfare protection, and no official representation. The share of total employment being absorbed by Viet Nam's formal business sector (private and FDI) covers more than 15% (Figure 1.8). However, there are some differences in geographic and gender-related characteristics of the employment structure. By nature, the share of wageworkers in nonagriculture sectors is significantly higher in cities and urban regions (e.g., 67.2% in Ho Chi Minh City) than in rural provinces (e.g., 15.1% in the Central Highlands), but this comes along also with slightly different shares of women being employed by wage contract in these sectors. In rural areas, men still dominate in such employment types (Figure 1.9).

Figure 1.8: Distribution of Employed Population by Type of Employment
(% of total employment)

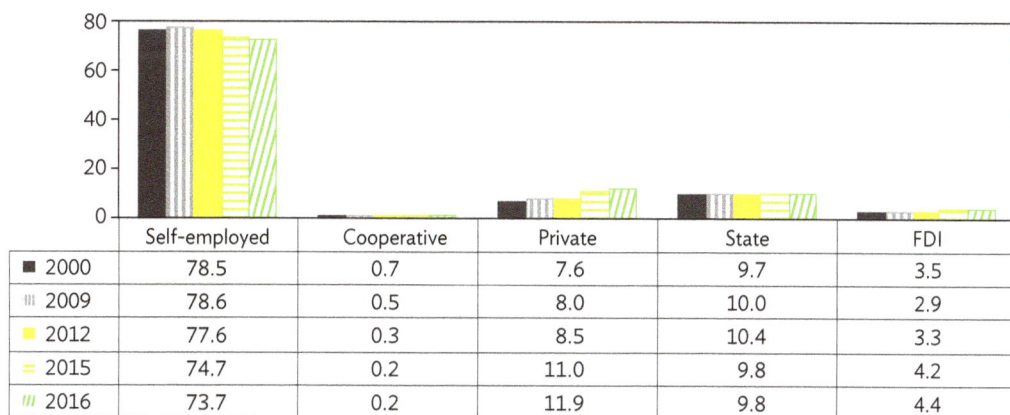

	Self-employed	Cooperative	Private	State	FDI
■ 2000	78.5	0.7	7.6	9.7	3.5
⦀ 2009	78.6	0.5	8.0	10.0	2.9
▩ 2012	77.6	0.3	8.5	10.4	3.3
≡ 2015	74.7	0.2	11.0	9.8	4.2
▥ 2016	73.7	0.2	11.9	9.8	4.4

FDI = foreign direct investment.
Source: General Statistics Office of Viet Nam. Report on Labor Force Survey 2016. Ha Noi.

Figure 1.9: Share of Wageworkers in Nonagriculture Sectors by Region and City, 2016
(in % to total employment)

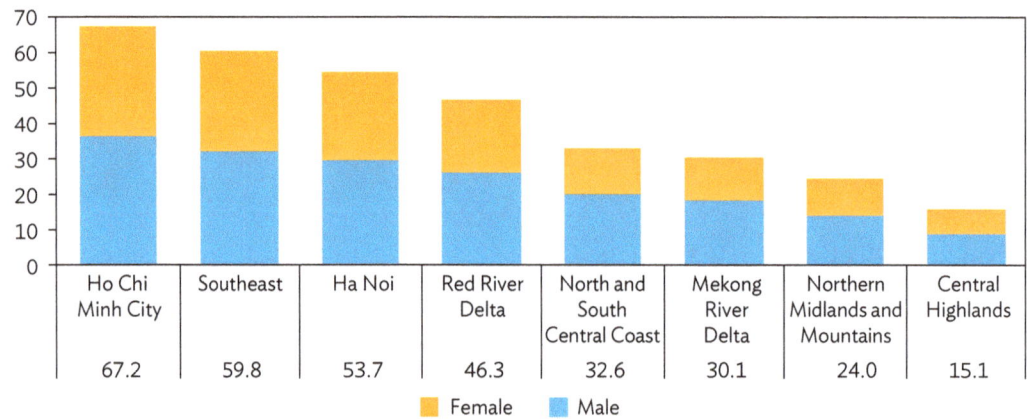

	Ho Chi Minh City	Southeast	Ha Noi	Red River Delta	North and South Central Coast	Mekong River Delta	Northern Midlands and Mountains	Central Highlands
	67.2	59.8	53.7	46.3	32.6	30.1	24.0	15.1

■ Female ■ Male

Source: General Statistics Office of Viet Nam. *Report on Labor Force Survey 2016.* Ha Noi.

10. **Women in the workforce.** Viet Nam has one of the highest labor force participation rates of females in the region. On average, women represent about 48% of those employed. Gender-related disparities are still salient when comparing different age groups in formal employment (Figure 1.10), yet disproportionalities are significantly decreasing among younger workers. More striking are disproportionate shares of women in particular occupations (Table 1.4). While female workers are well represented in white-collar professions, with a significant higher proportion in service-related occupations, they are still remarkably underrepresented in leadership positions. In addition, there are some peculiarities regarding female jobs in particular industry sectors (Figure 1.11). While the classic disproportion of women employed in the social sector (i.e., health and education) versus those working in heavy industries (e.g., mining, construction, transportation) does not really surprise, the relative high employment rate of women in the manufacturing sector is still because of Viet Nam's prevailingly huge textile and garment industry employing large numbers of (mostly low skilled) female

Figure 1.10: Share of Wageworkers in Nonagriculture Sectors by Age Group
(% to total employment) **and Gender Distribution, 2016**

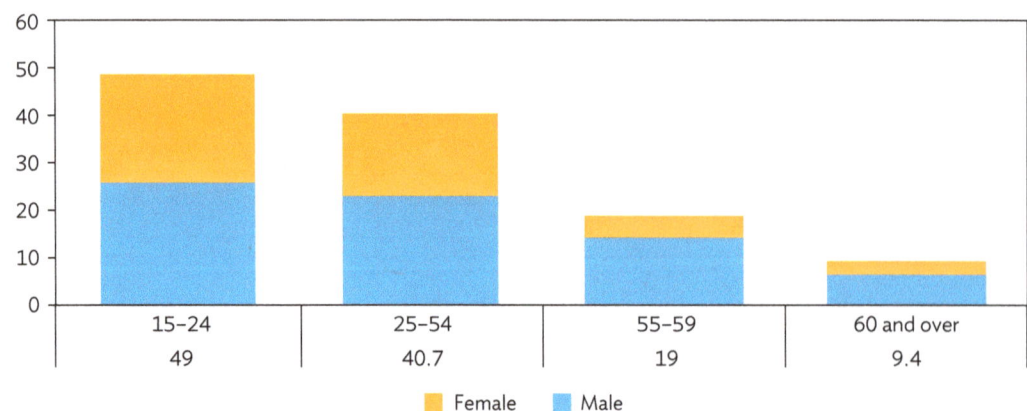

	15–24	25–54	55–59	60 and over
	49	40.7	19	9.4

■ Female ■ Male

Source: General Statistics Office of Viet Nam. *Report on Labor Force Survey 2016.* Ha Noi.

workers. A still unsolved issue seems to persist in the low shares of women working in the science and technology and the information and communication technology (ICT) sectors.[8]

Table 1.4: Number and Composition of Employed Population by Occupation and Sex, 2016

Occupation	Number of Employed Workers (1,000 persons)	Proportion (%)			% Female
		Total	Male	Female	
Total	**53,302.8**	**100.0**	**100.0**	**100.0**	**48.5**
1. Leader in all fields and levels	555.0	1.0	1.5	0.6	26.1
2. High-level professional	3,659.0	6.9	6.2	7.6	53.7
3. Secondary-level professional	1,639.0	3.1	2.7	3.5	55.6
4. Clerks	991.9	1.9	1.8	1.9	49.2
5. Personal services, protection, and sales	8,861.4	16.6	12.3	21.2	61.9
6. Agricultural, forestry, fishery occupation	5,470.9	10.3	11.9	8.6	40.4
7. Skilled manual workers and related ones	6,827.0	12.8	17.7	7.6	29.0
8. Assemblers and machine operators	4,493.8	8.5	10.2	8.2	42.9
9. Unskilled occupations	20,247.8	38.0	35.4	40.8	52.1

Source: General Statistics Office of Viet Nam. *Report on Labor Force Survey 2016*. Ha Noi.

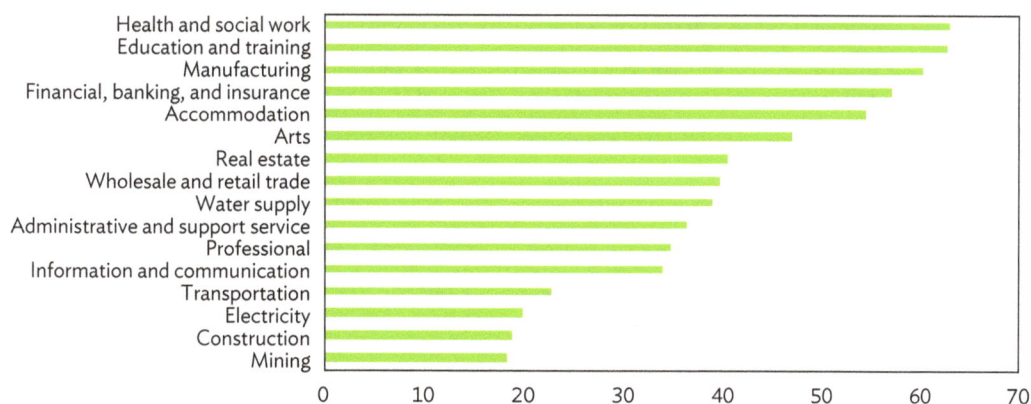

Figure 1.11: Share of Female Employees in Industry Sectors, 2016

Source: General Statistics Office of Viet Nam. Statistical Yearbook of Viet Nam 2017. Ha Noi.

11. **Wage levels.** Discrepancies are still evident in the salaries of women and men, even when they have the same qualifications (Table 1.5). The highest average income gap between men and women (almost 20%) applies to workers with university degrees and higher qualifications. Generally, having a professional qualification seems to pay off for Vietnamese employees by wage returns that were up to 45.6% higher than the total average monthly wage income in 2016. Among males, university graduates achieved almost double the income (187.2%) of those with no technical qualifications, while for female academics this difference was at least 163.4%. The wage return spread appears to

_____

[8]   According to ADB (2014), the reasons for low female participation rates in these areas are multifaceted: "Women face discrimination about their technical competency and ability to work long hours. However, they also tend to believe that there is a negative impact of computers on their reproductive health."

be less pronounced among workers with professional qualifications on different levels. Particularly for those obtaining a college diploma, there are only marginal differences to workers with secondary professional training, and both groups (except for females) seem to profit to a lesser extent from their qualifications than workers who completed a vocational training. However, such peculiarities might be also attributed to an unclear coverage of the General Statistics Office category "vocational training," particularly if it would comprise all levels and types of TVET certificates.

Table 1.5: Average Monthly Income of Wageworkers by Sex and Technical Qualification, 2016

Qualification	Average Monthly Wage Income in 2016 (D1,000)						Gender Gap
	Total		Male		Female		
Total average	**5,066**	**100%**	**5,304**	**100%**	**4,739**	**100%**	**10.7%**
No technical qualification	4,224	83.4%	4,367	82.3%	4,015	84.7%	8.1%
Vocational training	5,834	115.2%	6,009	113.3%	4,899	103.4%	18.5%
Secondary professional training	5,150	101.7%	5,568	105.0%	4,748	100.2%	14.7%
College	5,280	104.2%	5,809	109.5%	4,935	104.1%	15.0%
University and above	7,374	145.6%	8,173	154.1%	6,559	138.4%	19.7%

Source: General Statistics Office of Viet Nam. *Report on Labour Force Survey 2016*. Ha Noi.

12. **Skills levels.** National labor force surveys indicate that the proportion of workers who possess occupational certificates obtained through formal vocational training or at higher education levels has increased between 2011 and 2016 but still remains low compared with the number of employees working without professional qualifications (Figure 1.12). At the end of 2016, only 21% of the employed workforce nationwide possessed a certificate. The statistics show, however, significant variances between men (23.5%) and women (18.3%) as well as between urban and rural areas (37.9% versus 13.1%). The lowest rate of qualified employees pertains to female workers living in rural areas (10.7%), while more than 40% of male workers in urban areas possessed formal occupational qualifications.

Figure 1.12: Rates of Trained Labor Force, 2011 versus 2016
(%)

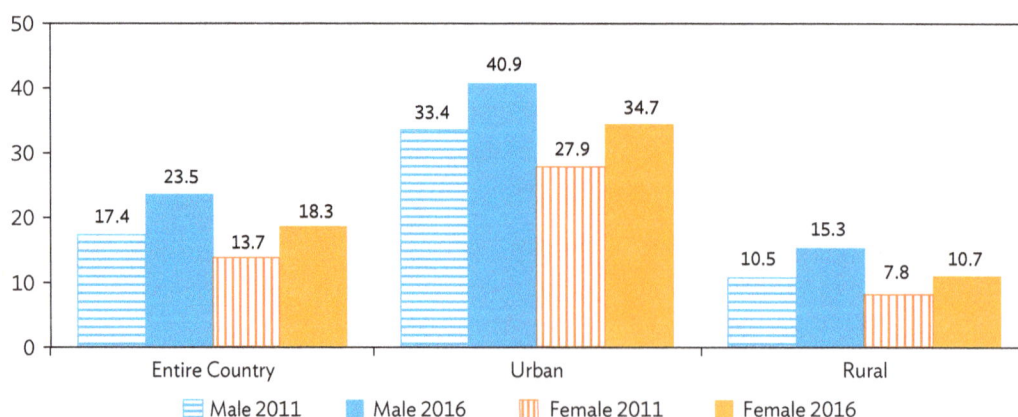

Source: General Statistics Office of Viet Nam. *Report on Labour Force Survey 2016*. Ha Noi. www.gso.gov.vn (accessed August 2017).

13. Even more disparities appear in the distribution of qualification types and levels (Figure 1.13). Most remarkable is the relatively large share of people with university degrees in Viet Nam's workforce, which even outperforms the share of employees with lower professional qualifications in urban regions. Countrywide, only 11.8% of the employed population aged 15 and above possessed such mid-level qualifications (14.4% male and 9.3% female). Qualifications subsumed under the "vocational training" category, which seems to comprise all levels of formal TVET certificates, cover only 5.3% of the employed population on a national scale and seem to be still a predominant characteristic of male employees (8.5% versus only 1.9% for females).

Figure 1.13: Distribution of Qualifications in Employed Population, 2016
(%)

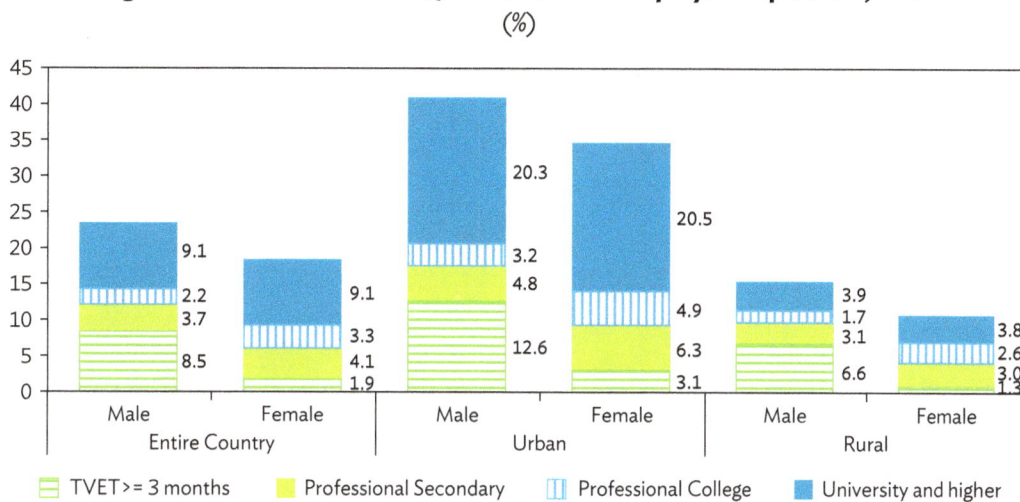

Source: General Statistics Office of Viet Nam. *Report on Labour Force Survey 2016*. Ha Noi. www.gso.gov.vn (accessed August 2017).

2. Socioeconomic Issues and Challenges

14. **Limited competitiveness.** As shown in the previous section, labor productivity in Viet Nam has been a major concern despite having increased in overall terms by structural employment shifts, as it has remained lower than other countries in the region.[9] In 2016, Viet Nam ranked 60th out of 138 economies on the Global Competitive Index[10] with a score of 4.3 out of 7 (Figure 1.14). The country's market size index factor ranked higher at 32nd but all other factors were lower, with "business sophistication" only at 96th, "technology readiness" at 92nd, and "higher education and training" at 83rd. At the same time, many neighboring countries have shown improvements in their competitiveness.

[9] In 2015, total annual labor productivity in Viet Nam (at current prices) reached $3,660, just equaling 4.4% of Singapore, 17.4% of Malaysia, 35.2% of Thailand, 48.5% of the Philippines, and 48.8% of Indonesia in the same year. See also General Statistics Office. Economic Growth. http://www.gso.gov.vn/default_en.aspx?tabid=622&ItemID=16194.

[10] The World Economic Forum (2016) ranks economies according to their competitiveness using a global competitiveness index comprising 12 main variables derived from more than 100 indicators. The variables are legal and administrative framework, transport and communications infrastructure, macroeconomic stability, health and primary education, higher education and training, market efficiency for goods, labor market efficiency, financial market development, technological readiness, market size, business sophistication, and innovation. This listing illustrates the complexity of the task of boosting national competitiveness and suggests multiple pathways to greater competitiveness.

Figure 1.14: Competitiveness and Labor Productivity

Global Competitiveness Index[a]

Singapore	2
Taipei,China	14
Malaysia	25
Korea, Republic of	26
PRC	28
Thailand	34
India	39
Indonesia	41
Philippines	57
Viet Nam	**60**
Sri Lanka	71
Cambodia	89
Lao PDR	93

Low Labor Productivity[b]

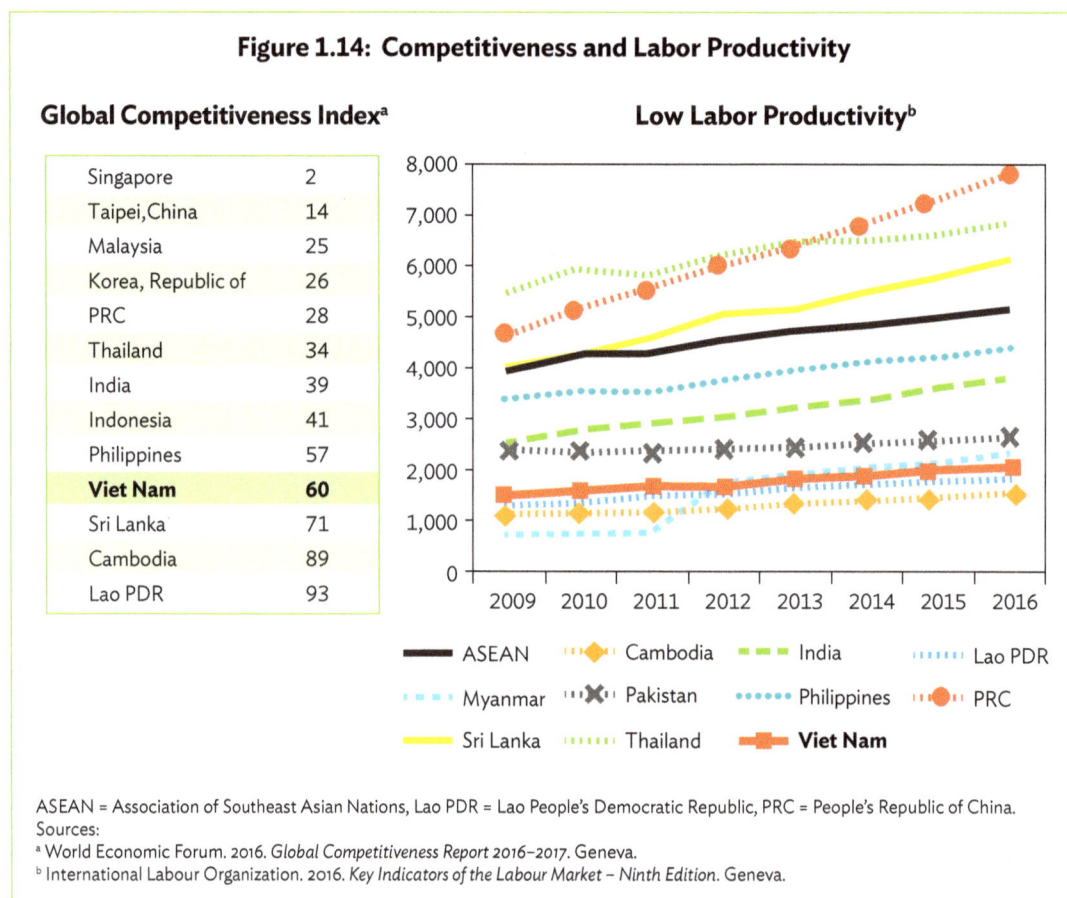

ASEAN = Association of Southeast Asian Nations, Lao PDR = Lao People's Democratic Republic, PRC = People's Republic of China.
Sources:
[a] World Economic Forum. 2016. *Global Competitiveness Report 2016–2017*. Geneva.
[b] International Labour Organization. 2016. *Key Indicators of the Labour Market – Ninth Edition*. Geneva.

15. From 2000 onward, relative annual productivity growth rates in most industry sectors in Viet Nam declined (Table 1.2), indicating that a growing amount of labor supply has not been efficiently combined with other important economic factors, such as sufficient capital endowment, state-of-the-art machinery equipment as well as technology and respective process innovation (World Bank and MPI 2016). As shown, the latter has had a persistently low share of Vietnamese employees with professional qualifications obtained through formal vocational training or at higher education levels (Figure 1.13). The ratio of graduates with academic degrees to those with college, professional secondary, or vocational training certificates also appears to be unfavorable to the demand of skilled labor in the manufacturing industry, which may be partly related to unbalanced wage returns for employees obtaining mid-level occupational certificates.

16. Key factors attributing to this situation have been identified in Viet Nam's prevailing structural economic settings. Deeply rooted in tradition, a centrally governed "socialist market economy" has led to big monopolistic but inefficient state-owned enterprises, a prevailingly weak and disadvantaged domestic private industry sector, as well as a huge but fragmented smallholder-dominated agriculture and informal business culture. Despite ambitious reform efforts during the past decades, state-managed human resources development (through higher education and TVET) and respective labor market support systems have remained weak, fragmented, and inefficiently funded, most of them still receiving low trust in performance and ability to adapt to changing market demands (VCCI and ILO Bureau for Employers' Activities 2016).

17. **Shortage of skilled labor.** Given that almost 80% of Viet Nam's working age population is actively involved in the labor market, the size of the country's talent pool is considerable. A challenge for enterprises, however, relates to the quality of workers and the issue of skills mismatch in the job market. Recent surveys among employers across different types of enterprises[11] indicate that it is still difficult to recruit workers who qualify for a specific sector, type, and level of work, a problem increasing with the demand for relevant higher-level job qualifications. The vast majority of firms in Viet Nam find it difficult or fairly difficult to recruit workers with qualifications for mid-level technical jobs (technical workers). For recruiting managers and supervisors this issue seems even more pronounced, while it appears to be relatively easy to recruit lower-skilled manual workers and, to a lesser extent, employees for mid-level white-collar jobs, such as accountants. Figures 1.15a–d show some remarkable differences across sectors and manufacturing subsectors regarding the difficulty to recruit technical workers and management staff. In its 2016 Labor Market Report (VCCI and ILO Bureau for Employers' Activities 2016), the Viet Nam Chamber of Commerce and Industry (VCCI) rated this trend as highly problematic adding to the concern that in Viet Nam "technical workers are in steady demand and there is often a competition among foreign and domestic enterprises to recruit them."

18. **Youth unemployment.** At the same time, statistics show that young workers aged 15 to 24 still have difficulty joining the labor market as they constitute almost half of the country's unemployed population. In 2017, youth unemployment was at 7.4% and, contrary to the general perception that higher education would give the added advantage in finding jobs, unemployment is high among young graduates with professional and tertiary certificates, particularly in urban areas. Surprisingly, a higher education level raises the chances of being unemployed after graduation (Table 1.6). The assumption that skills mismatches is one of the dominant factors contributing to this situation can be

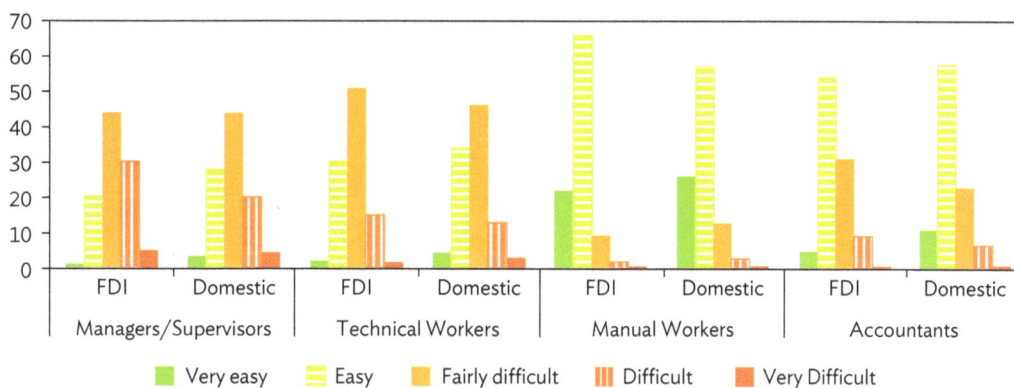

Figure 1.15: Ease of Staff Recruitment by Job Category and Type of Enterprise
(% share of responses)

FDI = foreign direct investment.
Source: Viet Nam Chamber of Commerce and Industry (VCCI) and International Labour Organization Bureau for Employers' Activities. 2016. VCCI Labour Market Report: Trends in the Workplace – Skills and Labour Productivity. Ha Noi.

[11] Surveys such as, for example, Viet Nam Chamber of Commerce and Industry. The Provincial Competitiveness Index (PCI) Survey 2015. www.http://eng.pcivietnam.org.

Figure 1.15a: Difficulty of Foreign Direct Investment Enterprises in Recruiting Technical Workers by Sector

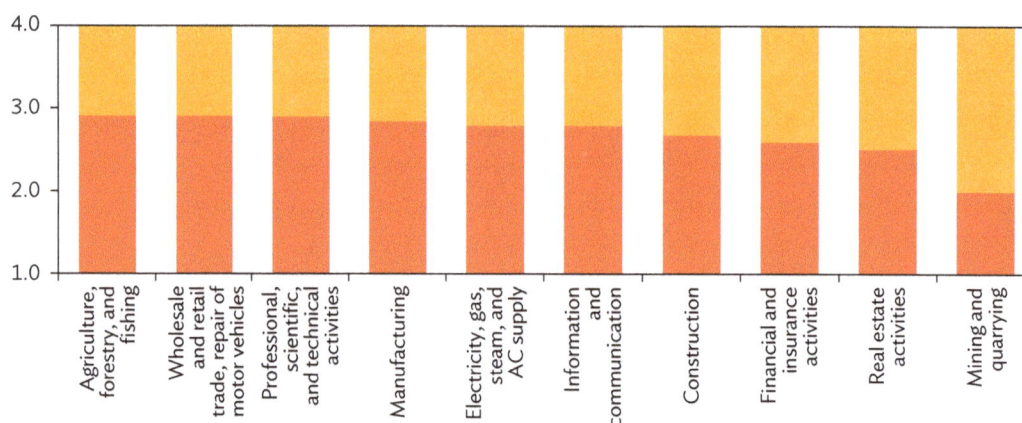

1 = easy; 4 = difficult.
Source: Viet Nam Chamber of Commerce and Industry (VCCI) and International Labour Organization Bureau for Employers' Activities. 2016. VCCI Labour Market Report: Trends in the Workplace – Skills and Labour Productivity. Ha Noi.

Figure 1.15b: Difficulty for Foreign Direct Investment Enterprises in Recruiting Technical Workers by Manufacturing Subsector

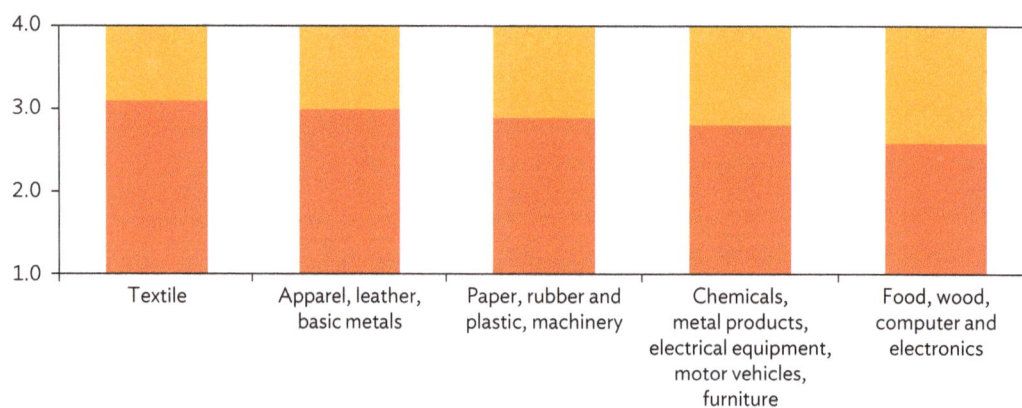

1 = easy; 4 = difficult.
Source: Viet Nam Chamber of Commerce and Industry (VCCI) and International Labour Organization Bureau for Employers' Activities. 2016. VCCI Labour Market Report: Trends in the Workplace – Skills and Labour Productivity. Ha Noi.

Figure 1.15c: Difficulty for Foreign Direct Investment Enterprises in Recruiting Managers and Supervisors by Sector

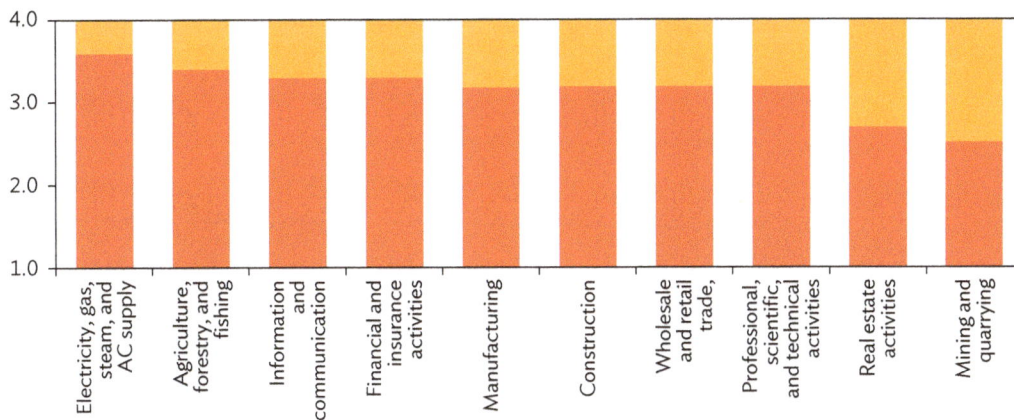

1 = easy; 4 = difficult.
Source: Viet Nam Chamber of Commerce and Industry (VCCI) and International Labour Organization Bureau for Employers' Activities. 2016. VCCI Labour Market Report: Trends in the Workplace – Skills and Labour Productivity. Ha Noi.

Figure 1.15d: Difficulty for Foreign Direct Investment Enterprises in Recruiting Managers and Supervisors by Manufacturing Subsector

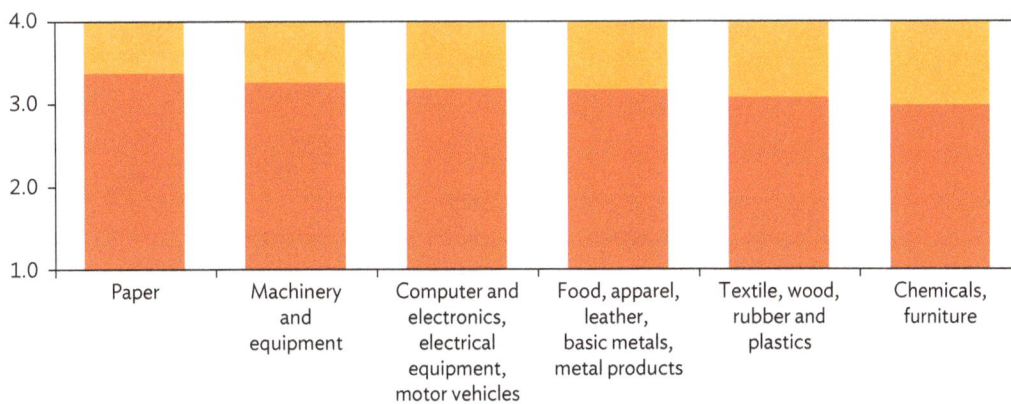

1 = easy; 4 = difficult.
Source: Viet Nam Chamber of Commerce and Industry (VCCI) and International Labour Organization Bureau for Employers' Activities. 2016. VCCI Labour Market Report: Trends in the Workplace – Skills and Labour Productivity. Ha Noi.

substantiated by the 34.3% of Vietnamese employees who answered yes when asked if their current job matches their field of study or occupational training. In total, 55.7% stated that they were not sufficiently trained (GSO 2017).

Table 1.6: Youth Unemployment Rate by Level of Education or Training
(%)

Level of Training	Whole Country	Male	Female	Urban	Rural
Total	**15.1**	**14.9**	**15.3**	**16.7**	**13.7**
Short-term TVET	7.7	8.7	0.0	7.3	7.9
Midterm vocational or professional training	9.0	9.1	8.9	11.4	7.5
College	10.1	12.9	7.9	12.0	8.4
University and higher	25.4	26.5	24.8	23.8	27.7

TVET = technical and vocational education and training.
Source: General Statistics Office of Viet Nam. 2017. Report on Labor Force Survey (Quarter 4, 2017). Ha Noi.

19. In 2017, 20.8% of about 918,000 underemployed workers were aged 15–24, although their share in the entire country's workforce accounted for only 13.8%. According to General Statistics Office (2017), underemployment (i.e., workers with education, experience, or skills beyond the requirements of their current job) is still a main issue in the agriculture sector, which covered 76.6% of all cases of underemployment, compared with 17.2% in the services sector and 6.2% in industry and construction.[12]

20. **Socioeconomic prospects.** While accounting only for 55% GDP growth in 2000–2013, macroeconomic projections show that, realistically, at least 90% of Viet Nam's future growth will emanate from its labor productivity. Since the contribution of structural transformation from agriculture to industry and services is expected to stabilize at around 20%, productivity growth in all major economic sectors would need to account for almost 80% of future labor productivity growth. And while capital deepening will continue to be essential to total factor productivity (TFP) growth, the country's human capital would need to contribute a three-quarter share to this increase (World Bank and MPI 2016).

21. Figure 1.16 reveals that the current employment structure in major industry sectors does not yet provide a promising picture of Viet Nam's preparedness for such a scenario. Particularly in its processing and manufacturing industry, which employs the vast majority of employees in Viet Nam's formal business sector, workers without or with noncertified technical qualifications comprise more than two-thirds (69.3%) of its current human capital stock. In the construction industry, Viet Nam's second largest formal employment sector, this share still accounts for almost 50%. An exception is the information and communication sector, which currently employs only about 1.3% of wageworkers.

22. Employers have constantly cited an inadequately educated workforce as one of the key obstacles to doing business in Viet Nam (see Bodewig et al. 2014). In the 2017 Executive Opinion Survey of the World Economic Forum, participants ranked this issue at the top of all business constraints (Figure 1.17a), while in the World Bank's 2015 Enterprise Survey for Viet Nam, only large companies with more than 100 employees ranked this issue among their top business environment constraints. The same World Bank survey, however, ranked the issue third in the top 10 constraints relevant to all firms (small, medium-sized, and large) (Figure 1.17b).

---

[12]   It should be noted, however, that the total rate of underemployment among Viet Nam's working age population decreased significantly from 5.41% in 2009 to only 1.66% in 2016 (GSO 2017).

Figure 1.16: Estimated Employment Structure of Enterprises of Selected Sectors as of 31 December 2016
(%)

Processing and manufacturing industry
(6,388,291 employees)

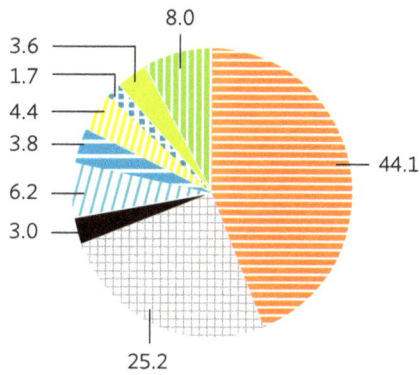

3.6
1.7
4.4
3.8
6.2
3.0
8.0
44.1
25.2

Information and communication
(165,239 employees)

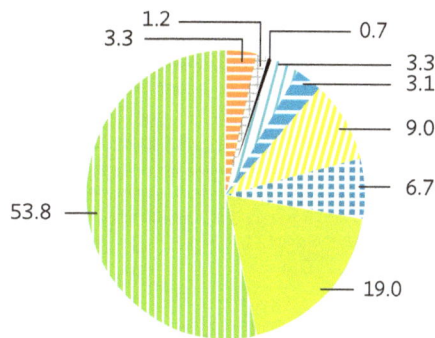

1.2
3.3
0.7
3.3
3.1
9.0
6.7
53.8
19.0

Agriculture, forestry, and aquaculture
(386,828 employees)

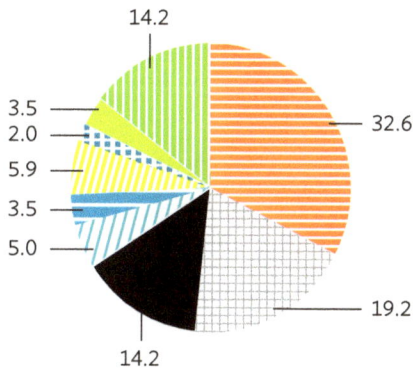

14.2
3.5
2.0
5.9
3.5
5.0
32.6
19.2
14.2

Construction
(1,718,521 employees)

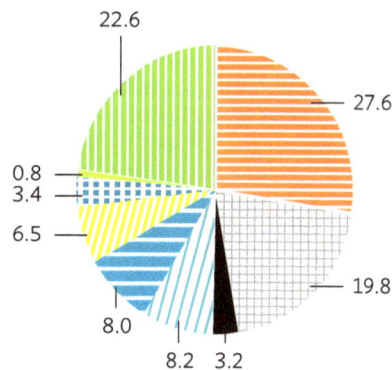

22.6
0.8
3.4
6.5
8.0
8.2   3.2
27.6
19.8

University or higher   Professional college diploma   Professional secondary   Technical qualification without certificate

TVET college diploma   TVET secondary level certificate   TVET certificate (3–12 months)   TVET certificate (<3 months)

No technical qualification

TVET = technical and vocational education and training.
Source: Ministry of Labour–Invalids and Social Affairs, Office of Employment. Investigation of Labour, Salary and Demand for Labour Use in Various Types of Enterprises in 2015. Ha Noi.

Figure 1.17a: Most Problematic Factors for Doing Business in Viet Nam

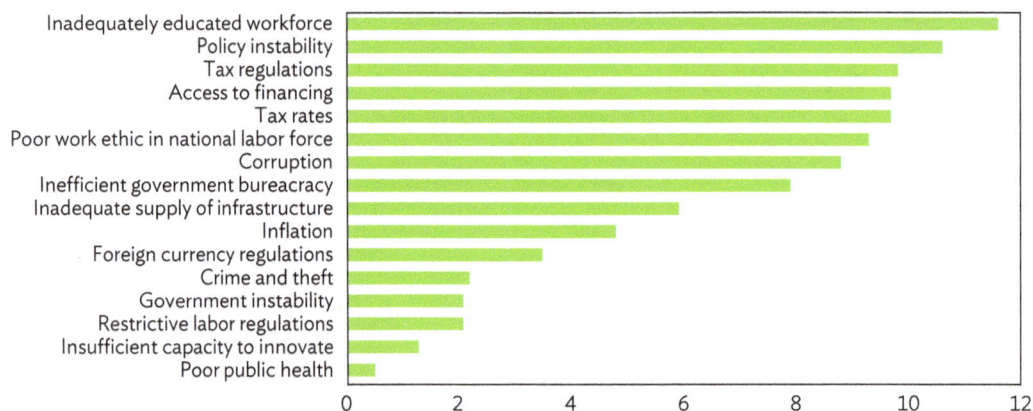

Note: From the list of factors, respondents to the World Economic Forum's Executive Opinion Survey were asked to select the five most problematic factors for doing business in their country and to rank them between 1 (most problematic) and 5. The score corresponds to the responses weighted according to their rankings.
Source: World Economic Forum. 2016. Executive Opinion Survey 2016. Geneva.

Figure 1.17b: Top 10 Business Environment Constraints
(percentage of firms)

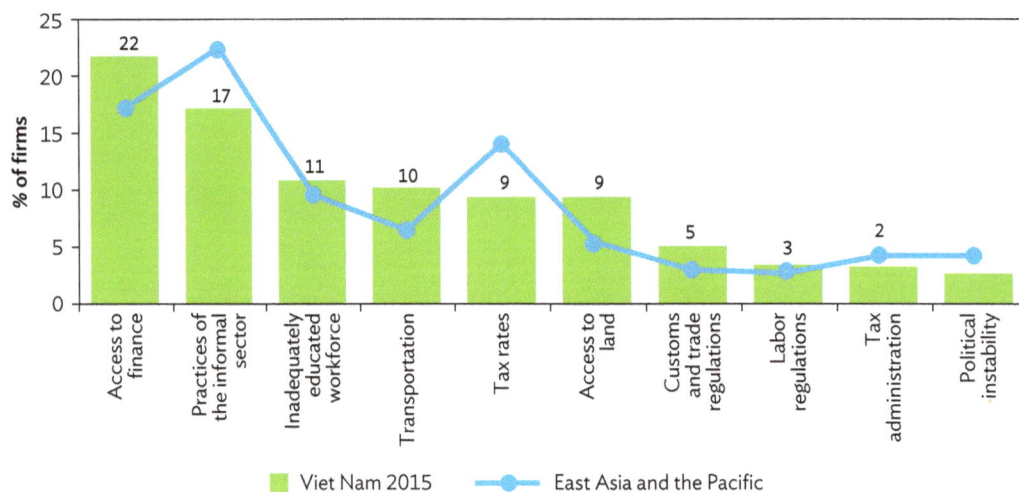

Source: World Bank. Enterprise Surveys. Washington, DC. www.enterprisesurveys.org (accessed December 2017).

23. In its long-term Socio-Economic Development Strategy 2011–2020 and subsequent Human Resources Development Master Plan, the Government of Viet Nam has recognized that substantial support in human resources development has highest priority, putting on the agenda rapid development of high-quality human resources through comprehensive renovation of the national education system. These plans focus on general education, higher education, and technical and vocational education and training (TVET) and are backed up by important amendments of respective

legal frameworks. So far, however, these reform efforts have not yet achieved a tangible breakthrough. Especially and particularly with regard to TVET, Viet Nam's industry and business community has remained largely critical.

24. Based on its 2015 surveys, the Viet Nam Chamber of Commerce and Industry (VCCI) presented enterprise ratings on the quality of vocational training (Figure 1.18a), with scores ranging between 2.03 and 3.52 depending on different locations (urban/rural) on a scale of 1 (very bad) to 6 (very good). Foreign enterprises gave the highest average score of only 2.57 (i.e., poor to slightly poor) for TVET in Ha Noi. In different industry sectors, ratings varied highly, with manufacture of textiles and wood processing scoring the lowest (Figure 1.18b).

Figure 1.18a: Industry Ratings of General and Vocational Educational Quality by Location
(1=very bad; 6=very good)

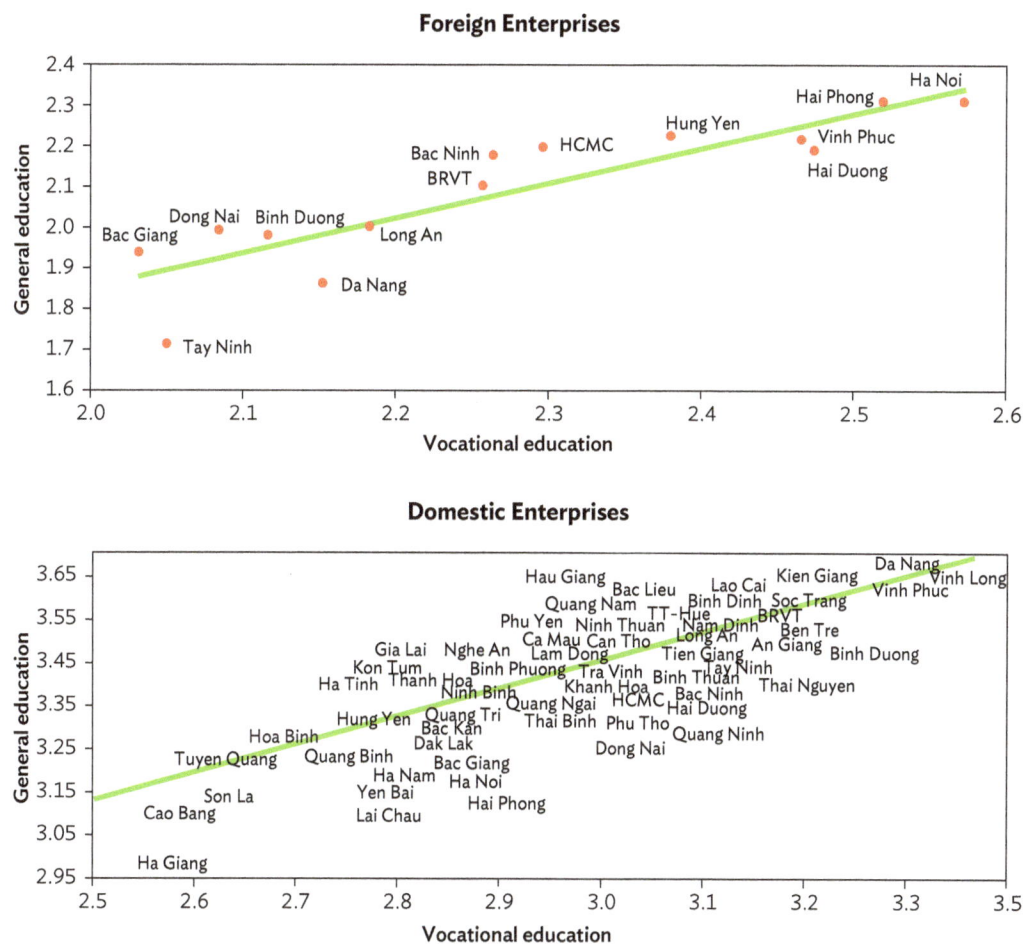

HCMC = Ho Chi Minh City.
Source: Viet Nam Chamber of Commerce and Industry (VCCI) and International Labour Organization Bureau for Employers' Activities. 2016. VCCI Labour Market Report: Trends in the Workplace – Skills and Labour Productivity. Ha Noi.

Figure 1.18b: Industry Ratings of General and Vocational Educational Quality by Sector
(1=very bad; 6=very good)

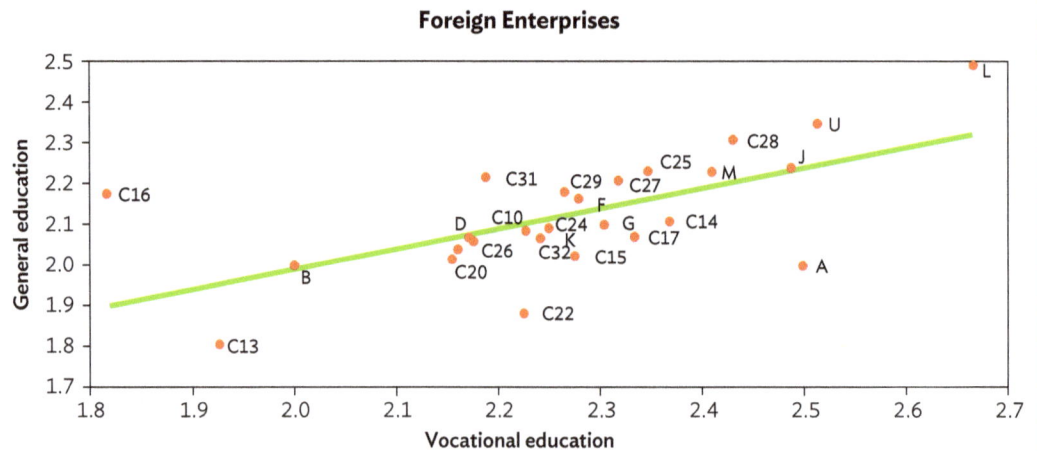

Foreign Enterprises

A	Agriculture, forestry, and fishing
B	Mining and quarrying
C	Manufacturing
D	Electricity, gas, steam, and air-conditioning supply
F	Construction
G	Wholesale and retail trade, repair of motor vehicles and motorcycles
J	Information and communication
K	Financial and insurance activities
L	Real estate activities
M	Professional, scientific, and technical activities
U	Activities of extraterritorial organizations and bodies

C10	Food
C13	Textile
C14	Apparel
C15	Leather and related
C16	Wood and related
C17	Paper
C20	Chemicals
C22	Rubber and plastic
C24	Basic metals
C25	Metal products
C26	Computer, electronics
C27	Electrical equipment
C28	Machinery and equipment
C29	Motor vehicles
C31	Furniture
C32	Others

Source: Viet Nam Chamber of Commerce and Industry (VCCI) and International Labour Organization Bureau for Employers' Activities. 2016. VCCI Labour Market Report: Trends in the Workplace – Skills and Labour Productivity. Ha Noi.

25. Earlier studies revealed that TVET graduates do not have enough industry-relevant occupational skills and lack fundamental soft skills such as working style, teamwork competence, and problem-solving abilities. Prevailing reasons for this relate to the TVET system's persistent focus on school-based training delivery with low involvement of enterprises and a wide range of system-immanent problems such as the lack of instructors with industry experience and practical skills, poor performance and output standards, lack of independent assessments of graduates as well as inefficient management and financing structures.

II. Skills Supply: Viet Nam's TVET System

1. System Structure, Governance, and Coverage

26. Over the past 4 decades, different agencies have supervised the technical and vocational education and training (TVET) system in Viet Nam (Figures 2.1a and 2.1b). In addition, a variety of education and training institutions have provided TVET, and multiple government and local organizations still administer TVET such as

(i) various line ministries (Ministry of Industry and Trade, Ministry of Agriculture and Rural Development, Ministry of Transport, Ministry of Construction, Ministry of Defence, and Ministry of Culture, Sports and Tourism, etc.);

(ii) education and labor ministries (Ministry of Education and Training [MOET] and Ministry of Labour–Invalids and Social Affairs [MOLISA]);

(iii) provincial, city, and district governments through their respective People's Committees;

(iv) enterprises and cooperatives; and

(v) social and economic organizations (e.g., Viet Nam Women's Union and the Viet Nam Labor Federation).

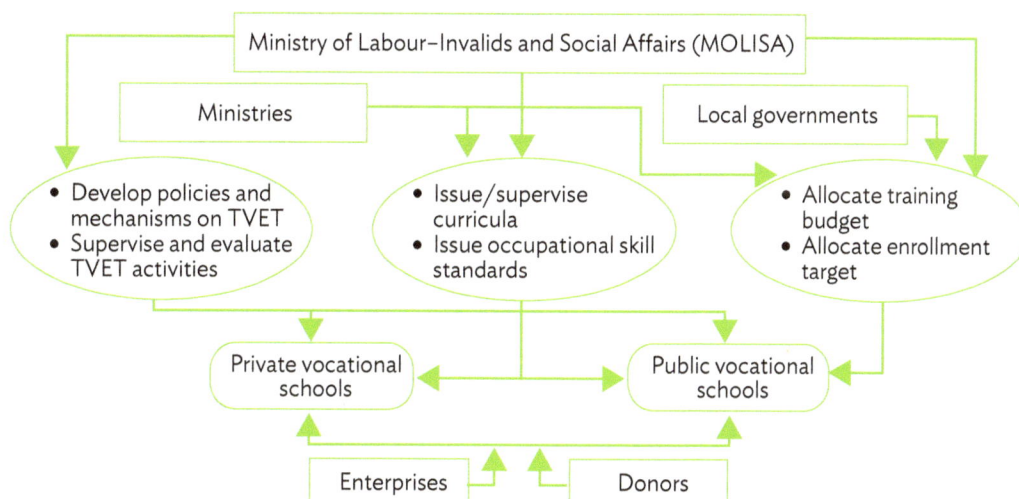

Figure 2.1a: Synopsis of TVET Governance in Viet Nam

TVET = technical and vocational education and training.
Source: Minh Thao Ta. 2017. Vietnam. In Economic Policy Forum. The Role of the Private Sector in Vocational and Educational Training: Developments and Success Factors in Selected Countries. *EPF Working Paper*. pp. 63–79.

Figure 2.1b: History of National Governance Bodies for Vocational Training 1953–2016

MOL	**Government**	**MOET**	**MOLISA**
Human Resource Management Department	General Directorate of Vocational Training (GDVT)	Department of Vocational Training	Directorate of Vocational Education and Training (DVET)

1953   1969   1978   1987   1990   1998   2016

MoL	**MOHVS**	**MoLISA**
General Department for Training of Technical Workers	Department of Vocational Training	Genral Directorate of Vocational Training (GDVT)

MOET = Ministry of Education and Training, MOHVS = Ministry of Higher Education and Vocational Services, MOL = Ministry of Labor, MOLISA = Ministry of Labour–Invalids and Social Affairs.
Source: Information provided by Phan Chinh Thuc, former Director General of the General Department of Vocational Training.

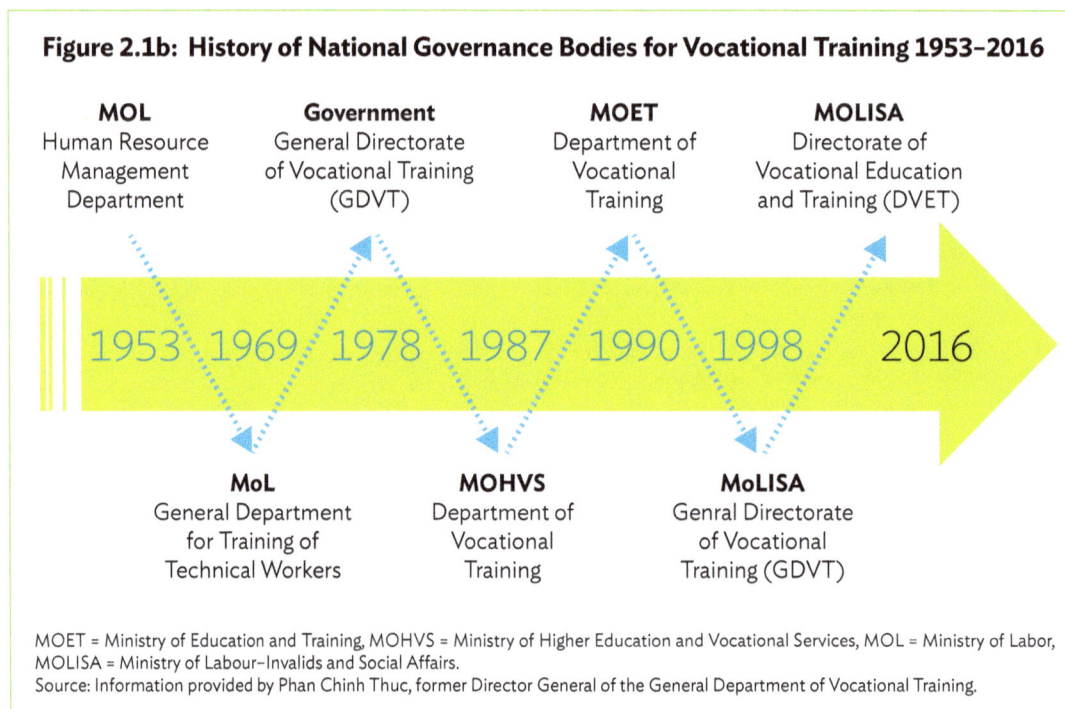

These organizations are responsible for "direct management" tasks, which not only include establishing, funding, and appointing management staff but also ensuring the quality of their vocational education and training (VET) institutions.

27. Up to the end of 2016, a dual structure offered two distinct TVET tracks in parallel (Figure 2.2):

(1) **Institutions supervised by MOLISA** offered formal TVET to three levels for secondary school graduates:

(i) Elementary TVET (3–12 months) at vocational training centers (VTCs);

(ii) Intermediate TVET (3–4 years or 1–2 years)[14] at vocational secondary schools (*Trung cấp nghề*);

(iii) Higher TVET (3 years) at vocational colleges (*Cao đăng nghề*); and

(iv) VTCs also offer short-term nonformal skills training (up to 3 months) for unemployed youth and workers.[15]

---

[14] Training is offered depending on entrance qualifications of students (lower secondary or upper secondary graduates).

[15] A significant scope of short-term courses is focusing on agricultural training for rural workers and are funded by a national target program of the government.

Figure 2.2 : Basic Overview of Viet Nam's TVET System and Different School Forms

Education System

School Forms in TVET

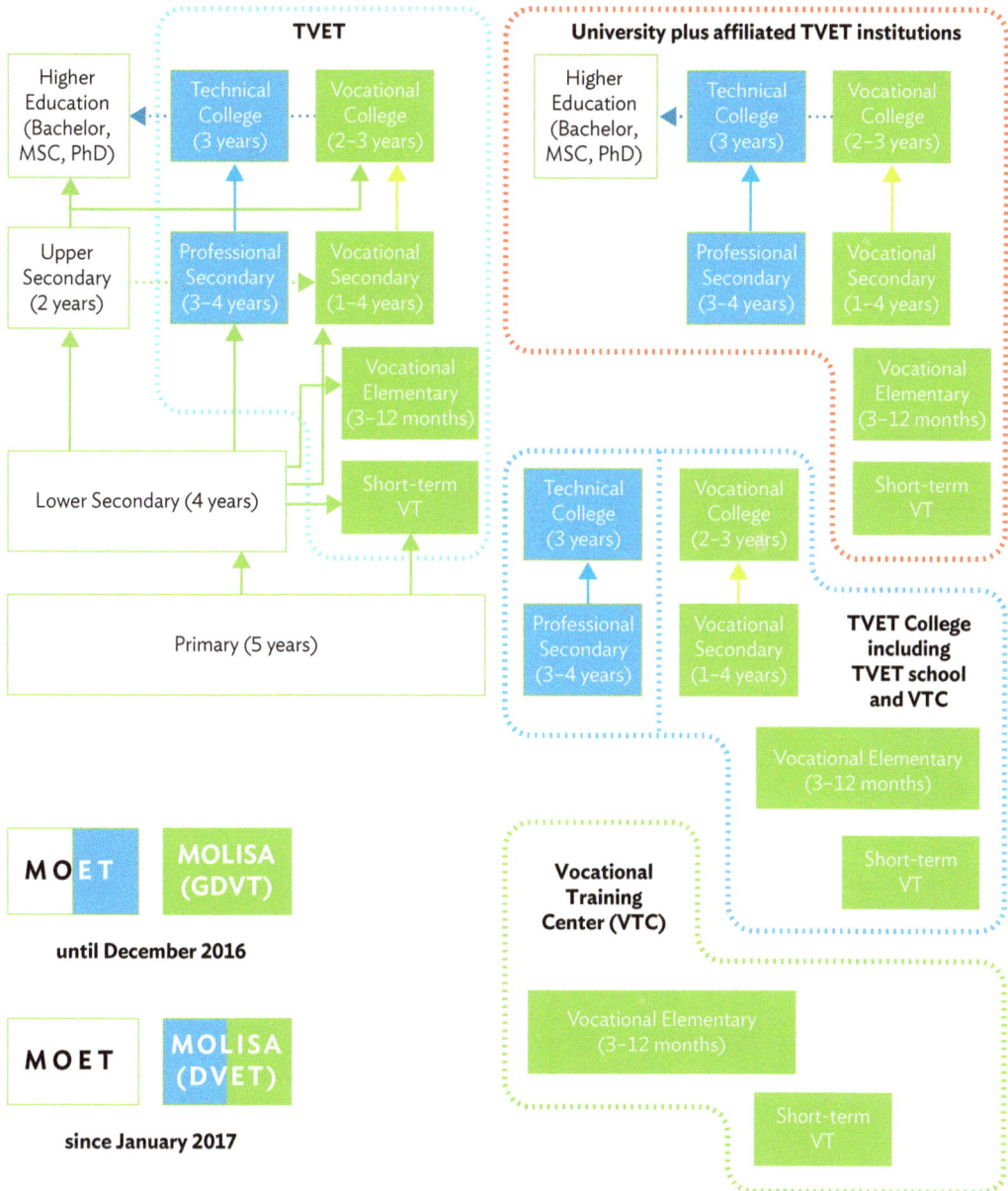

DVET = Directorate of Vocational Education and Training, GDVT = General Directorate of Vocational Training, MOET = Ministry of Education and Training, MOLISA = Ministry of Labour–Invalids and Social Affairs, TVET = technical and vocational education and training, VT = vocational training.
Source: Author.

Respective vocational certificates were awarded for training at elementary and intermediate level TVET, while a diploma[16] or an associate degree[17] is earned after training at vocational college level.

(2) **Institutions under the governance of the Ministry of Education and Training (MOET)** provided formal technical and professional education in professional secondary schools (*Trung cấp chuyên nghiệp*) and technical colleges (*Cao đẳng*) as well as some short-term training. In scope, these institutions covered more than half of the total number of TVET colleges and secondary schools (Figure 2.3). The main differences between the two streams under MOET and MOLISA were in the proportions of theory and practice in the curriculum of each stream and the orientation toward generic technical subjects versus more occupation-specific vocational skills. Previous rigid restrictions in the pathways between the two streams have been gradually removed[18] and the proportion of theory and practice has become more standardized across the two types of institutions.

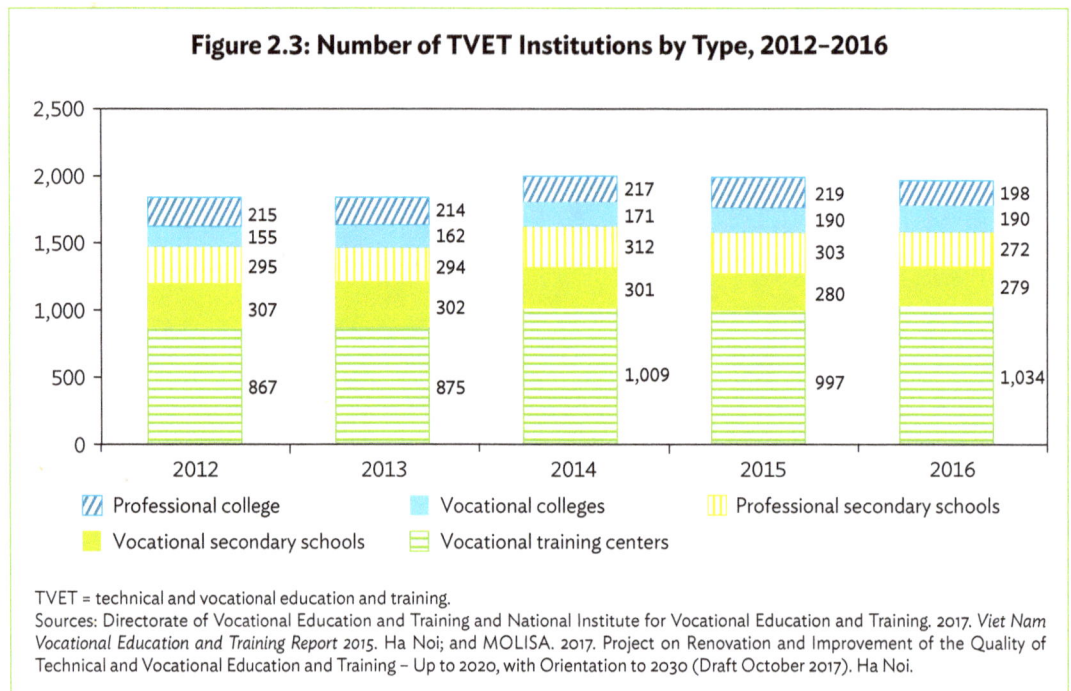

Figure 2.3: Number of TVET Institutions by Type, 2012–2016

TVET = technical and vocational education and training.
Sources: Directorate of Vocational Education and Training and National Institute for Vocational Education and Training. 2017. *Viet Nam Vocational Education and Training Report 2015*. Ha Noi; and MOLISA. 2017. Project on Renovation and Improvement of the Quality of Technical and Vocational Education and Training – Up to 2020, with Orientation to 2030 (Draft October 2017). Ha Noi.

28. In the wake of a new TVET law enacted in November 2014 (being effective in July 2015), both tracks have been legally merged into one system under MOLISA's Directorate of Vocational Education and Training (DVET), which now acts as the single central "state management" agency for TVET.[19]

---

[16]   Diploma programs require 1 to 2.5 years of full-time study after upper secondary school or 3 to 4 years after lower secondary school. Graduates may apply for admission to university.

[17]   Associates degrees require 2 to 3.5 years of full-time study (or 100 to 180 credits) at a college. Students must have completed secondary school and passed an admissions examination for entry. The curriculum tends to have a larger theoretical component than other vocational programs, but still retains a practical focus.

[18]   Previously, only graduates of professional secondary schools were eligible to enter colleges and universities, while graduates of vocational secondary schools could not enter a technical college and graduates of vocational colleges could not enter a university. Meanwhile, a graduate of a vocational college may proceed to university after having completed his/her study.

[19]   Government Resolution No. 76/NQ-CP of 3 September 2016 decided that MOLISA would be the state management agency on vocational education and the Ministry of Education and Training is the state management agency on pedagogical schools. Accordingly, 201 colleges and 303 professional secondary schools were handed over to MOLISA. From 2017 onward, these schools will admit learners based on the regulations promulgated in accordance with the Law on Vocational Education. GDVT's organizational structure is demonstrated in Appendix 2.

Operationally, the merger took effect in January 2017 and will lead to substantial alignments regarding school accreditation and program certification. Because of the diversity of institutions, the DVET has intensified its focus on stipulating standard procedures and criteria by issuing a torrent of circulars and decrees. All institutions must maintain thick books of orders and regulations they are supposed to follow. However, with each sector agency handling its own institutions, there is often little or even no coordination between national and provincial administrative levels and among ministries. Unfortunately, there is still no central database or management system providing consistent and reliable data on TVET institutions across all levels and agencies.[20]

29. In 2017, the central ministries owned almost a third (32%) of the institutions at the college level, while provincial People's Committees managed about 40% of them. At the intermediate level, the central government manages only 6% of the institutions, while 21% are known to be directly managed by People's Committees.[21] At the elementary level, local governments and sociopolitical organizations directly managed approximately 70% of the institutions (VTCs), while private owners (14%) or enterprises (17%) run more than 30%. Appendix 3 provides a synopsis of ownership distribution of Viet Nam's TVET institutions.

30. Since many institutions do not only offer programs from both tracks but also different levels of TVET courses at their facilities (Figure 2.2), obtaining a clear and accurate count of TVET institutions is complicated. As regulated by Article 23 of the TVET Law, higher-level institutions can and typically do offer lower-level training. For instance, some universities offer college-level as well as secondary-level TVET of both tracks (MOET and MOLISA) and provide even elementary-level training as well as short-term courses. Colleges tend to offer also intermediate-level TVET, elementary training, and short-term courses, while vocational secondary schools can also offer elementary-level courses and short-term training. Since teachers and lecturers of these institutions sometimes teach at more than one level, obtaining relevant statistical data on staff distribution is also difficult.

31. **Coverage.** Since 2011, the network of TVET institutes has expanded considerably and partly aligned to particular economic sectors, regions, and localities. For 2017, MOLISA reported a total number of 388 vocational and technical colleges (including 199 technical colleges formerly supervised under MOET), 22% (84) of them being private. On the secondary level comprising 279 institutions from MOLISA and 272 professional schools formerly supervised by MOET, 551 are intermediate vocational and professional schools, almost half of them (243) privately run. VTCs still make up the bulk of Viet Nam's TVET institutions accounting for a total number of 1,036, of which 240 are private.[22] Figures 2.3 and 2.4 show the changes in the number of TVET institutions between 2012 and 2016 and the regional distribution of TVET institutions in 2015.

---

[20] MOLISA is working on data collection from previous MOET institutions but announced during a meeting in July 2017 that respective data will be available only in 2020.

[21] The DVET could not clearly identify the ownership of about 50% of vocational secondary schools.

[22] These figures, however, should be taken with care, as they are not congruent with the actual number of TVET facilities, which often comprise institutional units on several TVET levels (cf. section above).

Figure 2.4: Number of Vocational Education and Training Institutions by Region, 2016

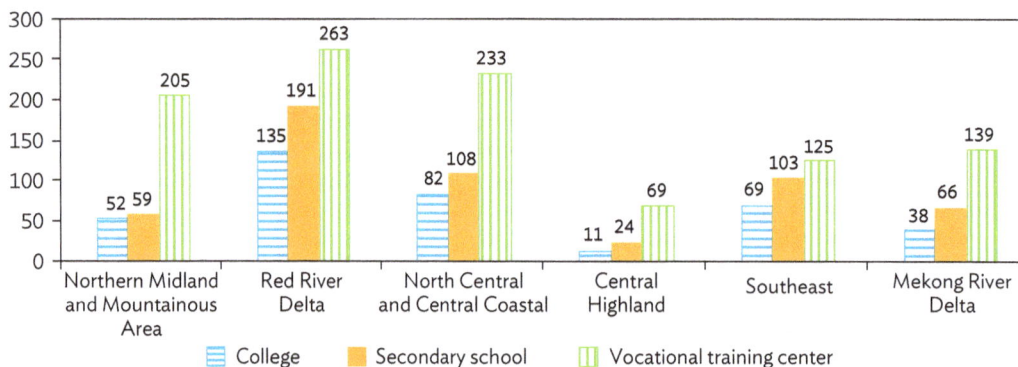

Source: Directorate of Vocational Education and Training and National Institute for Vocational Education and Training. 2017. *Viet Nam Vocational Education and Training Report 2016*. Ha Noi.

32. **Enrollments.** In 2016, 290,231 students were enrolled in Viet Nam's vocational and professional secondary schools, while vocational and technical colleges enrolled 241,411 students (Figure 2.5a). Yet, enrollments in both TVET subsectors were decreasing between 2011 and 2015, particularly in the professional secondary schools and technical colleges formerly governed by MOET (Figure 2.5b).[23]

Figure 2.5a: Number of Students Enrolled in Vocational Education and Training Institutions by Supervising Ministry, SY2011–2016

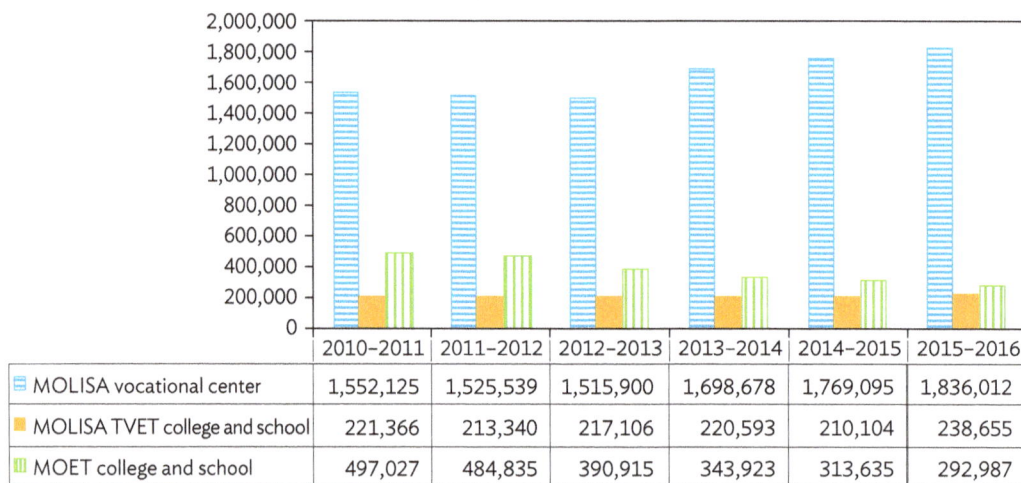

	2010–2011	2011–2012	2012–2013	2013–2014	2014–2015	2015–2016
MOLISA vocational center	1,552,125	1,525,539	1,515,900	1,698,678	1,769,095	1,836,012
MOLISA TVET college and school	221,366	213,340	217,106	220,593	210,104	238,655
MOET college and school	497,027	484,835	390,915	343,923	313,635	292,987

MOET = Ministry of Education and Training, MOLISA = Ministry of Labour–Invalids and Social Affairs, SY = school year, VET = vocational education and training.
Sources: Directorate of Vocational Education and Training and National Institute for Vocational Education and Training. 2017. *Viet Nam Vocational Education and Training Report 2016*. Ha Noi; and MOLISA. 2017. Project on Renovation and Improvement of the Quality of Technical and Vocational Education and Training – Up to 2020, with Orientation to 2030 (Draft October 2017). Ha Noi.

---

[23] In MOET's professional secondary schools during this period, annual student enrollments decreased by 35.6% and in its technical colleges 38.4%. At the same time annual enrollment in vocational secondary schools and vocational colleges under MOLISA decreased by 8.9% and 1.8%, respectively. One of the reasons reported for this is that many universities were newly established or upgraded from colleges before 2011, which competed with TVET schools in recruiting high school graduates. High unemployment rates of university graduates, however, seem to have shifted the preferences of high school graduates and their parents back to colleges to find jobs more easily after graduation.

Figure 2.5b: Development of Enrollments in Vocational Education and Training Institutions at Intermediate and Diploma Levels, SY2011–2016

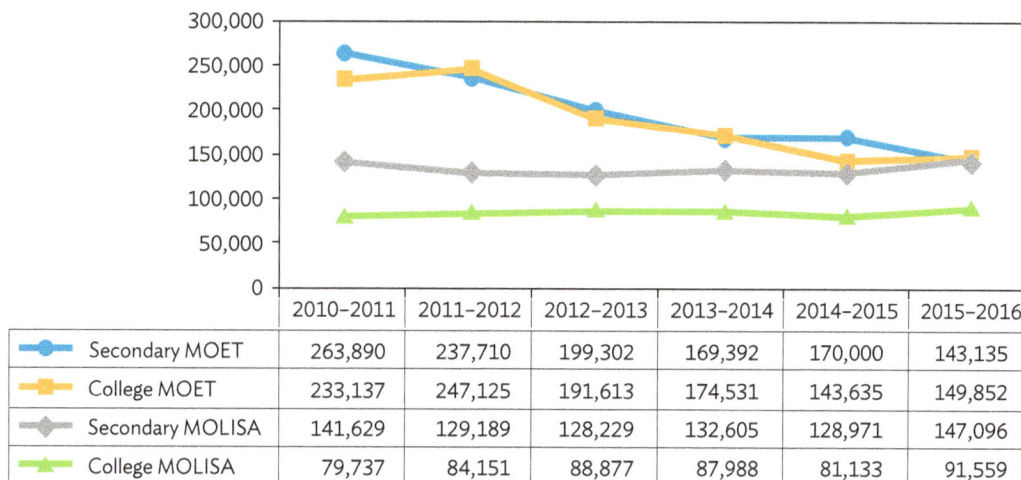

	2010–2011	2011–2012	2012–2013	2013–2014	2014–2015	2015–2016
Secondary MOET	263,890	237,710	199,302	169,392	170,000	143,135
College MOET	233,137	247,125	191,613	174,531	143,635	149,852
Secondary MOLISA	141,629	129,189	128,229	132,605	128,971	147,096
College MOLISA	79,737	84,151	88,877	87,988	81,133	91,559

MOET = Ministry of Education and Training, MOLISA = Ministry of Labour–Invalids and Social Affairs, SY = school year.
Sources: Directorate of Vocational Education and Training and National Institute for Vocational Education and Training. 2017. *Viet Nam Vocational Education and Training Report 2016*. Ha Noi; and MOLISA. 2017. Project on Renovation and Improvement of the Quality of Technical and Vocational Education and Training – Up to 2020, with Orientation to 2030 (Draft October 2017). Ha Noi.

33. A different situation applies to TVET enrollments at elementary level and in short-term courses offered by VTCs (1,836,012 in 2016). Between 2011 and 2015, total enrollments in VTCs accounted for a share of 88% of all TVET enrollments (7.8 million) in the country. In more than half of the cases (4.1 million), students were granted access to these types of training through the National Target Program for Rural Vocational Training (Project 1956) including financial support for over 2.7 million people. This led to a dramatic increase in the enrollments for short-term courses (under 3 months), while enrollments in formal elementary training (3–12 months) significantly decreased (Figure 2.6).[24] Moreover, MOLISA (2016) reported that some rural provinces have difficulty enrolling students in formal intermediate and higher-level TVET programs. Although, in recent reviews, MOLISA had to conclude that "vocational training for rural laborers was not really efficient,"[25] the program has continued in 2016 for another 1.72 million people and is expected to enroll a total of 5.73 million–7.9 million people between 2017 and 2020.

---

[24] According to MOLISA's recent review, the vocational training strategy for 2011–2015 was to train about 9.6 million people, of which the number of trained people at intermediate and college level should have been about 2.1 million people. By 2015, 9.1 million people had been trained, of which 1.1 million people were trained at intermediate and college level. The enrollment rate at intermediate and college level reached only 53% of the plan; the enrollment rate at intermediate professional level decreases by 15% per year and at college level by 18% per year (MOLISA 2017).

[25] According to MOLISA (2017), "the number of unemployed graduates was high (about 30%) and tended to increase." MOLISA (2016) indicates that the vast majority of training graduates (80%) become self-employed after the training, "the number of rural workers who, after the vocational training, were employed by enterprises through working contracts (...) by enterprises was still small. The number of workers studying nonagricultural occupations to change their jobs into industry and service sectors was low. Most of them participated in agricultural training and after the vocational training continued to work in agriculture sector. Due to difficult natural, socio-economic and trading conditions, their jobs were not sustainable."

Figure 2.6: Development of Enrollments in Vocational Training Centers by Type of Training, 2012–2015

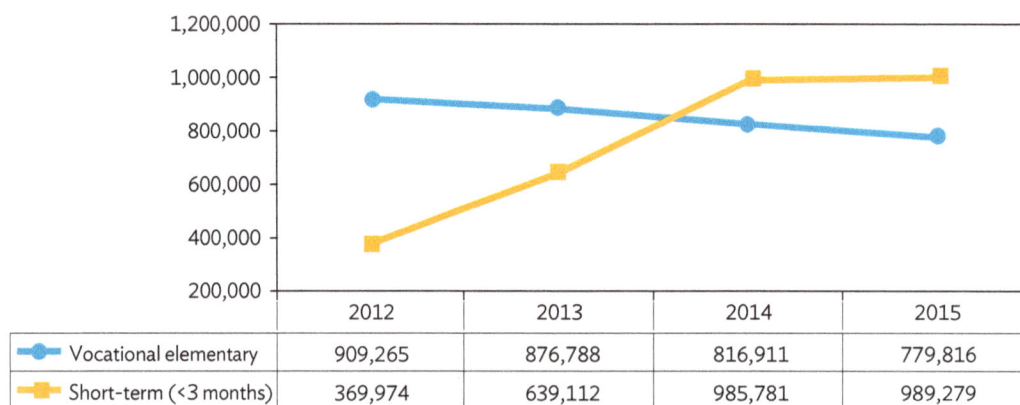

	2012	2013	2014	2015
Vocational elementary	909,265	876,788	816,911	779,816
Short-term (<3 months)	369,974	639,112	985,781	989,279

Source: Directorate of Vocational Education and Training and National Institute for Vocational Education and Training. 2017. *Viet Nam Vocational Education and Training Report 2015*. Ha Noi.

2. Access to TVET (Socioeconomic, Ethnic, and Gender-Related Conditions)

34. Statistical surveys consistently show large gaps by gender and geographic areas (urban/rural) in the share of the population with technical and professional training at all training levels, with no apparent trend of narrowing (GSO 2016a). Specifically, the proportion of the population in rural areas with college or lower levels of vocational education was almost half of that in urban areas. In 2015, still only 3.9% (1.7% female) had participated in vocational training, 3.1% were graduates of midterm professional training, and 2% have college qualifications. Only 3.8% have a university degree compared with 19.2% in urban regions (GSO 2015) (Figure 2.7).

35. Unfortunately, disaggregated data regarding socioeconomic background and ethnicity of TVET enrollments across different levels on a nationwide scale are still not available. Sample reports investigating the situation of TVET in specific socioeconomic regions provide only randomly selected information in this regard, e.g., by evaluating the effectiveness of activities under the national target program for rural workers, which basically focuses on pre-intermediate TVET and continuing training. According to MOLISA (2016), the majority of rural workers participating in such types of training in the Northern Midlands and Mountains between 2013 and 2015 were ethnic minority people (62%) and poor and near-poor people (19%). These reports do not provide disaggregated data on the enrollment structures of higher TVET levels.

36. For people in remote areas, few TVET institutions with boarding facilities,[26] which are mostly located in the provincial capital cities,[27] are generally the only option. Yet, promoting access to TVET

---

[26] In 2015, 16 TVET institutes countrywide specialized in vocational training for ethnic minority people (2 vocational colleges and 14 vocational secondary schools) and some vocational training faculties established for ethnic minority people at some vocational colleges (DVET and NIVET 2017).

[27] Government policies on national and provincial levels to merge the small TVET institutions spreading across districts into the bigger ones of capital cities to manage them more efficiently may further contribute to this constraint, rather than solve the issue.

Figure 2.7: Share of Trained Labor Force Aged 15+, 2015
(%)

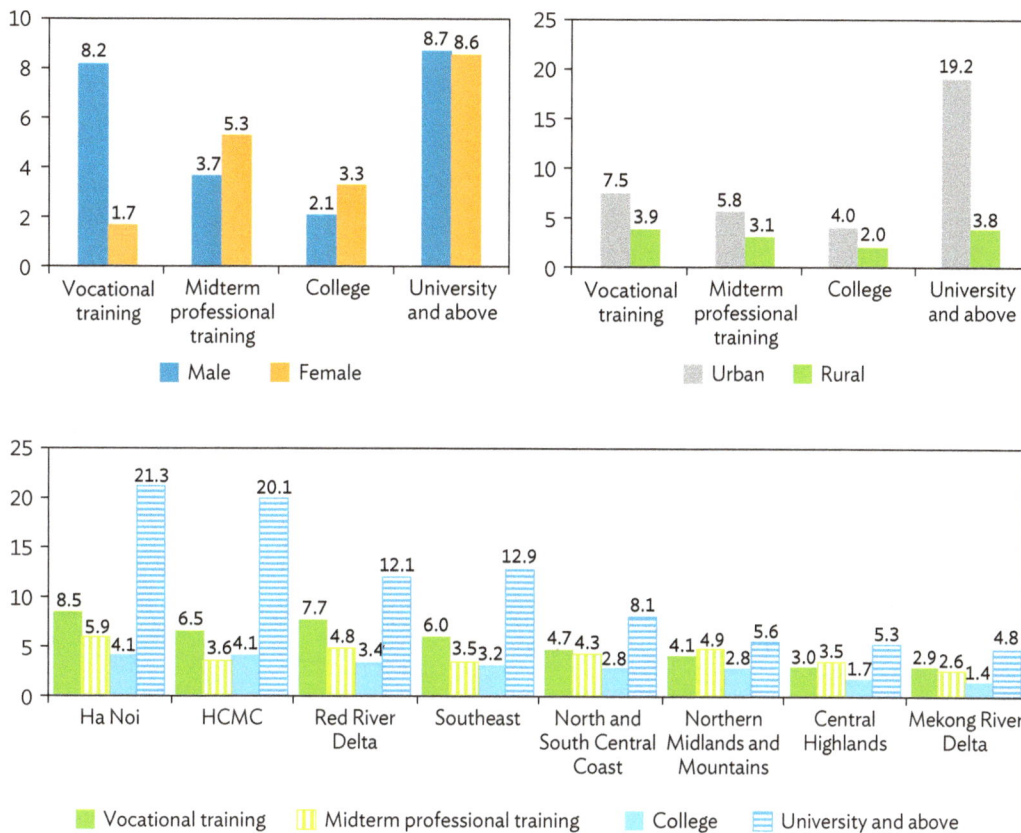

HCMC = Ho Chi Minh City.
Source: General Statistics Office of Viet Nam. 2016. *Major Findings – The 1/4/2015 Time-Point Population Change and Family Planning Survey.* Ha Noi.

remains prominent in Viet Nam's human resources development (HRD) policy framework, and is supported extensively by several policy propositions on TVET system development in the new TVET law and subsequent regulations. By stipulating exemptions from or reductions of tuition fees and granting other allowances[28] for ethnic minority students living in remote ("disadvantaged or severely disadvantaged") areas and/or from poor households[29] and for other disadvantaged groups (including disabled persons), the government stays committed to facilitate broad participation in TVET.

37. Decree No. 57 dated 9 May 2017 supports students from 16 ethnic minorities to proceed from lower secondary education to TVET institutions at basic and intermediate level and from high schools to enter TVET colleges and universities without taking entrance exams. It also regulates eligibilities of this group to receive financial support. Decree No. 86 dated October 2015 regulates tuition fees

---

[28]   Special government programs (e.g., 135 and 30a) provide financial subsidies to poor students.

[29]   Half of students living in poverty are from an ethnic minority, and most ethnic minority students live in remote rural areas. Poverty among ethnic minority groups is closely associated with low or limited access to educational and training opportunities (ADB 2016c).

and stipulates that 15 disadvantaged groups are exempted from paying fees to participate in training and education programs. Joint Circular No. 09 dated 30 March 2016 regulates tuition fees in public education and training institutions including fee exemptions for students from disadvantaged areas, ethnic minorities, poor households, and people with disabilities. Decision No. 971/QD-TTg dated July 2015 also stipulates that high-quality TVET programs should prioritize access to workers from poor and near-poor areas, members from ethnic minority households that depend on agriculture farming, and disabled people and fishermen.

38. To enter TVET at elementary level, a lower secondary education remains a prerequisite and still many young people among Viet Nam's disadvantaged populations are not achieving this status[30] (Table 2.1 and Figure 2.8). For these, the government provides the option to participate in an increasing number of nonformal short-term courses, which are largely subsidized through a respective national target program.[31] MOLISA (2016) reports that between 2010 and 2015 in the Northern Midlands and Mountainous Region, Viet Nam's poorest socioeconomic region,[32] 573,000 rural workers (7.6% of this region's total labor force in 2015) were trained through this program, 61.6% of them on agricultural occupations and 38.4% on nonagricultural occupations. In 2016, 65.2% of course participants were ethnic minority people, 9% were people from poor households, and 0.6% were people with disabilities (MOLISA 2016).

Table 2.1: Net Enrollment by Ethnic Group and Education Level, 2014

	Primary	Lower Secondary	Upper Secondary
Kinh	93.4	86.9	69.0
Tay	93.4	89.6	66.3
Thai	93.2	81.3	32.8
Hoa	95.6	90.3	65.0
Khome	89.1	59.9	24.1
Muong	89.2	90.3	62.7
Nung	96.5	89.2	51.2
H'mong	89.4	57.3	18.3
Dao	90.5	71.5	19.5
Others	90.5	66.7	32.9

Note: Relevant data for the technical and vocational education and training sector are not available.
Source: General Statistics Office of Viet Nam. 2016. *Major Findings –The 1/4/2015 Time-Point Population Change and Family Planning Survey.* Ha Noi.

39. Unfortunately, however, there are no clear arrangements yet showing how short-term course certificates are valued in the national qualification framework with regard to the option for further advancements (pathways) toward the formal TVET system. Comprehensive data disaggregating the socioeconomic background of students entering the formal TVET system and indicating how many

[30] According to the education sector assessment in ADB (2018), about 430,000 youths (240,250 boys and 189,750 girls) of lower secondary education age were not enrolled in SY2015/16.

[31] According to MOLISA's 2015 TVET Report, about 900,000 rural workers were trained under this program in 2015, of which about 550,000 benefited from state support (DVET and NIVET 2017).

[32] The region has 45 of the 63 poorest districts in the country. In 2015, this region had about 15% of poor households compared with the national rate of less than 10%.

Figure 2.8: Unequal Distribution of Students in Secondary and Tertiary Education

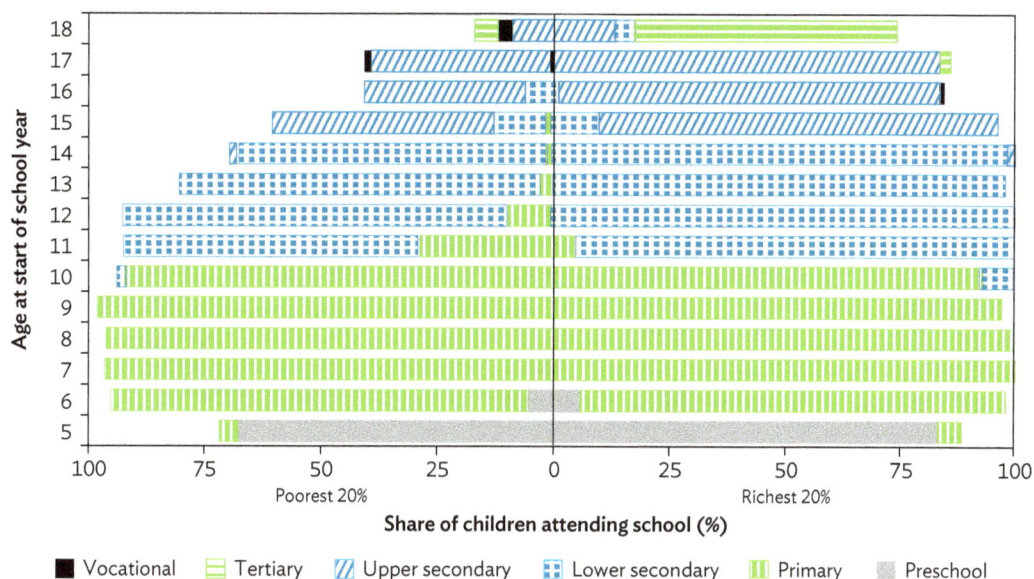

Source: World Bank and the Ministry of Planning and Investment of Viet Nam. 2016. *Vietnam 2035: Toward Prosperity, Creativity, Equity, and Democracy*. Washington, DC: World Bank.

of them are supported by state subsidies are not available. [33] Yet, despite government incentives to channel enrollments from lower secondary schools into formal intermediate TVET, Viet Nam citizens' preference for general education qualifications (upper secondary education/university) seems to strongly challenge the attraction to TVET. As Figure 2.9a shows, only about 4% of lower secondary graduates proceed annually to vocational secondary schools and less than 2% of them decide to continue their studies at professional secondary schools. Figure 2.9b shows a potential reason for this.

40. During the last 1.5 decades, admission of upper secondary graduates to higher education institutions has eased considerably as a result of increasing the number of places and lowering the aspiration level of entrance exams. At the same time, increasing tuition fees for vocational training programs at intermediate and college levels accompanied by unclear conditions regarding employment prospects and future wage returns for TVET graduates have made public TVET institutions unfavorable. Managers of TVET institutions complain about the limited interests students can pursue in classic vocational majors and the increasing struggle to maintain their annual enrollment targets.

41. To a significant extent also, TVET institutions and their management bodies can be made responsible for this situation. The Vocational Training Report 2013–2014 (NIVT 2015) stated, "the work of career guidance and streaming of secondary school graduates was not effective, resulting in a very low rate of lower secondary school leavers entering vocational training and technical secondary education. Materials for career guidance and consultation are not regularly updated; career guidance activities at secondary schools are largely superficial and usually integrated into other activities."

---

[33]　GSO's Household Living Standards Survey 2014 provides only general data on fee exemptions/reductions for education. According to this survey, the total share of people benefiting from school fee or contribution reduction or exemptions was 43.2% (GSO 2014).

**Figure 2.9a: Streams of Lower Secondary School Graduates
to Higher Secondary Schools, 2009–2012**

(%)

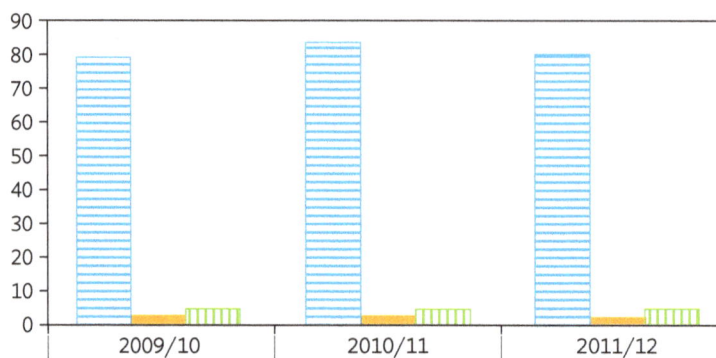

	2009/10	2010/11	2011/12
To general upper secondary school	79.15	83.65	80.36
To professional secondary school	2.09	2.18	1.88
To vocational secondary school	4.01	4.28	4.00

Source: General Department of Vocational Training and National Institute for Vocational Training. 2015. *Vocational Training Report – Viet Nam 2013–2014*. Ha Noi.

**Figure 2.9b: Number of Upper Secondary Graduates with Certificates for Higher
Education Studies Compared with the Number of Places Available in
Higher Education Institutions**

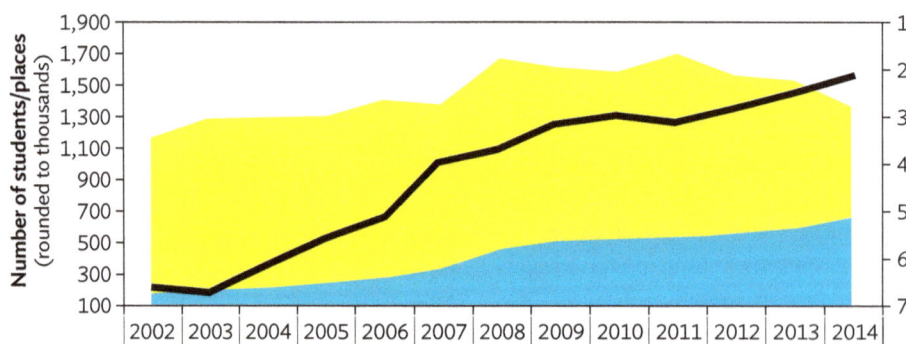

	2002	2003	2004	2005	2006	2007	2008	2009	2010	2011	2012	2013	2014
Number of certified graduates	1,162	1,287	1,301	1,300	1,397	1,368	1,664	1,615	1,589	1,698	1,564	1,528	1,372
Number of HE places	176	192	212	17.6	271	346	449	509	528	543	557	604	640
Admission rate (graduates per place)	6.62	6.71	6.13	27.3	5.16	3.96	3.71	3.17	3.01	3.12	2.81	2.53	2.14

HE = higher education.
Note: Right-hand scale: Rate of upper secondary graduates per study place.
Source: Author, based on Ministry of Education and Training data provided by Phan Chinh Thuc, former Director General of the General Department of Vocational Training.

42. **Gender equality.** A 2017 gender assessment study conducted by the Asian Development Bank (ADB) identified a lack of up-to-date and reliable information as a key constraint for clearly identifying gender issues of TVET in Viet Nam (ADB 2017b). Although the assessment report had to state that "there is insufficient data or evidence on which to base conclusions and recommendations," it illustrates and provides strong evidence on the need to improve technical capacity within Viet Nam's TVET sector to address gender inequality through policy, strategy, and implementation. Key findings relate to a range of issues:

(i) Key government policies are inadequately gender responsive, as they do not take account of differences between women and men. Although there is a National Strategy for Gender Equality (2011–2020),[34] its objectives and targets are not reflected in other key government policies and strategies, in particular the Vocational Training Development Strategy 2011–2020, or the Youth Development Policy and Strategy 2010–2020.

(ii) Within the National Strategy for Gender Equality, targets are not disaggregated by age. It is difficult to know whether the issues reported are the same for women across all age groups, or if women of specific ages should be targeted for special assistance.

(iii) The MOLISA's Gender Equality Department seems to have limited technical capacity and resources to implement the National Strategy for Gender Equality. Generally, there is a weak coordination with other ministries and the General Directorate of Vocational Training.

(iv) The Government of Viet Nam recently passed a state budget law that enables prioritization of budgets for women. However, weak technical capacity in gender-responsive budgeting indicates that it is unlikely to result in improved allocation of funds for women's activities.

(v) The TVET sector has only a few gender policies or other strategies and mechanisms to improve female enrollment, participation, graduation, and school-to-work transitions of women. Correspondingly, national TVET reports have limited data disaggregation by sex, ethnicity, disability, age, and socioeconomic status, making it difficult to determine (a) how many women who were trained in TVET graduated, (b) how many female TVET graduates gained employment after graduation, (c) how many women trained in TVET were part of intern programs, (d) the level of qualifications and certifications gained by women compared with those of men, (e) how many women are employed in management roles, and (f) the different levels of qualifications and skills of women and men employed in the TVET system and whether there is wage inequality between women and men.

(vi) Evidence from other sources shows that within the TVET sector, men dominate leadership and decision-making roles. While some women teach in male-dominated areas, they are reported to have few opportunities for advancement to senior roles.

(vii) Traditional social and cultural beliefs are strong, limiting women's participation in male-dominated areas of training and employment. Women's enrollment in TVET is concentrated in a narrow range of occupational areas such as tourism and social services. Even when women do study such disciplines, they specialize in areas that are seen as "culturally appropriate" and allow them to take responsibility for family.

(viii) Training offered through TVET institutions is often targeted at supply, while a focus on industry demand is needed. Hence, it is unclear how women might be encouraged to study also in male-dominated areas projected to be in demand in the labor market in the future. TVET institutions are not discouraged from developing training courses in areas they perceive women want to be trained in, even if there is no clear link to projected labor market demand.

---

[34] This strategy addresses the responsibilities of line ministries and stipulates that they increase the number of female leaders in key positions across all ministries, ministerial agencies, and agencies of the government and the People's Committees.

3.　Quality of TVET

43. Despite the government's considerable effort during the last decade to improve quality and relevance of Viet Nam's TVET system, the industry and business sector's perception of TVET performance and outcomes has remained critical (see section I.2 of this report). The TVET system focuses persistently on school-based training delivery with low involvement and participation of enterprises and, correspondingly, a wide range of system-immanent problems, such as the lack of instructors with industry experience and practical skills, poor performance and output standards, lack of independent assessments of graduates as well as inefficient management and financing structures.

A. Teacher Development and Qualifications

44. **Qualification standards.** According to the TVET law, teachers at vocational secondary schools and lecturers at TVET colleges must have at least a graduation diploma (bachelor's degree) from technical or specialized universities[35] plus a certificate on TVET pedagogy for teaching theory lessons, while instructors providing practical sessions in these institutions need only a TVET pedagogy certificate and "certificates of professional skills" in relevant occupational fields. Teachers and/or lecturers conducting both occupational theory and practice ("integrative teaching") are required to obtain both qualifications. Hence, the vast majority of teachers and lecturers in public TVET institutions are recruited from universities, colleges, and secondary schools, and not from industry.[36] All newly recruited TVET teachers and lecturers have to undergo a probation period of 12 months at secondary and college level or 6 months at elementary level, respectively (Figure 2.10).

45. **Preservice training for vocational education and training teachers.** Nationwide, there are 4 universities for technical education, 1 vocational teacher training college, and 45 training divisions for TVET pedagogy at universities and colleges. Most of these institutions provide both vocational preservice and in-service training. The majority of students enrolled in preservice programs at the four universities are graduates from general upper secondary schools (about 75%). Graduates from vocational and professional secondary schools account for only about 10%–25%, and only few graduates from vocational or technical colleges upgrade their diplomas into a bachelor's degree through a special bridging program. Programs on TVET pedagogy (module blocs) are conducted separately from the technical studies and, hence, can be delivered at a large scale also to non-academic trainees such as skilled professionals who want to become instructors for practical training sessions at TVET institutions. Graduates of these programs are awarded special teaching certificates at two levels depending on the institutional level of their training. As Table 2.2 shows, both programs cover a large share of theory topics. Modules on pedagogical practice account for only about 20% of credit points to be gained. A major weakness results from the exclusive preservice character of the training programs, which may widely support inert knowledge acquisition without linkages to professional experience to be gained during subsequent probation periods.

---

[35]　Including graduates from vocational and technical teacher training universities or at vocational and technical teacher training faculties at universities. The training duration of these teachers/lecturers depends on their entrance qualifications and takes up to 4.5 years (4 years of technical studies and 5 months for TVET pedagogy).

[36]　According to MOLISA's latest TVET Report (DVET and NIVET 2017), in 2015 42.77% of TVET teachers in 2015 were graduates from universities, colleges, and vocational colleges; 28.2% had a master's or higher degree; 9.13% were graduates from professional or vocational secondary schools; and 19.9% had other qualifications such as skilled worker certificates.

Table 2.2: Teacher Training Curricula

TVET Pedagogy Curriculum at University Level			TVET Pedagogy Curriculum at College Level		
	Modules	Credits		Modules	Credits
1	Logics of learning	3			
2	General psychology	2			
3	Occupational psychology	3	1	Occupational psychology	4
4	General school education	2			
5	Vocational school education	3	2	Vocational school education	4
6	Organization/management of the teaching process	2	3	Organization/management of the teaching process	2
7	Teaching skills	5	4	Teaching skills	5
8	Specialized teaching methods	3	5	Specialized teaching methods	3
9	Research methodology of professional education	2	6	Scientific research methods of education*	2*
10	Pedagogical communication*	2*			
11	Application of information technology in teaching*	2*	7	Application of information technology in teaching*	2*
12	Teaching technology*	2*	8	Teaching technology*	2*
13	Development of vocational training programs*	2*	9	Development of vocational training programs*	2*
14	Economics of education*	2*			
15	Pedagogical practice 1	2	10	Pedagogical practice	6
16	Pedagogical practice 2	6			
	Total	**36**		**Total**	**28**

TVET = technical and vocational education and training.
* Elective modules (2 of 5 modules selected at university level and 2 of 4 modules selected at college level).
Source: Author, based on information from Vinh University of Technology Education. http://vuted.edu.vn.

46. **Formal qualifications.** MOLISA's 2017 data indicate that some 87% of more than 40,000 lecturers at Viet Nam's vocational and technical colleges fulfill the standard requirements for teaching theoretical subjects. At intermediate level, this share is reportedly 77% in vocational secondary schools and almost 80% in professional secondary schools. Taking together the number of teachers and lecturers possessing college or other degrees and those who are eligible for "integrative teaching" in these institutions, the potential share of instructors for practical sessions may account for some 32% in vocational colleges and 53% in vocational secondary schools, respectively.[37] At elementary level, about 73% of the total 13,912 teachers are currently registered for "integrative teaching" but only 26.8% of teachers at this level have academic degrees and 53% possess less than a college degree.[38]

---

[37] The figures for the number of teachers/lecturers for "integrative teaching" (i.e., both theory and practice) are currently only available for institutions previously supervised by MOLISA and for technical colleges and professional schools formerly operating under MOET.

[38] According to the Law on Vocational Education and Training 2014, vocational teachers at elementary level must at least possess either a secondary level TVET diploma or "certificates of professional skills."

Table 2.3: Number of Teachers in Vocational Education and Training Institutions by Formal Qualification, 2015

	Subsector and Training Level	Total	Qualifications				Technical Skills	
			Postgraduate (Master's, PhD)	Bachelor's Degree	College Diploma	Others	Integrative Teaching Ability	
I	**MOLISA**	**39,152**	**7,342**	**17,430**	**4,962**	**9,418**	**16,052**	**41.0%**
1	Vocational colleges	15,986	4,670	9,246	1,271	799	3,053	19.1%
2	Vocational secondary schools (intermediate level)	9,254	2,406	4,720	925	1,203	2,797	30.2%
3	Vocational training centers (elementary level)	13,912	266	3,464	2,766	7,416	10,202	73.3%
II	**MOET**	**34,460**	**17,014**	**12,022**	**4,844**	**580**	**n/a**	**n/a**
1	Technical colleges	24,260	13,542	7,350	3,160	208	n/a	n/a
2	Professional secondary schools	10,200	3,472	4,672	1,684	372	n/a	n/a
	Total (MOLISA + MOET) 2015	**73,612**	**24,356**	**29,452**	**9,806**	**9,998**		

Note: Data on the number of TVET teachers disaggregated by sex are not available.
n/a = not available, MOET = Ministry of Education and Training, MOLISA = Ministry of Labour–Invalids and Social Affairs, TVET = technical and vocational education and training.
Sources: Directorate of Vocational Education and Training and National Institute for Vocational Education and Training. 2017. *Viet Nam Vocational Education and Training Report 2015*. Ha Noi; and MOLISA. 2017. Project on Renovation and Improvement of the Quality of Technical and Vocational Education and Training – Up to 2020, with Orientation to 2030 (Draft October 2017). Ha Noi.

47. **Occupational competence.** When interpreting TVET teacher qualification standards, the unclear definition of "certificates of professional skills"[39] as the only mandatory legal requirement for teaching practical lessons is a major concern. Awards of such certificates are often based only on some more or less preliminary exercises accomplished during formal vocational training (such as for obligatory short-term industry placements and internships); hence, they do not necessarily assert in-depth professional work experience and profound occupational competence. Beyond that, teachers can voluntarily sign up for a formal occupational skills assessment if their vocational majors belong to the 62 focal occupations that are regulated by national occupational standards for different competency levels and have been promulgated for corresponding examinations.[40] These examinations are conducted at 36 skills assessment centers that are mostly located in universities and vocational colleges[41] and certified for operation by the DVET. The assessment consists of a set

---

[39] For practical teaching at secondary and college levels this must be at least a national certificate of vocational skills level 2, or a worker's certification level 4/7, 3/6, or a certificate of meritorious artisan, meritorious artist, or meritorious doctor, or a certificate of vocational practice at vocational college level or vocational college's degree or junior college's degree or equivalent. For practical teaching at elementary level only a national certificate of vocational skills level 1, worker's certification level 3/7, 2/6 or an artisan certificate of province or central-affiliated city is sufficient (see also MOLISA Circular No. 08/2017/TT-BLDTBXH on Standards in Qualifications of TVET Teachers from March 2017).

[40] By 2015, a total of 83 occupations had national occupational skills examinations compiled. Of these, 21 occupations had not yet been appraised for promulgation (see also DVET and NIVET 2017).

[41] Currently, only one assessment center is corporate owned.

Figure 2.10: Training System for Vocational Education and Training Teachers and Lecturers

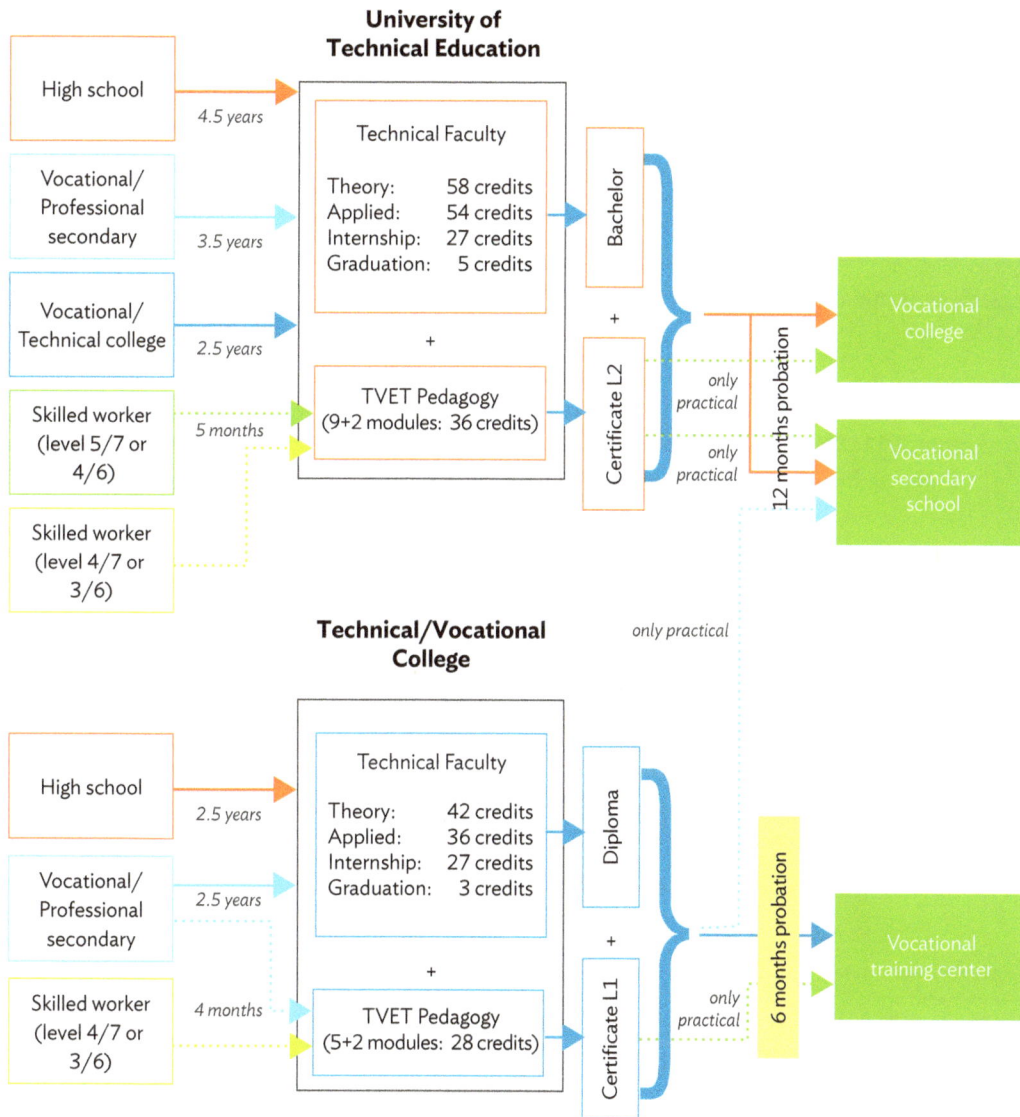

TVET = technical and vocational education and training. Source: Author, based on information provided by staff of Vinh University of Technology Education, Vinh City, Viet Nam.

of multiple-choice questions to test the understanding of essential knowledge and a practical skills test that evaluates the critical skills required for a certain level of occupational task performance as specified in Viet Nam's National Occupational Skills Framework (see section 3.D). To be recruited, assessors must have been trained, certified by the DVET for their job, and possess a decent track record regarding formal qualifications and professional experience.[42]

48. By 2015, however, only 120 persons nationwide fulfilled the requirements to become certified assessors, although a total of 1,785 candidates had been trained for this task since 2009. Correspondingly, the number of Vietnamese workers whose occupational skills were assessed still failed to meet the government's expectations,[43] and also TVET teachers with national skills certificates are still an exception. Surveys for MOLISA's 2013–2014 TVET Report, which were conducted among 40 TVET institutions earmarked to become high-quality schools, revealed that only 25.3% of lecturers teaching national key occupations were probably qualified in their occupational fields, while the vast majority of them had not participated in a formal skills assessment (NIVT 2015). GDVT statistics for 2015 confirmed these findings with slight deviations between TVET colleges and vocational secondary schools[44] (Figures 2.11 and 2.12).

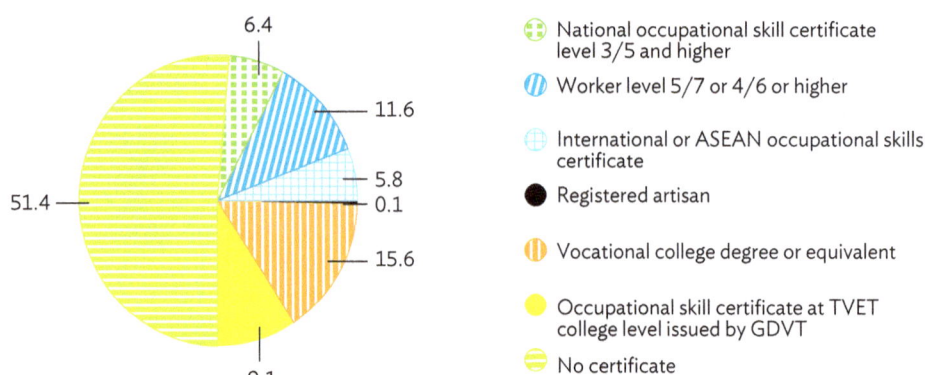

Figure 2.11: Share of Teachers at Selected High-Quality Vocational Education and Training Institutes (Colleges) Achieving Occupational Skills Conditions, 2015
(%)

Legend:
- National occupational skill certificate level 3/5 and higher
- Worker level 5/7 or 4/6 or higher
- International or ASEAN occupational skills certificate
- Registered artisan
- Vocational college degree or equivalent
- Occupational skill certificate at TVET college level issued by GDVT
- No certificate

Pie chart values: 6.4, 11.6, 5.8, 0.1, 15.6, 9.1, 51.4

ASEAN = Association of Southeast Asian Nations, GDVT = General Department of Vocational Training, TVET = technical and vocational education and training.
Source: Directorate of Vocational Education and Training and National Institute for Vocational Education and Training. 2017. *Viet Nam Vocational Education and Training Report 2015*. Ha Noi.

---

[42] To be granted an appraiser card for the full range of occupational skills assessments (from level 1 to level 5), a person must satisfy one of the following two conditions on skills, qualifications, and experience: (i) possessing a certificate of national occupational skills of level 5 in that occupation and having worked in that occupation for at least 3 years since obtaining the certificate; or (ii) holding a tertiary or higher degree in a discipline relevant to that occupation and having worked in that occupation for at least 15 years after graduation and currently engaging in training at collegial or higher level or working as a manager or supervisor at a health establishment or an enterprise (see also MOLISA Decree No. 31/2015/ND-CP dated March 2015).

[43] According to the Vocational Training Development Strategy 2011–2015, occupational skills assessment and certification were to be carried out for 2 million workers. Between 2009 and 2015, occupational skills assessment, although supported by state budgets in the majority of cases, was only conducted for a total number of 8,407 workers, of which only 49.7% met the requirements.

[44] A common problem of GDVT statistics is a persistent lack of reliable data. In the 2015 survey, for instance, only 37 out of 45 TVET institutes provided relevant information on the occupational skills of their teaching staff. Only 19 of these 37 schools had teachers teaching intermediate level.

Figure 2.12: Share of Teachers at Selected High-Quality Vocational Education and Training Institutes (Secondary Schools) Achieving Occupational Skills Conditions, 2015

(%)

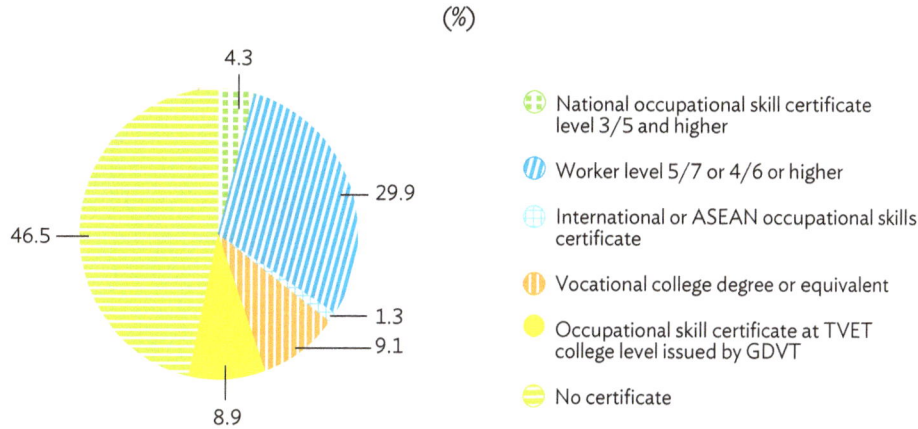

National occupational skill certificate level 3/5 and higher

Worker level 5/7 or 4/6 or higher

International or ASEAN occupational skills certificate

Vocational college degree or equivalent

Occupational skill certificate at TVET college level issued by GDVT

No certificate

ASEAN = Association of Southeast Asian Nations, GDVT = General Department of Vocational Training, TVET = technical and vocational education and training.
Source: Directorate of Vocational Education and Training and National Institute for Vocational Education and Training. 2017. *Viet Nam Vocational Education and Training Report 2015*. Ha Noi.

49. A crucial reason for this situation may be because voluntary compliance with desired qualification norms does not sufficiently pay off for public servants in TVET unless appropriate (potentially costly) incentives are given to attract candidates with proven occupational skills and work experience to join the teaching profession; such incentives would also commensurably motivate already employed teachers to continuously upgrade their occupational skills and qualifications. On 9 November 2015, the government promulgated Decree No. 113/2015/ND-CP on special allowances extending basic salaries of public TVET teachers for integrative teaching[45] for those with high levels of professional competence[46] who teach disabled students, and for those who perform their teaching duties under physical hardship and hazardous and/or dangerous conditions. While this regulation grants significant salary upgrades for the last two groups (e.g., allowances of up to 65% of base salary for full-time teachers of classes attended by disabled students), TVET teachers of normal classes providing certified evidence on high-level occupational skills are awarded an allowance of only 10% of their respective base salaries. Taking into account rather low base salary levels of young teachers employed in Viet Nam's public TVET institutions,[47] it remains questionable whether this measure will lead to a tangible breakthrough toward improvement of teacher qualifications or turn out to be a well-intended but widely ineffective paper tiger. Becoming eligible for this modest incentive appears to be somewhat incommensurable with actual career development efforts TVET teachers need to invest on to qualify for this.

---

[45]   Integrative teaching refers to teaching of theoretical and practical knowledge in a lesson/course/module/subject.

[46]   A person who has achieved a high level of professional competence refers to a person who has gained the national professional skill certificate at level 4 or higher, or level 5/6, 6/7, or higher.

[47]   The current salary level of Vietnamese teachers, particularly of those starting their career at public educational institutions (including TVET), is rather low. The minimum monthly pay for all civil servants and public employees is calculated by multiplying a low base salary with a coefficient determined by qualifications and years of experience. For new teachers who have worked less than 5 years, the average monthly salary ranges from only VND3.2 million ($142) to VND3.9 million ($173). Although this income may more than double after 15 to 25 years of teaching (e.g., up to VND8.5 million for university lecturers), a teacher reportedly needs to work at least 13 years before achieving more than the average wage level of other Vietnamese employees. According to a World Bank study, this highly seniority-based promotion scheme contributes to a very high ratio of salary levels of old teachers at the top of the scale to the starting salaries of younger ones, which is not an effective way to attract talented new teachers and incentivize good performance (World Bank and the Government of Viet Nam 2017).

50. **Regulations stipulating teaching quality and in-service training.** So far, the main regulatory instruments supporting compliance of training program delivery with national standards are an explicit provision of the duty to teach "modules or subjects as assigned in conformity with the given plan or program"[48] and a standard requirement to obtain at least "a certificate of vocational pedagogy" for the respective vocational level.[49] However, in its 2017 status quo review, MOLISA stated that "curricula are not in line with practical conditions of production, business and services; the number of teachers are inadequate and short of professional and pedagogical skills; pedagogical universities only trained vocational teachers for some occupations, capacity of vocational pedagogical faculties at colleges failed to meet requirements of further training on pedagogical skills and skill improvement for teachers; facilities and equipment failed to meet requirements of curricula and are often outdated compared to current technologies in production, business, services" (MOLISA 2017).

51. Article 55 of the new TVET law mandates vocational teachers "to participate in internship in enterprise in order to update (or) improve professional skills, and approach new technology as regulated." Yet, MOLISA's recent regulation on qualification standards still states rather unclear specifications of "regularly self-study" and "participation in advanced training courses."[50] Nevertheless, MOLISA has earmarked additional training budget from the National TVET Target Program[51] and established further training programs for teachers to (i) improve teaching techniques focusing on quality improvement of practical training in classrooms and workshops, (ii) improve technical knowledge and practical skills of teachers, and (iii) improve English language skills. So far, about 6,000 teachers received training on these topics. Compared with this modest figure, MOLISA's plan for teacher training activities envisaged for 2017–2020 appears to be ambitious (Table 2.4). Developing High Quality TVET institutes as hubs for practice oriented in-service training in combination with pedagogical and theoretical training at Universities of Education could be a model that helps to achieve the MOLISA's plan.

---

[48] See MOLISA Circular No. 07/2017/TT-BLDTBXH on Working Regime for Vocational Education Teachers.

[49] See MOLISA Circular No. 08/2017/TT-BLDTBXH on Standards in Qualifications of Vocational Education Teachers. Between 2011 and 2015, MOLISA has trained 1,896 teachers in pedagogical professional knowledge and 4,070 teachers in occupational skills and evaluation of occupational practice skills. Training for a total of 20,000 teachers in both areas shall be delivered until 2020.

[50] MOLISA Circular No. 06/2017/TT-BLDTBXH.

[51] Based on MOLISA Decision No. 562/2016/QD-TCDN dated 19 December 2016, VND35 billion have been allocated to provide training for vocational teachers on professional skills, pedagogical skills, foreign languages, and information and technology skills.

Table 2.4: Envisaged Training in MOLISA's Project for TVET Reform 2020/2030

Type of Training or Related Intervention Envisaged	Number of Participants Targeted				
	Total	2017	2018	2019	2020
Train teachers overseas for occupations adopted from foreign countries	1,000	400	300	300	–
Train TVET teachers to meet standards in 50 training programs for TVET teachers adopted from overseas	9,000	–	3,000	3,000	3,000
Train and further train teachers of focal occupations in specialized English and informatics	16,000	3,500	4,000	4,000	4,000
Develop further training programs and materials in professional pedagogy for three levels (elementary, intermediate, and collegial)	3	2	–	–	–
Train and further train teachers in professional pedagogy	20,000	5,000	5,000	5,000	5,000
Develop training programs and materials in occupational skills for teachers of national focal occupations and occupations not selected as focal occupations	100	20	30	30	20
Train and further train teachers in occupational skills and evaluate occupational practice skills	20,000	4,500	5,000	5,000	5,000
Train and further train teachers in specialized English	40,000	10,000	10,000	10,000	10,000
Develop further training programs and materials in new technologies for teachers	100	20	30	30	20
Further train teachers on new technologies	24,000	6,000	6,000	6,000	6,000
Further train teachers in business startup and international integration	40,000	10,000	10,000	10,000	10,000
Foster credit-based training by developing integrated lesson plans and teaching activities for competence-based training and assessments; conduct training on soft skills for teachers	25,000	5,000	5,000	5,000	5,000
Offer further training for vocational trainers in teaching skills, knowledge of business and enterprise startup for rural laborers	4,000	1,000	1,000	1,000	1,000

MOLISA = Ministry of Labour–Invalids and Social Affairs, TVET = technical and vocational education and training.
Source: Adapted from MOLISA. 2017. Project on Renovation and Improvement of the Quality of TVET – up to 2020 with Orientation to 2030, (Draft October 2017).

B. Management Staff at Vocational Education and Training Institutions

52. Managers of vocational training institutions are heads and rectors of vocational institutes, members of school management boards as well as staff of school departments for training support including student affairs and admission, finance and accounting, facilities management, corporate relations, and academic research. Some teachers are also in charge of management tasks including section heads, faculty deans, etc. Teachers are entitled to additional allowances for such jobs.

53. In 2016, the total number of management staff in vocational training institutions under MOLISA was 10,534,[52] of which almost 40% were at vocational colleges, 22.1% were at secondary vocational schools, and 37.1% were at vocational training centers. In 2015, a total of 27.3% of TVET school managers were female.[53]

54. While the total number of TVET school managers increased by more than 60% between 2011 and 2016, this increase was mainly related to the number of managers in vocational colleges (which more than tripled) as well as in VTCs (plus 57.2%) and a decrease in the number of management staff in vocational secondary schools (–14.2%).[54] This resulted in a remarkably inverse shift in management staff distribution between secondary vocational schools and TVET colleges (Figure 2.13). The share of TVET school managers also performing teaching tasks ranges from less than 38% in VTCs to about 60% and 62.4% in vocational secondary schools and colleges, respectively (DVET and NIVET 2017).

Figure 2.13: Development of Enrollments in Vocational Training Centers by Type of Training

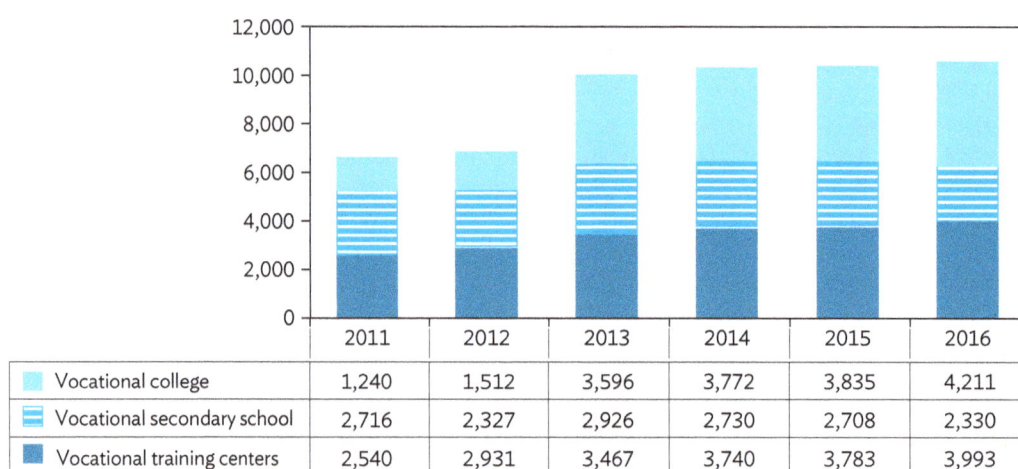

	2011	2012	2013	2014	2015	2016
Vocational college	1,240	1,512	3,596	3,772	3,835	4,211
Vocational secondary school	2,716	2,327	2,926	2,730	2,708	2,330
Vocational training centers	2,540	2,931	3,467	3,740	3,783	3,993

Source: Ministry of Labour–Invalids and Social Affairs. 2017. Project on Renovation and Improvement of the Quality of Technical and Vocational Education and Training – Up to 2020, with Orientation to 2030 (Draft October 2017). Ha Noi.

55. **Qualifications of management staff.** The TVET Law 2014 specifies minimum qualification requirements for rectors of colleges and secondary schools and for directors of VTCs. A college rector needs a master's or higher degree, a rector of a secondary school needs at least a university degree, and the minimum qualification requirement for a vocational training center (VTC) director is a college diploma. In addition, the law mandates that rectors and directors "have been trained, fostered on vocational education and training management."[55]

---

[52] Figures on management staff in technical colleges and professional secondary schools are currently not available.

[53] According to DVET and NIVET (2017), the proportion of female managers in TVET colleges was 24.1%, in vocational secondary schools 28.8%, and in vocational training centers 29.9%.

[54] For the same period the number of TVET colleges and VTCs increased only by 39% and 22%, respectively, while the number of secondary vocational schools under MOLISA decreased by only 9%.

[55] TVET Law 2014, Article 13 and 14.

56. According to MOLISA's 2015 TVET Report, most managers of TVET institutes fulfilled those basic qualification requirements with almost 50% of managers at vocational colleges possessing a bachelor's degree and 46.9% having a master's degree or PhD. At vocational secondary schools, the vast majority of managers had bachelor's degrees (70%) and 20.9% had a master's degree or PhD. Most managers of vocational training centers surpassed the minimum qualification requirement, as 77.5% of them possessed a bachelor's or higher degree. However, also 12.3% of VTC managers possessed only secondary school or other certificates (Figure 2.14).

Figure 2.14: Qualification Structure of Managers at Vocational Education and Training Institutions, 2015

(%)

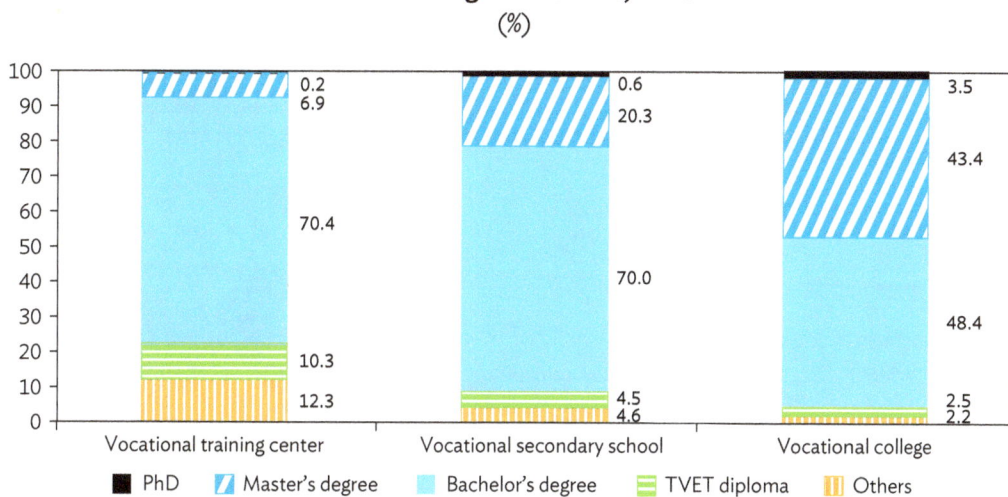

TVET = technical and vocational education and training.
Source: Directorate of Vocational Education and Training and National Institute for Vocational Education and Training. 2017. *Viet Nam Vocational Education and Training Report 2015*. Ha Noi.

57. A less promising picture appears in MOLISA's statistics recording the status of TVET school managers' professional management skills. In 2015, only 22.4% of them held professional certificates for education management or vocational training management, with the lowest share (only 17.1%) recorded for managers of vocational secondary schools (Figure 2.15). This situation is all the more precarious as the current government policy strongly demands fundamental changes in the governance structure of public institutions by gradually shifting the responsibility for key administrative duties (including organizational and financial management, staff recruitment and development, effective service delivery and quality assurance) from state agencies to institutions. MOLISA's draft reform plan envisages that by 2025 at least 20% of all TVET institutions shall be granted full autonomy status after being assessed for compliance with a comprehensive set of quality accreditation criteria and standards. However, investigations revealed that even among 45 TVET institutions invested to become high-quality schools less than 50% of managers had such certificates. In more than half of these institutes (26) the share of managers having professional qualifications was only 20%–30% (DVET and NIVET 2017).

58. To further improve management performance in TVET institutions, MOLISA issued new accreditation criteria, which (inter alia) stipulate that managers and administrators of TVET institutions shall be "appointed and dismissed in accordance with regulations," "meet professional

Figure 2.15: Share of Vocational Education and Training School Managers with Management Certificates, 2015

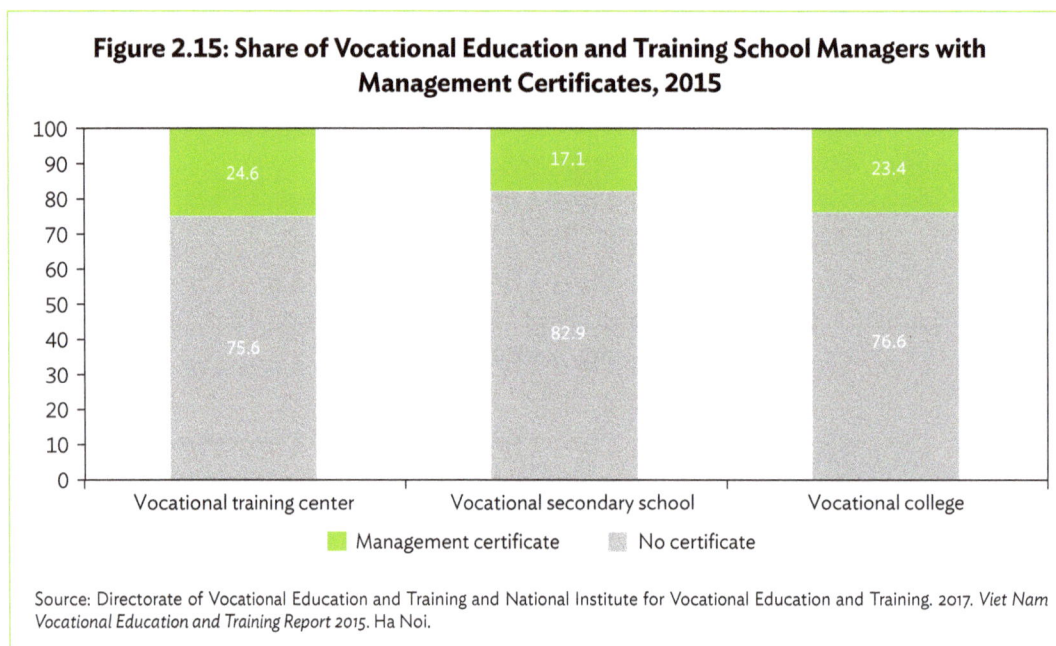

Source: Directorate of Vocational Education and Training and National Institute for Vocational Education and Training. 2017. *Viet Nam Vocational Education and Training Report 2015*. Ha Noi.

standards for knowledge and skills," and shall "properly perform assigned authorities and tasks."[56] Yet, measurable indicators specifying how compliance with respective qualification/performance standards will be assessed as well as tangible procedures stipulating interventions for remediating noncompliance are still missing.

59. **Training on management skills.** By 2015, 2,010 TVET school managers participated in domestic courses delivered under an International Labour Organization program, while 45 managers from high-quality TVET institutes were sent to training abroad (Australia). In addition, MOLISA's TVET report for 2013/14 mentions that 3,953 VTC managers participated in a special training course on "organization and implementation skills for the project of vocational training for rural laborers." The number of school managers trained between 2011 and 2016 on administrative standards in local and overseas training has been reported as accounting for in total 3,180 persons in 2015. A smaller number of managers (1,650) also received further training on TVET equipment, and 1,200 managers on "soft skills necessary for officers in charge of student affairs." In addition, 2,900 "officers in charge of foreign relations, archives and diplomas" were trained during this period. Until 2020, MOLISA plans to extend the training scopes considerably. According to its draft project plan, about 11,500 TVET managers shall be trained annually on school management standards regarding these topics during the next 4 years.[57]

60. **Information and communication technology and language skills.** In addition, national regulations[58] stipulate that examinations be conducted on foreign language skills and computer skills as basic requirement for staff recruitment in public institutions. Heads of agencies competent to recruit public employees can decide on the form and content of such examinations to meet requirements of working positions. For each skill domain, certificate levels (A, B, and C) will be awarded. In 2015, 12.5%

---

[56]   MOLISA Circular No. 15/2017/TT-BLDTBXH dated 18 June 2017.

[57]   MOLISA's draft plan for TVET reform until 2020/30 envisages by 2020 to offer training or further training for 70% of managers at all levels and for 10% of teachers in TVET institutions engaged in management and quality control. By 2030 training and further training shall be provided for 80% of managers at all levels and 20% of teachers in TVET institutions.

[58]   Decree No. 29/2012/ND-CP on Recruitment, Employment and Management of Public Employees.

of management staff in TVET schools did not have any degree or certificates in foreign languages and 10.3% of managers had no certification in basic computer skills. However, formally meeting certification requirements does not guarantee real world proficiency in these skills. Field trips and a series of workshops conducted with managers and teachers of more than 30 TVET colleges, which had been proposed to participate in an upcoming Asian Development Bank (ADB) project, indicated rather modest accomplishments, both in the ability to apply basic conversation patterns in English and to use basic software applications like MS Excel in a reasonably professional way.

61. Between 2011 and 2016, only 940 teachers participated in training on specialized English and informatics for teachers in key investment occupations (MOLISA 2017). In 2013–2014, 140 managers participated in information technology (IT) training for vocational training management (NIVT 2015). Although MOLISA plans to modernize IT infrastructure in 63 provinces and cities to serve management and operation of TVET institutions,[59] the draft plan does not yet contain specific propositions on respective IT qualification and training requirements for school managers, let alone a concept for establishing respective long-term support structures to help school managers gradually improve their professional capabilities and performance.[60]

C. School Facilities and Training Equipment

62. Apart from teachers lacking industry-relevant practical skills, outdated or insufficient training facilities appear to negatively affect employer ratings of Viet Nam's TVET system. Although MOLISA (2017) stated that "the facilities and equipment of vocational education institutions have been invested to meet the training requirements," sample reports of TVET institutions give cause to concerns that "technical facilities and means of teaching and learning do not meet the requirements for high-quality training" and/or are not sufficient in scope to conduct decent hands-on training activities for all students enrolled in a course. Even comparatively well-equipped colleges report that they are facing "challenges in improving and innovating training programs in key technical industries due to difficulties in practice equipment."[61] In other surveys, students reported that they had to take turns when doing practice at college workshops and only worked at a machine about once or twice during five practical learning sessions. Although there were 9 machines, only 4 or 5 functioned properly for one group of 6 to 10 students (Ho and Reich 2014). Similar findings have been collected during field visits to TVET colleges during the preparation of this report. Even the University for Technical Education in Vinh City reported to have regularly conducted night shifts for practical workshops in teacher training programs to overcome strong limitations in the availability of appropriate training facilities.

63. A 2017 empirical study on the situation of TVET financing in Viet Nam (MDRI and NEXIA STT 2017) has revealed that the rate of investment in machinery and equipment of training facilities fluctuates very sharply even among high-level TVET institutions operating in the same field of disciplines and with remarkable differences in the structure of recurrent expenditures, including those that cover wages and wage-like expenses (Figure 2.16).

---

[59] The draft accreditation system for high-quality schools even includes the standard: "Management activities of TVET institutes are computerized." See Appendix 5.5.

[60] Decision No. 899/QĐ-TTg sets the target: To modernize IT infrastructure (means and teaching equipment for management, teaching, and learning activities) so as to strive to have at least 50% of vocational education establishments having information technology infrastructure by 2020.

[61] See also proposals of 10 TVET colleges applying for support through a proposed ADB TVET Program.

Figure 2.16: Expenditure Structures of Sample Vocational Education and Training Colleges by Type of Ownership and Field of Disciplines

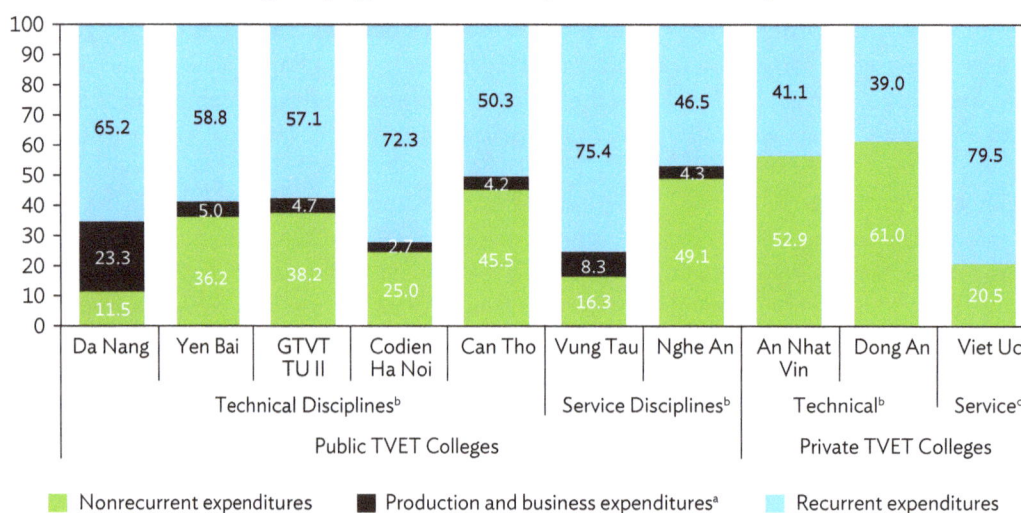

Codien Ha Noi = Ha Noi College of Electrical Mechanics, GTVT TU II =Central Transport College No.2, TVET = technical and vocational education and training, Viet Uc =Viet Nam–Australia.
a Accounted within recurrent and nonrecurrent expenditures in nonpublic vocational training institutions.
b Automotive, industrial electrics, and electronics.
c Hospitality management, cooking technique.
Source: Mean expenditure structures calculated for the period 2012–2014 by Mekong Development Research Institute and NEXIA STT. 2017. *Recommendation for an Effective Financial Model: Program's Cost Norms Study – Final Report.* http://mdri.org.vn/publication/recommendation-for-an-effective-financial-model-programs-cost-norms-study/.

64. The high variance among TVET institutions' infrastructure conditions is mainly because the rate of investment in machinery and other nonrecurrent expenditures depends largely on the investment priorities and available funding of different governing bodies.[62] Over the last 5 years, government funds of national target programs have contributed considerably to infrastructure upgrades of some TVET institutions, particularly in training centers located in rural areas. However, as ADB (2014) revealed, allocations per institution for facilities and equipment were set before training programs and equipment requirements had been identified.[63]

65. **Technical and vocational education and training resource management** in Viet Nam, particularly for covering recurrent expenditures of TVET institutions, is still largely input based.[64] State funding does not take into account specific training costs of different majors and varies remarkably by governing agencies depending on their spending capabilities and priorities, which remain widely opaque.[65] High variances in government budget support schemes could be observed among TVET institutions operating at similar levels under the same agency (Figure 2.17).

---

[62] MDRI and NEXIA STT (2017) mention that the TVET institutions in the sample showing low proportions of recurrent expenditures received large investment funds in machinery and infrastructure from 2012 to 2014. All public TVET institutions in the sample were selected to become high-quality schools in 2020. Therefore, the study suggests that the average ratio of nonrecurrent expenditure over recurrent expenditure of institutions outside of its sample could be much lower.

[63] This finding could be exemplarily verified during field visits to TVET institutions in the preparation phase of this report.

[64] The current state funding allocation to TVET institutions under ministries is determined based on four criteria: (i) income-expense situation of the previous year; (ii) duty assigned by the ministry for the following year (expected school's admission quota); (iii) number of staff, teachers, and officers approved by authority; and (iv) current regime of spending.

[65] TVET institutions under ministries and central agencies tend to receive more state budget per capita than the provincial TVET institutions under provincial People's Committees. In addition, the determination of actual training costs in public schools has numerous limitations because accounting systems are not yet required by any policy to record specific costs for each field of training (see also MDRI and NEXIA STT 2017).

Figure 2.17: Revenue and Expenditure Structures of Vocational Education and Training Colleges under the Ministry of Industry and Trade, 2015

(D million)

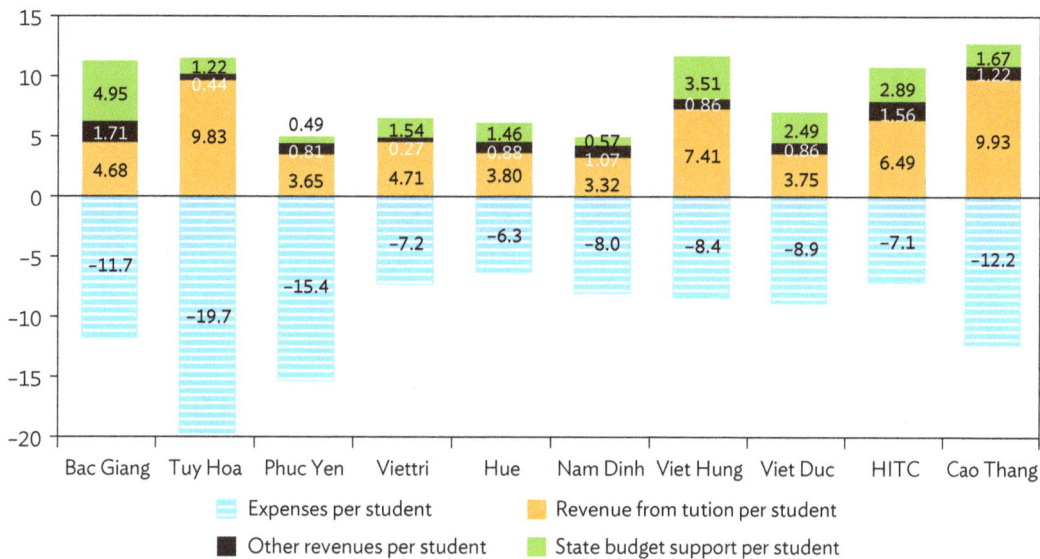

HITC = Ho Chi Minh City Industry and Trade College.
Source: Calculations of ADB team based on data collected from selected vocational education and training colleges in November 2017.

66. Strategically, government-regulated tuition fee margins (see also section II.4 on Financing TVET) are seen as the key means to offset the increasing gap between state budgets and actual costs of training delivery. This shall give institutes greater autonomy in operating efficiently[66] and allow for a stepwise redeployment of state budget support schemes from regularly financing recurrent expenditures to targeted nonrecurrent infrastructure investments, particularly in TVET institutions earmarked to become "high-quality schools."[67] However, survey findings give cause to concerns that this strategy may not necessarily help eliminate ineffective factors in the current expenditure structures of public TVET institutions, as long as it does not also provide enough incentives to improve management's efficiency and performance. Sample investigations show that often the proportion of wages paid directly to teachers is low, even among public TVET institutes that were chosen to become "high-quality schools."[68] Apparently, too many schools operating under state governance are maintaining a bulky resource management system with larger-than-necessary regular expenses for administrative tasks (Figure 2.18).[69]

---

[66] The government has issued four legal documents on tuition rates of public vocational training institutions, including Decision No. 70/1998/QĐ-TTg dated 31/03/1998, Decision No. QĐ-TTg dated 21 August 2009, Decree No. 49/2010/NĐ-CP dated 15 May 2010, and Decree No. 86/2015/ND-CP dated 2 October 2015.

[67] This option finds its legal basis in the new TVET Law (cf. Articles 6 and 25) and is further elaborated in Decree No. 16/2015/ND-CP dated May 2015 Stipulating the Mechanism for Exercising the Autonomy of Public Administrative Units.

[68] All public TVET institutions investigated in MDRI and NEXIA STT (2017) were selected because of this status.

[69] According to MDRI and NEXIA STT (2017), it should be acknowledged that public VTIs have difficulty in maintaining an efficient wage structure due to problems in government policy, i.e., public institutions cannot fire tenured teachers. Another problem in adjusting direct wage expenditures is that some members of administrative staff also participate in teaching but receive salary for only one task; there has been no mechanism to allocate wages for these employees based on their direct teaching hours.

Figure 2.18: Structure of Wage and Wage-Like Expenditures in Sample Vocational Education and Training Colleges by Type of Ownership

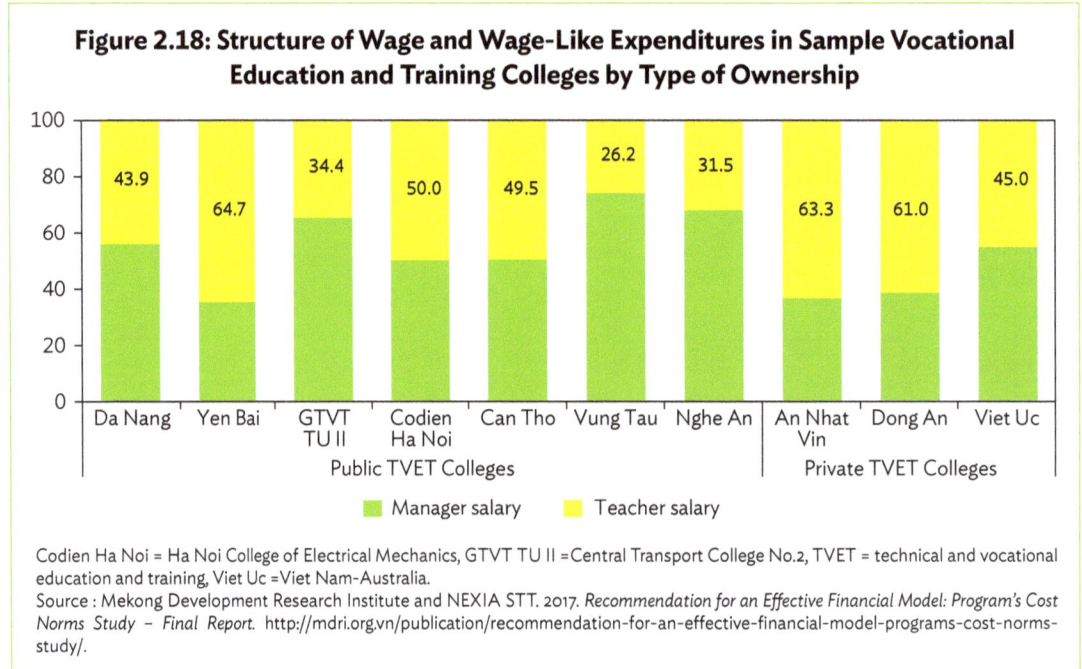

Codien Ha Noi = Ha Noi College of Electrical Mechanics, GTVT TU II =Central Transport College No.2, TVET = technical and vocational education and training, Viet Uc =Viet Nam-Australia.
Source : Mekong Development Research Institute and NEXIA STT. 2017. *Recommendation for an Effective Financial Model: Program's Cost Norms Study – Final Report.* http://mdri.org.vn/publication/recommendation-for-an-effective-financial-model-programs-cost-norms-study/.

67. **Practice materials.** School managers also report that because of shortage of funds, savings often have to be made by reducing expenses in direct training costs (equipment, materials), which inevitably results in low quality of training (i.e., less opportunities for occupation-relevant practical learning) in these schools. Yet, also in this area, expenditure structures in Viet Nam's TVET institutions are varying highly, not only between institutions with different faculty and qualification profiles but also among institutes with similar training portfolios (Figure 2.19).

Figure 2.19: Proportion of Expenditures for Practice Materials in Total Recurrent Expenditures of Sample Vocational Education and Training Colleges

(%)

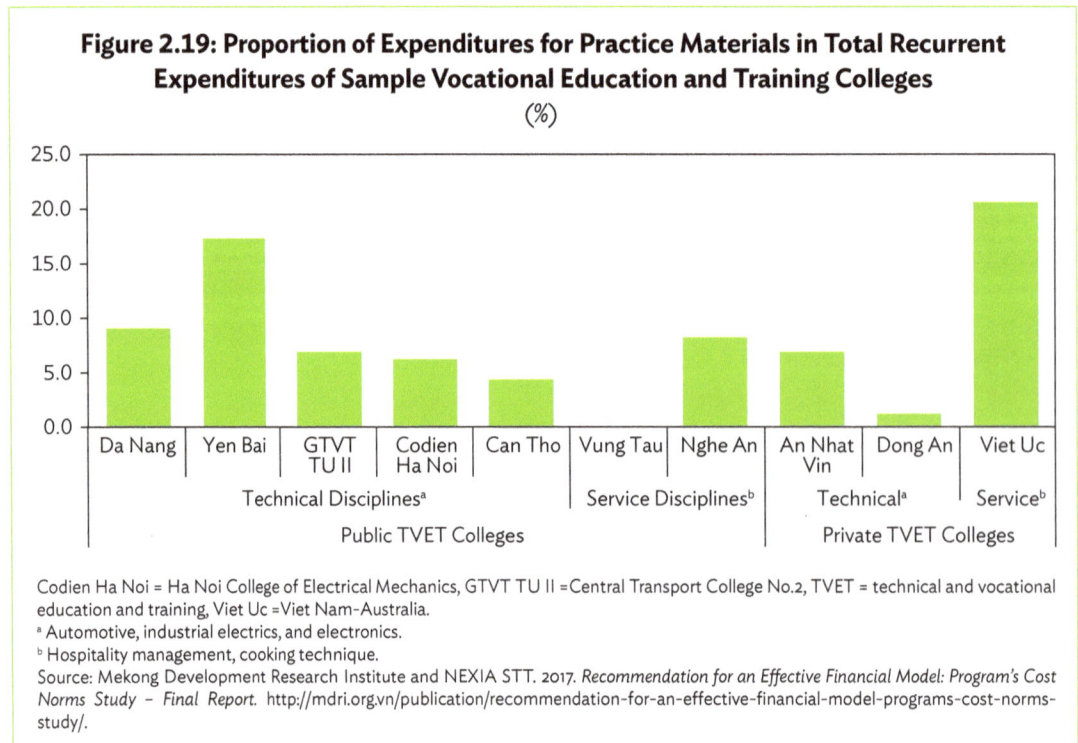

Codien Ha Noi = Ha Noi College of Electrical Mechanics, GTVT TU II =Central Transport College No.2, TVET = technical and vocational education and training, Viet Uc =Viet Nam-Australia.
[a] Automotive, industrial electrics, and electronics.
[b] Hospitality management, cooking technique.
Source: Mekong Development Research Institute and NEXIA STT. 2017. *Recommendation for an Effective Financial Model: Program's Cost Norms Study – Final Report.* http://mdri.org.vn/publication/recommendation-for-an-effective-financial-model-programs-cost-norms-study/.

68. Most remarkable are TVET institutions with zero funding for practice materials (such as the public TVET College for Tourism in Vung Tau) where students pay for these materials in addition to their tuition. Some private TVET colleges also have extraordinarily low expenditures for this purpose. In one case, however, the school (i.e., Dong An Vocational College) reportedly saved on expenditures for practice materials by sending both teachers and students to firms' production units to practice. The only public TVET institution in the sample that had relatively high expenditures for practice materials (Yen Bai Vocational College) received an explicit state budget for the purpose, which was allocated separately from the budgets for wages and other recurrent expenses.

69. MOLISA is working on "economic-technical cost norms," which public TVET institutions are to follow for aligning expenditures and revenues after 2020.[70] However, the current regulation stipulates only "educational institutions that exercise financial autonomy in terms of recurrent expenditures and investment" to adjust their fees to such norms. All others "shall determine tuition fees according to the State's grant and learners' contribution according to the decline in State's subsidies."[71] What is still missing are sound and feasible concepts that guide institute managers to review their current income and spending patterns and provide reasonable benchmarks for aligning future expenditure structures to realistic (major specific) unit cost standards for quality-oriented training. Such standards should not only include decent direct and indirect cost relationship patterns but also relate to specifications on physical facilities and respective fixed asset depreciations as well as on equipment and material expenses required for single training occupations and levels. Such specifications are usually included in well-designed training curricula but need to be thoroughly costed before they are imposed to become the guiding tool for training planning and delivery in TVET institutions. The Mekong Development Research Institute and NEXIA STT (2017) study on TVET financing and program cost norms, which was developed under ADB's Skills Enhancement Project, has provided a valuable set of relevant tools, operational guidelines, and training resources (see also Chapter III of this report).

D. National Skills Standards, Skills Assessment, and Certification

70. Prime Minister Decision No. 1982/QD-TTg approved in October 2016 a **National Qualification Framework** (NQF), which specifies eight levels of qualifications (for three vocational certificates and five academic degrees) by generic work–task-related descriptions of competencies (outcomes) and minimum academic loads (credit points) for each level to achieve them (Table 2.5). The framework provides the essential basis for mapping recognized occupations and respective skills standards to regulative arrangements that stipulate minimum outputs and outcomes of vocational training programs consistently at different institutional levels and, hence, will have a fundamental impact on future skills assessments and certifications. Currently, such regulations are largely input oriented by prescriptions of training objectives, content, methods, and unit duration in curricula to be followed by teachers and used for school-based student assessments.[72]

---

[70] Government Decree No. 16/2015/NĐ-CP dated February 2015 specifies the road map for the future pricing of public administrative services funded by the state budgets. It stipulates that by 2020 calculation of charges for public services shall be based on the full amount of salary costs, direct expenses, managerial and fixed asset depreciation costs (see also section II.4 on Financing TVET).

[71] Government Decree No. 86/2015/ND-CP dated October 2015 on Mechanism for Collection and Management of Tuition Fees.

[72] Although, reportedly, the development of such curriculum frameworks has also been based on an "extensive analysis of occupational requirements," these frameworks specify 70% of the content and time requirements of respective training programs.

Table 2.6: Synopsis of Core National Qualification Framework Specifications

Level	Learning Outcomes (Requirements on Knowledge and Understanding/Skills/Autonomy and Responsibility for Learners Completing a Training Course)	Minimum Academic Load	Qualification Type
1	Basic and general knowledge and basic practice skills to carry out one or a number of simple and repeated tasks of a field of work or study in an unchanged working context under the supervision of instructors.	5 credits	Certificate I
2	Factual and theoretical knowledge about tasks of a narrow scope in a field of work or study; general and basic knowledge about nature, culture, society and law; practical skills in standard techniques to perform a number of repeated tasks in contexts with very little change under the supervision of instructors; ability of self-control in a number of specific activities.	15 credits	Certificate II
3	Factual and theoretical knowledge about a number of contents in a field of work or study; general knowledge about nature, culture, society and law; basic information technology knowledge; awareness, professional skills, and communicative skills required to carry out tasks or solve problems independently in stable and familiar contexts.	25 credits	Certificate III
4	Factual and theoretical knowledge in a field of work or study; general knowledge about politics, nature, culture, society, law and information technology; awareness, professional skills, and communicative skills required to carry out frequent or complicated tasks; ability to work in groups or work individually in known and changeable contexts, disposition to take personal responsibility and responsibility toward own groups; capacity to instruct and supervise the ordinary tasks of others.	35 or 50 credits* * Depending on graduation from upper or lower secondary schools	Associate degree
5	Comprehensive, factual and theoretical knowledge about a discipline; general knowledge about politics, nature, culture, society, law and information technology; awareness, professional skills, and communicative skills required to solve complex tasks or issues; ability to work in groups or work individually in known and changeable contexts; disposition to take personal responsibility and responsibility for providing guidance; capacity to supervise and evaluate the ordinary tasks of own groups.	60 credits	College degree
6	Firm practical and comprehensive theoretical knowledge about a field of work or study and general knowledge about social science, politics, nature, culture, society, law and information technology; awareness related to criticism, analysis, and consolidation; professional skills and communicative skills required to solve complex tasks or issues; ability to work in groups or work individually in changeable contexts; disposition to take personal responsibility and responsibility for providing guidance and disseminating knowledge in the field of study; capacity to supervise ordinary tasks of others.	120–180 credits	Undergraduate degree
7	Comprehensive, practical and theoretical knowledge to master the knowledge in a field of study; skills in argumentation, analysis, and consolidation of data and information scientifically and creatively; skills in research to develop, innovate, and use suitable technologies in the field of study or work; skills to disseminate knowledge in profession; ability to self-orient and adapt to changeable professional contexts; ability to guide other people to carry out their tasks; capacity of management, evaluation, and innovation to increase the efficiency of work.	30–60 credits	Master's degree
8	Advanced, comprehensive factual and theoretical knowledge of a field of study; skills to consolidate and analyze information, discover and solve problems creatively, to shape thinking and conduct research independently and creatively, and to disseminate knowledge and formulate national and international cooperation networks in management and control of specialized activities; creativity and ability of self-orientation and professional instruction; ability to make professional conclusions and scientific suggestions.	90–120 credits	Doctoral degree

Note: Appendix 4 provides a more detailed structure of the National Qualification Framework.
Source: Compiled and slightly adapted from Decision No. 1982/QD-TTg of the Prime Minister dated 18 October 2016.

71. **National skills standards.** Based on provisions in the 2006 TVET Law,[73] the Viet Nam government launched the development of national skills standards already in 2008 by establishing a lead agency for this task in MOLISA's General Department of Vocational Training (GDVT) and by endorsing respective regulations, which specified key agents including diverse line ministries and employer representatives and guided the processes, operative procedures, and expected outcomes of this endeavor. A major achievement was the establishment of national skills standards development committees and national skills standards appraisal subcommittees initially enjoying active participation of industry representatives and employers. However, a GDVT study (MOLISA and BMZ 2012) reported as early as in 2012 that active participation in these committees had basically shrunk to contributions of training institutions, "whereas the role of enterprises is passive and dim." The study concluded that the quality of these standards would be "limited in terms of relevance for labor market." As Figure 2.20 shows, the process has significantly slowed over the past years, while parallel initiatives, supported by the Australian Government and the Asia-Pacific Economic Cooperation, focused on the development of common competence standards for selected occupational fields across different Asian countries.[74]

Figure 2.20: Number of National Occupational Skills Standards Established between 2008 and 2015

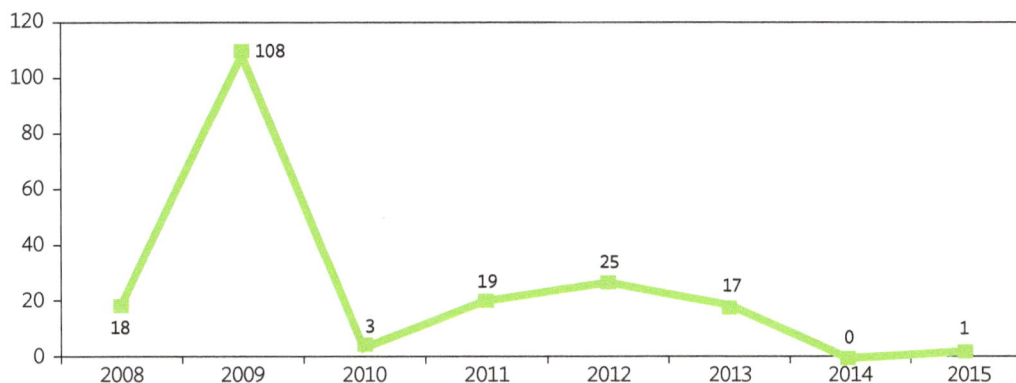

Source: Directorate of Vocational Education and Training and National Institute for Vocational Education and Training. 2017. *Viet Nam Vocational Education and Training Report 2015*. Ha Noi.

72. According to MOLISA's 2015 TVET report (DVET and NIVET 2017), 191 national occupational skills standards (NOSS) have so far been established and promulgated for 189 occupations,[75] 36 centers for assessment and certification of NOSS were granted certificates, a respective contingent of accreditors was developed, occupational skills assessment for workers was tested for 22 national occupations and 4 occupations following Japanese standards (Figure 2.21). By 2015, a total of 83

---

[73]   The ADB 2014 TVET Assessment Report for Viet Nam provides detailed descriptions of the legal framework for developing a national skills standard system.

[74]   Under the project "Development and Comparison of TVET Standards" within the Australian–Vietnamese Government Partnership Program for Development, three countries—Viet Nam, the Philippines, and Australia—cooperated to establish common competency standards in the four fields of automobile (auto mechanics), agriculture (aquaculture team leader), construction (elementary engineering), and manufacturing (mechanics and welding). Within the framework of the Asia-Pacific Economic Cooperation project "Comparing the Training Levels in Transportation and Logistics," five countries—Australia, the People's Republic of China, Indonesia, the Philippines, and Viet Nam—developed generic competency standards for five occupations of the logistics sector: warehouse operator, logistic administrative officer, freight forwarder, warehouse supervisor, and supply chain manager.

[75]   Further 275 standards shall be developed from 2016 to 2020 while 264 shall be updated during this period.

occupations had also national occupational skills examinations compiled but only for 62 occupations those examinations could be deployed, as the rest had not been appraised for promulgation. Hence, by the end of 2015, occupational skills assessment could be conducted only for a total number of 8,407 workers; only less than half of them (49.7%) actually met the assessment requirements.

Figure 2.21: Number of National Occupational Skills Standards Promulgated until 2015 by Sector

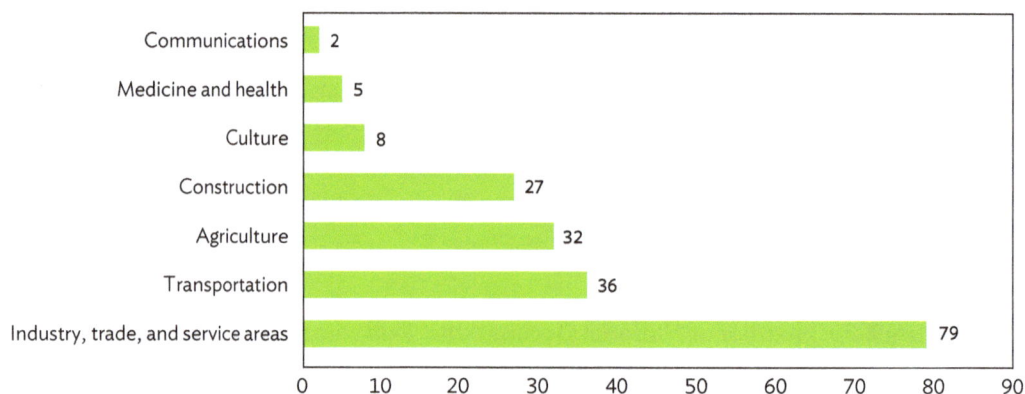

Source : Directorate of Vocational Education and Training and National Institute for Vocational Education and Training. 2017. *Viet Nam Vocational Education and Training Report 2015*. Ha Noi.

73. Yet, it is still unclear whether these accomplishments have spurred also tangible changes toward outcome orientation of vocational curricula and institutional profiles and how congruence shall be achieved between the qualification levels (eight for the NQF, and five for NOSS) and task/competence descriptors of the NQF and the NOSS[76] (Table 2.6).

74. MOLISA's 2015 TVET report provides more indications for a piecemeal perpetuation of the traditional input-oriented approach by stating that only "some parts of the training curricula were developed on basis of occupational skills standards" and adding that "for international focal occupations" 8 curricula from Malaysia, 12 curricula from Australia, and some programs from Germany were transferred, partly piloted, and tested at some colleges. Teachers are currently being trained in Germany (July/August 2019), however the implementation remains a challenges, as the training programs have not been adapted to the local conditions and the requirements of the industry. How these foreign curricula will comply with national occupational standards and compete with national certificates on the labor market remains unclear. Managers of TVET colleges predestined to implement those curricula assumed that the actual cost of course delivery at this level will be about seven times higher than the current D14 million–D16 million, which the Prime Minister has endorsed for three pilot TVET colleges as the maximum limit of tuition fees to be charged from students per academic year.[77]

---

[76] MOLISA's Circular No. 03/2017/TT-BLDTBXH prescribing the Procedures for Design, Evaluation and Issuance of the Training Program leaves the orientation of training curricula to skills standards to "Executive Boards" or a "Group of Designers" at the institutional level to "define objectives of the training program, minimum requirements concerning knowledge and competency that students may attain after graduation from their respective training industry or occupation." It rather unclear specifies that such definitions should also be "based on vocational skill standards and learning outcomes at the corresponding qualification level of training industry and occupation."

[77] Prime Minister Decisions No. 538, 539, and 540 issued on 4 April 2016 approve a pilot project for the period 2016–2019 that provides autonomy to three colleges (HCMC Technical College, LILAMA 2 Industrial College, and Quy Nhon Vocational College) and includes the establishment of independent fee structures and college management.

Table 2.6: Levels, Performance Criteria, and Competence Descriptors of National Occupational Skills Standards

Level	Framework of National Occupational Skills Standards (Criteria regarding nature and extent of required jobs, scope and situation in which jobs are performed, level of flexibility and creativity in performing the jobs, and level of coordination and responsibility in carrying out the job)
1	(a) Perform simple tasks, repetitive tasks in fixed situations. (b) Have the basic knowledge of the profession and understanding of the activities of the profession in limited areas; be able to use the knowledge and understanding to carry out the work as being instructed. (c) Be able to receive, record, and communicate required information; be able to participate in teamwork; be partly responsible for the results of work.
2	(a) Perform routine tasks and some complicated tasks in certain situations. (b) Have professional knowledge and understanding of a wide range of tasks in many areas; be able to apply knowledge and understanding to solve common technical problems and some complex issues but need guidance when performing tasks. (c) Be able to reason, judge, and explain information; be self-controlled in teamwork and able to work independently in some cases when performing tasks; be mainly responsible for the results of work.
3	(a) Execute most of the complicated tasks, the tasks which have many options in many different situations. (b) Have professional knowledge, basic knowledge of principles and theory, and extensive knowledge of the activities of the profession in various fields; be able to apply gained knowledge and understanding to come up with solutions for complicated professional problems and to meet the management's requirements while performing the job. (c) Be able to identify, analyze, and evaluate the information from many different sources; work independently as well as guide others in the group while performing the job; take responsibility for the quality of the results/products according to the prescribed standards and take partial responsibility for the results of work that other members of the team execute.
4	(a) Do most of the complex work and work that includes decision-making in many different situations. (b) Have specialized professional knowledge, deep knowledge of principles, theory, and extensive knowledge of the activities of the profession in various fields; be able to apply gained knowledge and understanding to come up with solutions for complicated professional technical problems as well as manager's requirements while performing the job. (c) Analyze and evaluate information from various sources and use the results of such analysis and evaluation to provide opinions and recommendations for management and research purposes; work highly independently and have high self-management; be able to manage and lead teams in the process of performing jobs; take responsibility for the quality of work results and products according to the prescribed standards and take responsibility for the results of work or products made by other members of the teams.
5	(a) Perform the complex work and work that includes decision-making in all situations. (b) Have specialized professional knowledge, deep knowledge of principles, theory, and extensive knowledge of the activities of the profession in various fields; be able to analyze, consider, diagnose, and design solutions to solve complex technical and professional problems and to meet the management's requirements in a wide range of work. (c) Analyze, evaluate, and generate information to form ideas and initiatives; work independently and have high self-management; be able to manage and lead teams in the process of performing jobs; take responsibility for the quality of work results and products and take responsibility for the results of work or products made by other members of the teams according to the prescribed standards.

Source: Directorate of Vocational Education and Training and National Institute for Vocational Education and Training. 2017. *Viet Nam Vocational Education and Training Report 2015*. Ha Noi.

75. Moreover, the new TVET law no longer contains specifications on NOSS and its systemic relation to the national qualification framework. According to new regulations,[78] the development, assessment, and certification of national occupational skills are now to be adjusted in accordance with the Employment Law. While MOLISA appreciates this as a "positive change in the perception of the role and position of occupational skills assessment in the world of work" and expects that it will make "the assessment and certification of occupational skills more practically relevant," severe structural challenges concerning the future alignment of NOSS and the NQF can be imagined from another casual remark: "The Law on TVET identified three training levels of the TVET system, however, compared with the labor market demand and the national education system structure framework as well as the national qualifications framework, this revealed shortcomings" (MOLISA 2017).

76. MOLISA's Circular No. 15/2017 on Criteria and Standards for Quality Accreditation of Vocational Education envisages the need for NQF and NOSS alignment of vocational training programs only in its enhanced requirements for program accreditation at elementary level. Colleges and intermediate schools are apparently not (yet) subjected to such regulations (see next section).

E. Quality Assurance and System Accreditation

77. The adoption of TVET curricula from abroad follows the government's policy objective for 2020 to obtain around 70 high-quality vocational schools certified for training in some vocations that are recognized by the advanced countries in the ASEAN region or in the world.[79] This shall contribute "to the basic and comprehensive innovation of vocational training in Viet Nam" and meet "the requirement of high quality human resources for socioeconomic development of the country."[80]

78. By law, all institutions delivering TVET in Viet Nam need to be licensed and registered by competent authorities acting on behalf of public and private bodies that are granted ownership of these institutions. MOLISA, through its DVET as the central state management agency for TVET, stipulates criteria, legal conditions, and procedures to be followed for this and, jointly with its satellite departments at provincial level, shall monitor their implementation and compliance with legal requirements, including the fulfillment of a wide range of duties that specify the quality of training organization and delivery in these institutes.[81]

79. Although quality assurance and quality accreditation are now mandatory elements of these duties, which apply to all TVET institutes,[82] the new TVET law includes a particular chapter that specifies also the requirement of program accreditations concerning "national focal occupations and TVET

---

[78] Government Decree No. 31/2015/ND-CP regulating the details of the implementation of a number of articles in the Employment Law regarding the assessment and certification of National Occupational Skills; and MOLISA Circular No. 56/2015/TT-BLDTBXH dated 24 December 2015 guiding the formulation, appraisal, and promulgation of the NOSS.

[79] As mentioned in the previous section, it is still unclear how these foreign curricula will comply with national occupational standards and compete with national certificates on the Viet Nam labor market. In addition, there is yet no evidence on the awareness that those imported curricula and standards need to be continuously updated and renewed in parallel to respective processes in the partnering countries to ensure that respective qualifications will be recognized by them also in the future.

[80] Prime Minister Decision No. 761/2014/QD-TTg Approving the High Quality Vocational School Development Project by 2020.

[81] Cf. Law on Vocational Education and Training (2014), Article 23.

[82] Unlike the previous law, which did not contain such detailed specifications but only set the framework for quality accreditation without binding conditions for its implementation at institutional level. Hence, formal accreditation was basically perceived as voluntary and provided no clear incentives to many TVET institutions for participation (see also ADB 2014).

programs for occupations approaching regionally, internationally advanced levels"[83] as well as those "on fields, trades serving the state management."[84] Apart from this, the chapter provides the legal basis for organizing and managing quality accreditation, defines the duties and rights of institutes during its implementation, and issues some specifications on the benefits of and implications after status recognition.

80. According to MOLISA (2017), 25% of vocational colleges, 10% of vocational secondary schools, and 3.5% of vocational training centers have been subject to formal accreditation and recognition.[85] These accreditations were based on a set of nine quality criteria with 50 standards (Table 2.7) covering key input factors such as management, staff, pedagogy, facilities, services and finances, and measure 150 indicators specific for each institutional level. Accreditations were to be conducted through a three-stage approach, comprising initial self-assessment, an expert-guided internal assessment, and potentially in addition, also a fully independent external assessment. The first two stages resulted in awards of sophisticated score-based quality levels, which categorize an institution's quality status either as not yet sufficient (level 1), satisfactory but with the need of improvement (level 2), or fully compliant to the national quality standard (level 3).

Table 2.7: Criteria, Standards, and Benchmarks for Vocational Education and Training School Accreditation (2008–2010)

	Criteria		Standards	College	VTC
				Score Σ=100	
1	Mission and goals	1.1	Mission and objectives clearly defined, approved, and published	6	6
		1.2	Mission and objectives established to meet the needs of labor market and learners in accordance with actual local conditions		
		1.3	Mission and objectives periodically reviewed and adjusted		
2	Organization and management	2.1	Regulations on the organization and management mechanism regularly reviewed, evaluated, and adjusted	10	8
		2.2	Logical structure in accordance with national regulations as well as with objectives of school resulting in high effectiveness		
		2.3	Development of teachers and school managers		
		2.4	Organization of Viet Nam Communist Party and other social organizations		
		2.5	Monitoring activities regularly implemented and improved		
3	Teaching and learning activities	3.1	Enrollment work effectively implemented in compliance with regulations of MOLISA	16	16
		3.2	Diversifying of training forms and establishment of relationships with enterprises		
		3.3	Planning of training logically designed, effectively implemented; organization of teaching and learning in accordance with requirements of the actual occupation		
		3.4	Continuing training programs		
		3.5	Training in compliance with approved contents		
		3.6	Teaching methods in orientation of active learning		
		3.7	Process-based evaluation giving feedback to learners, in accordance with form of training		
		3.8	Scientific research and international cooperation		

continued on next page

---

[83] Key occupations selected for training at international, regional and national level include automobile engineering, industrial electronics, metal cutting, industrial electrical engineering, electro-mechanics, welding, and refrigeration and air-conditioning technology.

[84] Law on Vocational Education and Training (2014), Article 65.

[85] However, only 52.4% of these colleges were granted certificates, while this applies to 91% of institutions, which were invested to become high-quality TVET institutes.

Table 2.7 continued

4	Teachers and management staff	4.1	Quantity and organizational structure of teachers	16	18
		4.2	Qualification and competence of teachers		
		4.3	Teachers' performance		
		4.4	Training for teachers		
		4.5	Qualification, competence, and ethics of principal and vice-principal		
		4.6	Quantity of management staff		
		4.7	Qualification of management staff		
		4.8	Quality of technical staff and office staff		
5	Program and curricula	5.1	Curriculum in accordance with national program framework	16	18
		5.2	Coherence of various levels of training; involvement of enterprises		
		5.3	Clearly defined learning outcomes, standards of knowledge and skills, methods of training and evaluation		
		5.4	Curriculum adjusted and improved based on reference to curriculum of developed countries and feedback from stakeholders		
		5.5	Curriculum with training modules and subjects		
		5.6	Training modules and subjects with learning materials		
		5.7	Innovative syllabus		
		5.8	Clarification of requirements of knowledge, skills, attitudes		
6	Library	6.1	Quantity of books, journals matching trained occupations	6	2
		6.2	Computers and internet		
		6.3	Support for readers		
7	Facilities, equipment, and teaching aids	7.1	Convenient location of school	14	18
		7.2	General design of campus		
		7.3	Technical infrastructure		
		7.4	System of classrooms, lecture halls, laboratories, workshops, classrooms		
		7.5	Operating conditions of the workshops		
		7.6	Quantity and quality of equipment		
		7.7	Preservation and storage of equipment		
8	Financial management	8.1	Assurance of financial resources	10	8
		8.2	Standardization and transparency of financial management		
		8.3	Financial estimation		
		8.4	Rationality, transparency and effectiveness of using finance		
		8.5	Financial reporting		
9	Services for trainees	9.1	Providing information about trained job, training courses, and other school rules for learners	6	6
		9.2	Ensuring the conditions on accommodation and health care for learners		
		9.3	Providing information about labor market and job recommendation for graduates		

MOLISA = Ministry of Labour–Invalids and Social Affairs, VTC = vocational training center.
Note: Based on Decision No. 02/2008/QD-BLDTBXH and Circular No. 19/2010/TT-BLDTBXH.
Sources: Directorate of Vocational Education and Training and National Institute for Vocational Education and Training. 2017. *Viet Nam Vocational Education and Training Report 2015*. Ha Noi; and P. C. Diep. 2016. Substantial Policies and Measures to Promote Quality Assurance of TVET in Vietnam Towards Mutual Recognition of Qualifications in ASEAN. Viet Nam: Ho Chi Minh City University of Technical Education. http://www.tvet-online.asia/issue/7/diep (accessed November 2017).

81. So far, prioritization of school accreditation on voluntary basis has yielded positive results, particularly among selected colleges and secondary schools that were invested to become high-quality institutions. By the end of 2015, from a total of 239 applicants, 184 vocational institutions had been quality accredited at minimum level 2 (Figure 2.22). Of these, 113 institutions (78 colleges and 22 secondary schools) were granted valid certificates at level 3. Less promising are the results for vocational training centers (VTCs). Only 323 (11.2%) of a total of

2,893 VTCs that were asked between 2013 and 2015 to conduct a self-evaluation actually submitted respective reports on their school quality. Apparently, none of them has so far achieved a certification by the GDVT, as MOLISA reported only 13 from a total of 28 VTCs, which had been fully accredited between 2010 and 2013.

Figure 2.22: Quality Accreditation Results of TVET Institutes, 2008–2015

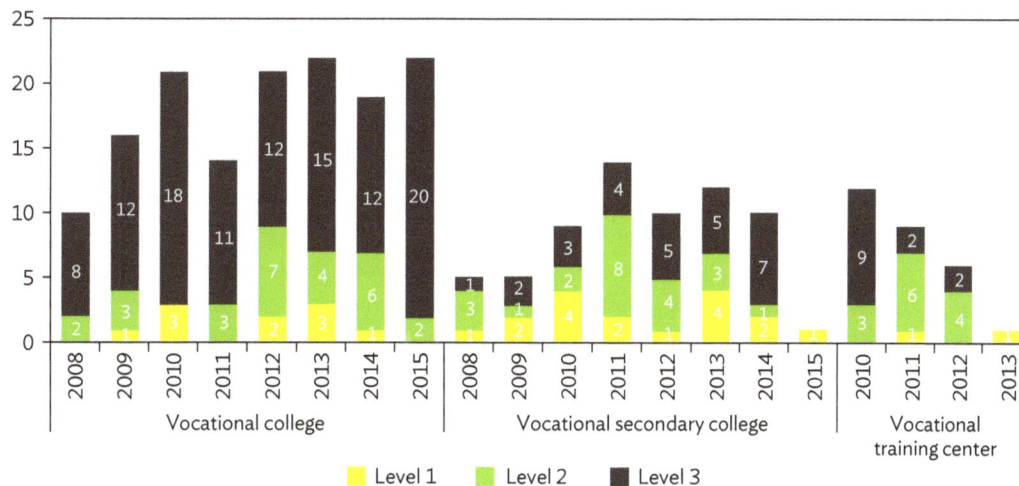

TVET = technical and vocational education and training.
Source: Directorate of Vocational Education and Training and National Institute for Vocational Education and Training. 2017. *Viet Nam Vocational Education and Training Report 2015*. Ha Noi.

82. **New quality accreditation model.** Meanwhile, MOLISA has revised its quality accreditation model considerably. In June 2017, it launched a circular on quality accreditation of vocational education[86] promulgating a new set of criteria and standards as well as a more nuanced but simplified evaluation system for this. Criteria and standards have been refined and streamlined into a more reasonable structure and now comprise specific sets of requirements differing substantially between VTCs and colleges and secondary schools. In addition, there are now detailed prescriptions for the accreditation of training programs, which are specific for two vocational levels (see also Appendix 5).

83. Measurable process standards now clearly stipulate the involvement of enterprises in program design, implementation, student assessment, and training evaluation. Mandatory requirements for teachers not only include continuous training on their professional knowledge and skills but stipulate also that they perform practice sessions in industry facilities "to update their understanding of technologies and methods of production management."[87] Standards for training facilities and equipment now address the requirement to fulfill minimal quality standards relevant for each discipline and stipulate that institutions apply cost norms for materials essential for learning activities in different majors. Moreover, the performance of internal quality assurance has also become a separate criterion comprising different sets of standards that define measurable outcome indicators regarding ambitious

---

[86] MOLISA Circular No. 15/2017/TT-BLDTBXH on Criteria and Standards for Quality Accreditation of Vocational Education which came into force on 24 July 2017.

[87] Footnote 86.

employment rates of graduates[88] as well as employer feedback on school graduates' performance after employment.

84. A peculiarity still appears in specifications prescribing the quality of training program curricula for different vocational levels. While VTCs will have to explicitly align their programs to the NQF and NOSS to become accredited, those delivered by colleges and intermediate schools only need "to ensure the achievement of vocational education objectives." However, unlike VTCs, higher-level TVET institutions have to involve at least two employer representatives "in the process of formulation and appraisal of training programs."[89]

85. **Accreditation standards for high-quality vocational education and training institutions.** Apart from enhanced quality standards for all TVET institutions and programs, the demand for quality accreditation has become even more ambitious with Prime Minister Decision No. 761/QD-TTg in May 2014 Approving the High Quality Vocational School Development Project by 2020. This decision stipulates a set of higher standards for institutions to be recognized as "high quality vocational schools" by introducing criteria that also largely focus on measurable outcome and output performance of vocational programs (such as employment of graduates and their proficiency levels regarding NOSS, ICT, and English language abilities), especially for those that are based on regional and international curriculum standards.

86. According to the results of a 2015 survey GDVT conducted in 45 vocational schools, some of these criteria were rated as difficult to be applied to a total of 70 schools envisaged to achieve this status by 2020. Consequently, MOLISA through its GDVT launched in 2016 a pilot project, which tested a set of modified but more elaborated criteria, standards, and indicators for high-quality performance of TVET institutes and centers of excellence in five selected vocational colleges (Appendix 5). Gesellschaft für Internationale Zusammenarbeit (GIZ) and the Korea International Cooperation Agency conducted workshops to develop the quality criteria, standards, and indicators; developed guidelines for evaluation; conducted training on self-evaluation in five partner schools and for external review teams; and compiled the final results. Apart from demanding input and output criteria, strong emphasis was put on a range of process standards addressing market-demand-oriented training implementation as well as close cooperation with enterprises in program design and delivery.[90] The test was successfully completed in July 2017 by a Directorate of Vocational Education and Training (DVET) workshop demonstrating appropriateness and applicability of the approach. The DVET announced to submit a set of revised criteria and standards to the Prime Minister for approval after a final appraisal on the results and issue a circular on the accreditation of selected 70 high-quality schools by the end of 2017.

87. In parallel, the DVET is working on special criteria and standards for the accreditation of training programs in national, regional, and international focal occupations that have been piloted for 44 programs and which shall be extended to 1,500 others by 2020. Although the accelerating dynamics in developing and improving TVET quality standards reflect the central government's strong will to establish fundamental system reforms, how the addressees and beneficiaries of these interventions will be able to cope with the implementation challenges remains to be seen. The risk is that sophisticated

---

[88] Generally only for intermediate schools and colleges, but also a requirement for program accreditation of VTCs.

[89] MOLISA Circular No. 15/2017/TT-BLDTBXH.

[90] Such criteria and standards were only marginally covered in the previous quality accreditation scheme but are partly included in the new QA model recently stipulated by MOLISA Circular No. 15/2017/TT-BLDTBXH.

drawing board constructs well adopted from international models but created with little consideration of actual training conditions (particularly regarding management capacity and financial implications) might be perceived as obstructive regulations rather than as constructive means to improve training quality and labor market orientation of individual TVET institutions that struggle for their existence. To avoid such a dilemma, more work has to be done in establishing effective (financial) support structures and confidence-building advisory services that persistently coach and guide the staff of TVET institutions (preferentially by good practice examples) toward incremental enhancements of their business processes and quality assurance.

F. Private Sector Involvement

88. Involvement of Viet Nam's enterprises in TVET delivery has become a more prominent aspect in quality accreditation, especially in ongoing efforts to establish a network of high-quality schools. Basically, the approach holds all TVET institutions responsible for engaging employers to deliver training and quality assurance and for establishing and developing respective enduring relationships. Field visits show that some TVET colleges have already managed to establish intensive and highly productive relationships with enterprises in their vicinity. MOLISA's 2015 TVET report refers to three successful pilot models of cooperative training within the frame of the Vietnamese–German Programme Reform of TVET in Viet Nam including training of in-company trainers, flexible arrangements of training programs, and internship phases in accordance with operational plans of the enterprises (Box 2.1).. Highly effective models of tripartite partnerships between government agencies, TVET institutes, and Japanese enterprises have also been reported in the Japan International Cooperation Agency study (JICA 2014).[91]

89. However, comprehensive data on a nationwide scale regarding school collaborations with industry partners are lacking. A representative employer survey conducted in 2011 revealed that industry cooperation with Vietnamese TVET institutions has been largely confined to graduate recruitment procedures and internship provision to students. Only 10% of employers stated an involvement in curriculum development and only 5% took part in student assessments (World Bank and CIEM 2012). What is still missing are reasonable strategies and incentives for employers to support and collaborate also with TVET institutions that do not yet perform well in the demand orientation of their training delivery because of various organizational and financial constraints. MOLISA's new quality accreditation model seems to emphasize unilateral obligations for TVET institutions to solve this chicken-and-egg-problem. However, unless public TVET suppliers gain the basic capacity (including appropriate training facilities and equipment as well as competent staff) to make themselves more attractive, the demand side will likely remain skeptic and stay reluctant with regard to active contributions.

90. In its Vocational Training Development Strategy 2011–2020, the Viet Nam government sees further TVET development as the "responsibility of the entire society" and mandates the collaboration of a broad range of government and nongovernment stakeholders including employers and employees to meet the country's labor market demands. Accordingly, the new TVET law 2014 dedicates Chapter IV to "Rights and Obligations of Enterprises in TVET." Rights basically cover eligibilities to establish and conduct own TVET institutions; cooperate with TVET institutions in a range of program-relevant tasks, including curriculum design and outcome assessment; and receive tax reductions for such

---

[91] In JICA (2014), the Japan International Cooperation Agency had to admit that because of various constraints, the approach could be applied only in a few TVET institutions.

Box 2.1: Common Features of Piloted Cooperative Training Models in Viet Nam

Cooperation Approach:

Training cooperation between a technical and vocational education and training (VET) institute and an enterprise focuses on the improvement of the quality in teaching occupational knowledge and skills as well as work skills and attitudes at the workplace. The main characteristics of such partnerships are as follows:

- The TVET institute takes the lead management position. Cooperating partners are enterprises.
- The enterprises are responsible for implementing a defined part of the training program, which is based on occupational standards jointly developed by the TVET institute and the business sector.
- There are two learning venues: at the TVET institute (classrooms and practical workshop) for building knowledge and basic occupational skills and at the enterprises for building production skills in the production and work process.
- Assessment of learning achievement is implemented jointly by the TVET institute and the enterprises.

The cooperation process includes the following three basic steps:

1. Preparation Phase

- Enterprise survey: Study the demand for technical skills in selected occupations, identify the current state of the local technology in these occupations, and derive orientation for the development of appropriate training programs.
- Adoption of occupational standards: TVET institute, partnering enterprises, business associations, and DVET jointly develop an agreement on level and local relevance of occupational standards (national, regional, or international) to be addressed by the training program.
- Development of training program modules and training materials: Objectives and structure of training programs follow agreed occupational standards, consistently link theory to work-relevant practice activities and specify expected learning outcomes in clear and measurable performance indicators.
- Conclusion of cooperation agreements with partnering enterprises: Cooperating enterprises are selected based on agreed criteria. A memorandum of understanding on training cooperation will be signed. A training cooperation contract specifies the number of students to be sent to study at enterprises, clarifies the responsibilities of each party as well as the specific contents of each practical training period, and identifies personnel (coordinators, training staff, teachers) who will conduct the different training activities.
- Training of in-company trainers: A training-of-trainers course will be developed and conducted for the enterprise coordinators and trainers including topics on teaching methodology, training organization and methods, monitoring and evaluation activities, and the coordination of tasks and activities among partners.

2. Training Phase

- Active coordination: The TVET institute is active in the organization and coordination of cooperative activities. Both partners follow the contract provisions on training content, duration, and the model of cooperative training.
- Monitoring: Management and monitoring the delivery of cooperative training activities should be carried out persistently and effectively to optimize the quality of learning experiences and training outcomes.
- Commitment in sharing resources: TVET institutes must be flexible in adjusting their training plans to the production requirements and work conditions of enterprises. Preferentially, teachers and training coordinators of TVET institutes should have gained in-depth experience on this through preceding work placements or internships.

3. Assessment and Evaluation

- Assessment: Tests of theory knowledge (examinations) are conducted at the TVET institute; practical learning assessments are conducted at the enterprises. Trainers of the enterprises and teaching staff of TVET institutes are members of examination councils both at the enterprise and at the TVET institute. Certificates are granted by the Directorate of Vocational Education and Training and (optionally in addition) also by enterprises.
- Evaluation: Evaluation is carried out regularly after each training module. The evaluation shall be comprehensive and cover all aspects including the training program quality and the coordination and implementation process. It is necessary to obtain feedback from representatives of both enterprises and trainees and to make timely adjustments that improve the effectiveness and efficiency of the training.

Source: Adapted from Directorate of Vocational Education and Training and National Institute for Vocational Education and Training. 2017. *Viet Nam Vocational Education and Training Report 2015.* Ha Noi.

activities. Obligations comprise the tasks of providing information on training needs and employment structures, placing orders to train workers, and cooperating with registered TVET institutions by visiting factories as well as conducting practical training and (paid) internships for TVET teachers and students.[92] Moreover, Article 52 clause 8 of the TVET law directs employers to employ only trained workers and those possessing relevant professional certificates.

91. Although the national TVET development strategy includes considerations to "form a vocational learning support fund" for "contributions of enterprises and other (financial) sources for vocational training development," no specifications for such a fund have been made, either in the new TVET law or in MOLISA's draft project plan for the upcoming years. Financial contributions of enterprises are commonly negotiated through school partnerships.

92. The TVET law only marginally covers the establishment of an enduring institutional framework for private sector involvement in the following areas:[93]

- formulating strategies, plans, master plans, and policies for TVET development;

- developing occupational standards and relevant standards in TVET and training programs;

- participating in training and fostering teachers and learners to participate in national, ASEAN, and international skills competitions;

- establishing departments/units to coordinate operation and consultation of state management agencies and representatives of TVET institutions at all levels with enterprises, employers, the Viet Nam Chamber of Commerce and Industry, and trade unions on a part-time basis;

- piloting the establishment of sectoral skill councils in a number of priority areas; and

- developing models of public–private partnership in TVET (MOLISA 2017).

93. As already mentioned in ADB (2014), such preliminary goodwill gestures might become virtually ineffective unless major stakeholder associations are equipped with respective representative functions, and unless the envisaged bodies will have real authority to make decisions. This would not only require appropriate legal provisions but also binding commitments of relevant stakeholder representations to take over an institutionalized (not only part-time) role in such fields.[94]

94. So far, the Viet Nam Chamber of Commerce and Industry (VCCI), seems to perform well in "amplifying the voices heard in the private sector." It periodically publishes important relevant data on the labor market and recommends the fundamental TVET sector improvements to the government. However, apart from a general statement in its latest labor market report "to play a leading role to ensure successful implementation of a second major economic reform," no clear proposals on VCCI's potential contributions could be identified that would also go beyond the preliminarily intention "to propel tripartite dialogue or policy debates among the Government, employers and business

---

[92] Article 52 Clause 5 of the TVET Law states: "Pay wages for learners and teachers participating directly or working to produce products which meet technical specification requirements during training, practical training, internship in enterprises under the agreement by the parties."

[93] It states in its general section that "the Vietnam Chamber of Commerce and Industry, business associations, professional associations are responsible for participating in formulation, appraisal of vocational education and training program framework."

[94] The gradual retreat of industry and employer representatives from active participation in National Skills Standards Development Committees (see section II.3) proves that there is an urgent need for this.

membership organizations as well as workers' organizations." Recommendations for actions to "enhance workforce quality in terms of skills and productivity" in this report are described solely as government-related duties and tasks (VCCI and ILO 2016).

G. Information Technology and Information and Communication Technology

95. As with most other components building essential factors for quality assurance and relevance of Viet Nam's TVET system, investigations about the status of information and communication technology (ICT) that is deployed and used for governing, managing, and administrating the overall system as well as for facilitating training delivery by modern software applications and tools (e-learning) reveal a rather uneven picture. It can be briefly characterized by a prevailing contrast between highly ambitious government visions and largely poor and fragmented accomplishments regarding their actual realization, both in the operative clarity of MOLISA's TVET reform strategy and at the operational level of TVET institutions utilizing respective tools and technologies.

96. Although the government's Socio-Economic Development Plan up to the year 2020 demands to "accelerate the application of information technology in the operation of state agencies and the provision of public services and e-government deployment" and has given priority to the development of and investment in human resources in high-quality service sectors including information technology and automation, the implementation of corresponding measures does not seem to follow a comprehensive master plan.[95] Regarding education and training, several ICT initiatives over the last decade have been spreading among different ministerial bodies and agencies, however with limited or at least opaque outcomes.

97. As early as 2005, the Ministry of Education and Training (MOET) already introduced some visionary concepts such as "e-Vietnam," "e-Government," "e-Citizenship," and its ICT-in-Education Plan for 2001–2005, laying out long-term goals toward the following direction: (i) to meet the demand for IT human resources, facilitate building up the IT industry and establish broad IT applications to promote the country's socioeconomic development; and (ii) to meet the demand for educational reform with regard to innovation in content, teaching, and learning methods, as well as in educational management. In 2007, MOET announced that 2008/09 would be the "Year of ICT" in Vietnamese schools and started a program to equip all schools with basic internet access. In parallel, several research studies were launched to investigate the government's ICT policy and its penetration in Viet Nam's education system. Key findings revealed that, though enhancements in the physical access to ICT resources in the country's schools could be identified, having computers, projectors, and internet access would not be enough to transform education also toward higher quality since in practice, ICT was mainly used to replace existing teaching practice, in a very limited way (Peeraer and Van Petegem 2011). Despite such disillusioning findings, activities addressing ICT utilization in MOET's reform strategy up to the year 2020 remain rather unclear though it comes up with some ambitious quantitative targets.[96]

---

[95] On 24 July 2015, the Viet Nam government approved its "Program of Public Telecommunications Services Supply by 2020 (see Decision No. 1168/QD-TTg), which mainly shall improve Viet Nam's communication infrastructure (including fiber-optic internet access, mobile broadband, and satellite TV) and contains key investment areas, main beneficiaries (including educational institutions), and budgets for this.

[96] By 2015 and 2020, all university and collegial lecturers, and all vocational education and general education teachers, shall respectively apply ICT in training and compile and use e-training manuals and e-textbooks.

98. Blurred boundaries between state management and direct management tasks are manifesting in an Advisory Report for Viet Nam's Ministry of Industry and Trade, which focuses on a Road Map for Enterprise Resource Planning/Enterprise Performance Planning/E-Learning for Viet Nam's Higher Education System (MOIT unpublished). Analyzing the state of IT and ICT systems in higher education in Viet Nam through a series of surveys and workshops, the report concludes that investment in core IT systems would be needed urgently "to enable Vietnamese educational institutions to fulfill its mission in preparing current and future students to be valuable and productive leaders in business, government and education." Key features forming the foundation of such systems should focus on two elements that would connect universities, colleges, and schools under the Ministry of Industry and Trade with its Human Resources Department and among each other: (i) an information-reporting web portal serving as a single point of access to information systems, tools, and processes and providing a "one stop shop" for students, faculty, and staff to engage in necessary interactions with partner institutions and the government management level; and (ii) an integrated data warehouse/exchange system enabling the collection of currently disparate raw data from this portal and other sources to be compiled and organized into a tool for data-driven decision-making for the Ministry of Industry and Trade. While the report already comes up with a detailed list of functional requirements and procedural tasks for establishing such system(s) through a 7-year project, it does not reflect potential linkages to future systems of superordinate state management agencies under MOLISA and MOET.

99. Indeed, MOLISA's 2015 TVET Report (DVET and NIVET 2017) shows similar, though not very concrete, accomplishments in this area. According to this, an "electronic information portal" on vocational training was set up along with a "vocational training database." Software for managing the training of rural workers as well as "technical support and online training" on its utilization was provided. In addition, MOLISA reports that "national vocational training software" has been developed and "will be used by vocational training institutes nationwide" after this activity was initially implemented in 26 out of 45 TVET institutes. According to the report, the pilot included a number of "electronic lessons" (107 "electronic lessons" and 70 "practical lessons") and simulation tools (2D/3D simulation) to be used in training for such occupations as metal cutting, automobile technology, mechanical engineering, industrial electrics, welding, and computer repair and assembling.

100. MOLISA's main policy instrument to promote IT/ICT utilization in the TVET system is its national project no. 1,982. However, so far not much is known about its concrete directions, let alone its accomplishments regarding tangible interventions in this complex field of technical and administrative reform. Statements from DVET officials collected during the fieldwork mission for this assessment indicated a range of substantial limitations and weaknesses in this project:

(i) Activities concerned with collecting and processing data from TVET colleges and schools (particularly from TVET institutions formerly managed under MOET) are slow, mainly because of severe budget and capacity constraints.

(ii) There is no specific project budget yet for TVET system-relevant IT/ICT components; funding of initial accomplishments so far had to be covered by regular DVET funds.

(iii) The DVET has no specific official plan or strategy for IT/ICT in TVET; the current approach is to publish basic information about TVET institutions on the DVET website, but there are still only separate one-way communication structures (DVET provides top-down information to schools and schools send information through traditional channels [data in Excel sheets through e-mail, contact by phone calls] on individual request).

(iv) It is largely unclear how data on the TVET system collected and processed by the DVET are used for developing the government's policy and strategy. Statements of diverse stakeholders interviewed indicate that basic considerations to improve the data and information collection process is at a starting point and utilization of the data and information for policy making is still on the waiting list.

(v) Although the project comprises also components addressing the application of ICT in the training process (e-learning), there are no clear specifications (let alone standards) on this, except some pilot programs targeting a number of selected schools (see above). Also, this pilot had to be funded by regular DVET budgets. Reportedly, several individual programs of schools are supported by official development assistance or private contributions, but there is neither a specific evaluation nor statistics on this.

101. As with other policy interventions, MOLISA seems to follow an IT/ICT approach that mainly addresses TVET institutions in their responsibility and tasks for management improvements and quality assurance. MOLISA's draft Project Plan for TVET Reform Up to 2020 with an Orientation to 2030 demands the following: By 2020, 50% of colleges, 30% of intermediate level institutions, 10% of TVET centers, and by 2030, 100% of colleges, 100% of intermediate level institutions, and 30% of TVET centers, "shall have advanced and modern internal quality control and management systems," "apply information technology to build a management information system," and "improve the capacity of administrators and teachers in charge of management and quality assurance through training." How this will be linked to and coordinated with MOLISA's overall ambition to "build national TVET information management systems ensuring the connectivity between state management agencies in charge of vocational education at all levels and vocational education institutions" has not yet been further specified.

102. Although some high-level TVET institutions have established special IT departments and data analysis teams that perform regular surveys on job opportunities for graduates and collect, analyze, and report information also in other domains useful for developing policies, strategies, and plans of these schools, it remains highly questionable whether and how such proprietary approaches can be integrated into a nationwide strategy that can spur not only (one-way) publication of school-relevant information but also supports interaction and information sharing, both at horizontal (among schools, teachers, and students) as well as at vertical levels (between TVET institutions and their diverse management agencies).

103. The same applies to MOLISA's visions regarding the "application of simulation software in teaching activities" only vaguely complemented by stipulating "access to open e-learning materials centers." Experiences from other countries show that the establishment of respective learning resource centers requires not only significant investments in appropriate technologies such as an advanced digital library/repository system (including sources that will cover recurrent costs of its operation and maintenance), but also important initial consideration on legal aspects concerning options for accessing relevant content and copyright issues. Moreover, there needs to be advanced ICT knowledge and local capacity to design and configure, maintain and promote the usability of such system, by adopting and adapting international standards of e-learning technologies and specifications such as the learning objects metadata standard and other guiding instructional (system) design processes and the complex administration of advanced learning management systems.

4. Financing TVET

104. Reflecting the importance of developing higher quality human resources, the Viet Nam government's target is to spend 20% of its total budget on education and training (Government of Viet Nam 2012b). Although the share of the government budgets for this sector has been constantly increased during the last years, it still reached only 15.9% in 2015. Significant expenditure growth rates in 2012 and 2013 have meanwhile declined, following the government's overall policy to reduce high public debt. Nevertheless, the proportion of public spending on education and training to (inflation-adjusted) gross domestic product (GDP) increased from 3.6% in 2011 to 4.5% in 2015, which was a rate comparable to many other middle-income countries and to the regional average of East Asia and the Pacific (Table 2.8).

Table 2.8: Trends in the Financing of Education in Viet Nam, 2011–2015

Item	2011	2012	2013	2014	2015
Government total annual expenditure (VND billion)[a]	787,554	978,463	1,088,153	1,103,983	1,177,100
Expenditure on education and training (VND billion)[a]	99,369	127,136	155,603	174,777	187,653
Share of education and training expenditure in total expenditure (%)	12.6	13.0	14.3	15.8	15.9
Annual growth of total government expenditure (%)		24.2	11.2	1.5	6.6
Annual growth of education and training expenditure		21.8	18.3	11.0	6.9
Total Viet Nam GDP (VND billion, current price)[a, b]	2,779,880	3,245,419	3,584,262	3,937,856	4,192,862
Annual nominal growth rate of GDP (%)		16.7	10.4	9.9	6.5
Annual inflation rate (%)[c]	18.7	9.1	6.6	4.1	0.6
Annual real GDP growth (%)		7.6	3.8	5.8	5.9
Proportion of education and training expenditure to GDP (%)	3.6	3.9	4.3	4.4	4.5

GDP = gross domestic product.
Sources:
(a) General Statistics Office of Viet Nam. https://www.gso.gov.vn/default_en.aspx?tabid=775 (accessed January 2018).
(b) International Monetary Fund (IMF). International Financial Statistics. http://www.imf.org/en/Data (accessed January 2018).
(c) IMF. 2017. *World Economic Outlook, October 2017*. Washington, DC.

105. **Government expenditure for technical and vocational education and training.** According to MOLISA's latest TVET Report (DVET and NIVET 2017), the annual government budget for vocational training also increased steadily between 2010 and 2014, from VND8,937 billion to VND14,308 billion (Table 2.9). However, comparing these figures with recent General Statistics Office statistics shows that the relative share for this subsector in the total government expenditure on education and training actually would have declined during this period[97] (Figure 2.23). With average shares of about 1.2% of total government expenditures and a mean average of 0.35% of GDP during this period, this would be a rather low rate compared with the average government spending for TVET of around 1% of GDP in many European countries but matches the rates of some other countries in the Southeast Asian region (Wright 2017).

---

[97] While it had increased from 4.9% to 9.0% between 2001 and 2010.

Table 2.9: Government Expenditure for Vocational Training for 2010–2014

Item	2010	2011	2012	2013	2014
Government budget for vocational training (VND billion)[a]	8,937	9,800	10,746	11,784	14,308
Vocational training budget in total government expenditure (%)[b]	1.38	1.24	1.10	1.08	1.30
Vocational training budget in total government expenditure for education and training (%)[b]	11.43	9.86	8.45	7.57	8.19
Proportion of total government vocational training expenditure to GDP (%)[b]	0.41	0.35	0.30	0.33	0.36

GDP = gross domestic product.
Sources:
(a) Directorate of Vocational Education and Training and National Institute for Vocational Education and Training. 2017. *Viet Nam Vocational Education and Training Report 2015*. Ha Noi.
(b) Calculations based on data of General Statistics Office of Viet Nam and IMF (cf. Table 15). Note: Calculated figures deviate from MOLISA's 2015 TVET Report calculations due to different reference values for GDP data (current prices versus constant 2010 prices used by MOLISA.

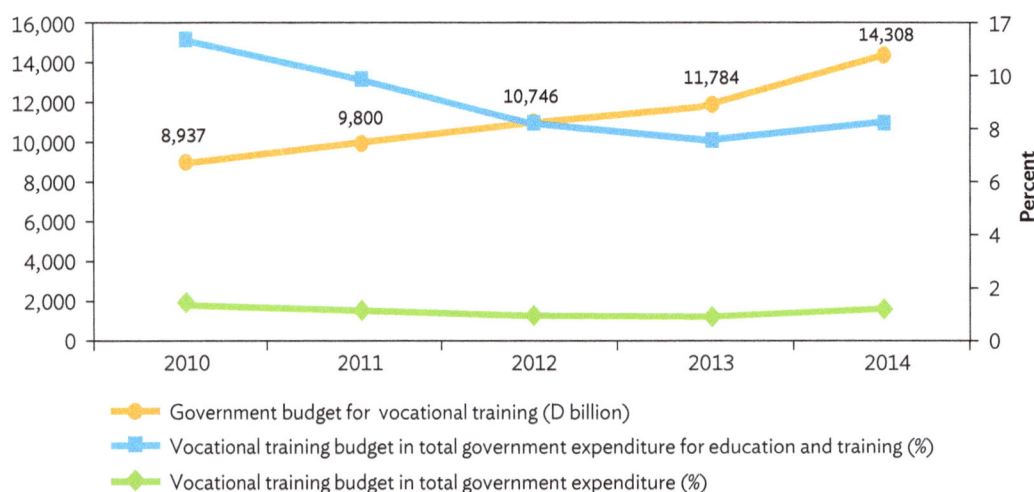

Figure 2.23: Trend of Government Expenditure for Vocational Training, 2010–2014

Sources: Directorate of Vocational Education and Training and National Institute for Vocational Education and Training. 2017. *Viet Nam Vocational Education and Training Report 2015*. Ha Noi; and Calculations based on data of General Statistics Office of Viet Nam and the International Monetary Fund (cf. Table 16).

106. Yet, these figures should be taken with care as they do not reflect, for instance, funds allocated to the 522 TVET institutions formerly supervised by MOET. In addition, individual funding mechanisms for the almost 2,000 TVET institutes running under dispersed governance of 13 line ministries, 63 provincial people's committees, diverse social-political organizations, and private owners remain widely opaque and, hence, make it difficult to compile comprehensive and consistent data on actual TVET financing in Viet Nam. In its 2015 TVET Report, MOLISA informed, "the current budgeting mechanism makes it difficult (...) to obtain specific information and report on financing of vocational training, especially due to additional program and project funding from local sources. Furthermore, the state budget category of Vocational Training (...) is included in one category of Education and

Training (...) in the existing 'Index of State Budget Items', which makes it difficult to account for and manage the financial aspects of vocational training" (DVET and NIVET 2017).[98]

107. **TVET funding from private resources.** As for most countries in the East Asia and Pacific region, government budgets are also the most significant source for financing TVET in Viet Nam (Wright 2017). Private training providers, however, which have been growing in number during recent years, do not receive any regular state budgets; instead tuition fees are their main source of funding. In addition, about 22% of firms (mostly big state-owned enterprises) offer self-funded formal vocational training to their future employees, which is a rate significantly lower than the average of 32.2% in the East Asia and Pacific region.[99] Unfortunately, for both areas no statistical data regarding total scope and relative distribution of financial contributions are available. Like most of its neighboring countries (Cambodia, the Lao People's Democratic Republic, and Myanmar) and unlike most of the wealthier nations in the region (such as the People's Republic of China, the Republic of Korea, Malaysia, Singapore, and Thailand), Viet Nam also has no private sector-financed training fund.

108. The government's 2014 Household Living Standards Survey (GSO 2016c) shows that private contributions to TVET paid by the country's citizens have more than tripled during the last decade and reached more than 15% of the government's per capita spending for students enrolled in this sector, with slight differences in socioeconomic and regional diversification (Figures 2.24a–c).

Figure 2.24a: Average Expenses of Viet Nam Households on Education and Training per Schooling Person, 2004–2014, by Level of Education (VND million)

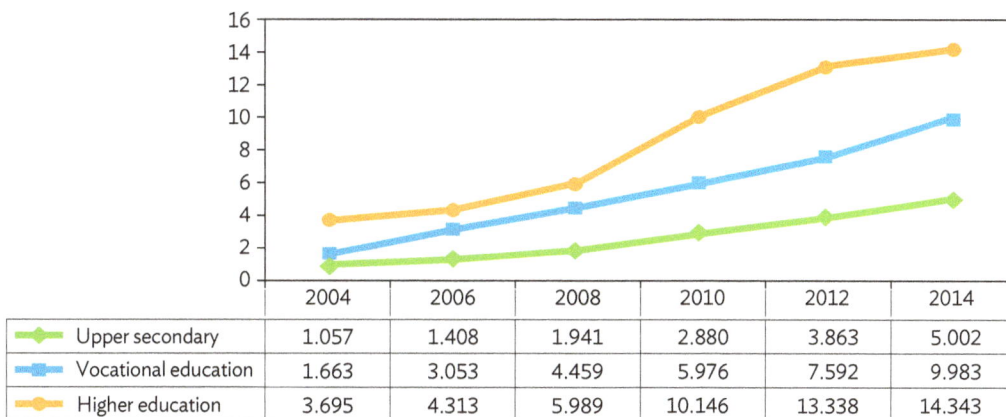

	2004	2006	2008	2010	2012	2014
Upper secondary	1.057	1.408	1.941	2.880	3.863	5.002
Vocational education	1.663	3.053	4.459	5.976	7.592	9.983
Higher education	3.695	4.313	5.989	10.146	13.338	14.343

Note: Average values do not distiguish between expenses for public and nonpublic schools. The latter have been estimated for being more than 3 times higher than expenses for public schools.
Source: General Statistics Office of Viet Nam. 2016. *Result of Viet Nam Household Living Standards Survey 2014.* Ha Noi.

[98] In the full report version (DVET and NIVET 2017), MOLISA further complements this by stating: "Under the current mechanism of spending the state budget on vocational training, MOLISA is only allowed to participate in the process of estimating and allocating the state budget for the national target programs in vocational training. MOLISA is not allowed yet to get involved in the estimation and allocation of the state budget for recurrent expenditures and infrastructure of vocational training, leading to the lack of related statistic updates for the year of 2015." (See also Appendix 6 for an overview on the flows of education financing).

[99] World Bank Group. Enterprise Surveys: Viet Nam (2015). http://www.enterprisesurveys.org/data/exploreeconomies/2015/vietnam#workforce (accessed January 2018).

Figure 2.24b: Average Expense on Vocational Training per Schooling Person, 2014, by Income Group
(VND million)

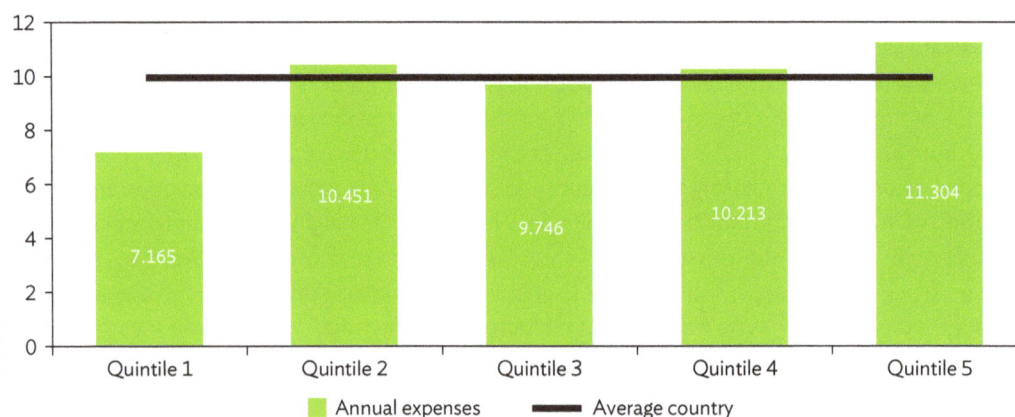

Source: General Statistics Office of Viet Nam. 2016. *Result of Viet Nam Household Living Standards Survey 2014.* Ha Noi.

Figure 2.24c: Average Expense on Vocational Training per Schooling Person, 2014, by Socioeconomic Region
(VND million)

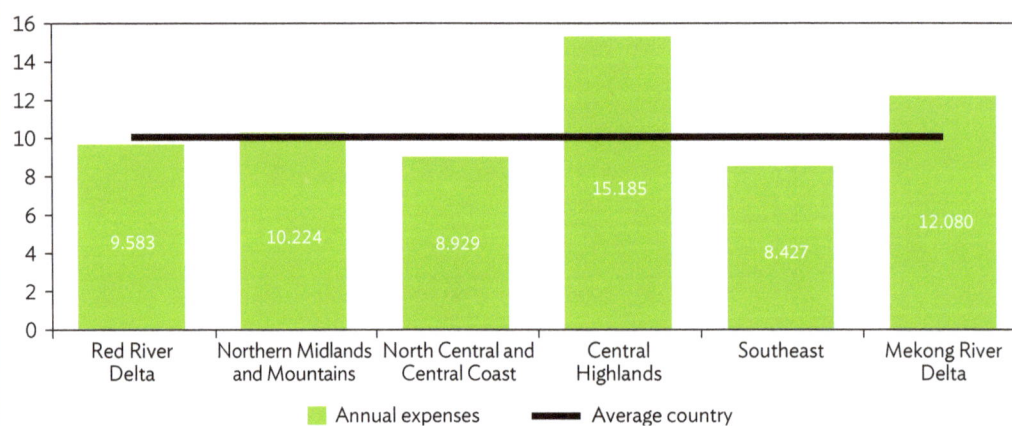

Source: General Statistics Office of Viet Nam. 2016. *Result of Viet Nam Household Living Standards Survey 2014.* Ha Noi.

109. **Structure of state funding in TVET.** State budget funds for TVET consist of three types: regular funding, capital construction investment, and national target programs. The latter are the main sources for financing the government's TVET reform agenda. In fact, substantial financial means for TVET system reform components were included in the National Target Program on Jobs and Vocational Training 2012–2015, which was approved by Prime Minister Decision No. 1201/QD-TTg in August 2012. It specified budgets of almost VND26 trillion for implementing the Rural Vocational Training Program during this period. For the project, Renewal and Development of Vocational Training, the program designated an estimated aggregate budget of VND18,946 billion. The new

Target Program on Vocational Education, Employment and Occupational Safety for the Period 2016–2020, which was approved in June 2017 by Prime Minister Decision No. 899/QD-TTg, has earmarked in total VND12,197.2 billion for MOLISA's project, Renovating and Improving the Quality of Vocational Education.[100]

110. During 2010–2014, the state budget allocated to vocational training under the responsibility of MOLISA was in total D55,575 billion, equivalent to $2.54 billion (DVET and NIVET 2017). Funds for recurrent expenditures accounted for 37.4% of this budget, funds for capital construction investment had a share of 40.81%, and 21.79% of the TVET budget was allocated for national target programs (DVET and NIVET 2017).[101] In its TVET report, MOLISA identified a "declining trend in the funding for the national target programs, while the funding for recurrent expenditures of vocational training remained unchanged, and the funding for capital construction investment increased relatively rapidly." The report concluded, the latter reflects "that funding focused on an intensive investment in infrastructure of (…) newly upgraded and established TVET institutes." For the decline in the funding of national target programs considerable gaps between planned targets and actual budget allocations have been made responsible (DVET and NIVET 2017).[102] The funding structure in these programs shows also a remarkable difference in the proportions of funding expected from the national state budget, local state budget, and official development assistance sources (DVET and NIVET 2017).[103]

111. The three funding schemes are specified by different laws and regulations. TVET institutions, through their different owners, need to follow complex procedures and responsibility settings at central and local levels involving the Ministry of Finance and the Ministry of Planning and Investment for negotiating and allocating annual budgets and program funds. Since fund allocations for regular expenditures of TVET institutes are based only on a generic per-capita-quota system,[104] they do not take into account specific training costs of different majors.[105] In addition, the financial resources for TVET institutions vary remarkably by governing bodies and line agencies. TVET institutions under ministries and central agencies tend to receive more state budget per student than the provincial TVET institutions under provincial People's Committees. Appendix 6 provides a schematic overview on the dimensions and flow of education financing in Viet Nam.

112. **Financial autonomy of vocational education and training institutions.** Apart from state budgets, revenues from tuition and admission fees and, to a smaller extent, contributions from

---

[100] Prime Minister Decision No. 899/QD-TTg dated 20 June 2017 Approving the Target Program on Vocational Education, Employment and Occupational Safety for the Period 2016–2020.

[101] However, the report qualifies also these statements by admitting that "reported figures on basic construction investment for vocational training are often inaccurate and incomplete, sometimes overlapping with other capital sources of investment nature" (DVET and NIVET 2017).

[102] The overall funding allocated for the Reform and Development of Vocational Training Project in the period of 2011–2015 consisted of only 40.8% of the approved funding plan. The total project budget allocation for the Project for Vocational Training for Rural Workers reached 70% of the funding plan for 2010–2015.

[103] Funding from the local state budget source accounted for only 5% of the total funds received while 17% was planned for the whole period. Funding from other mobilized sources was 0% while it was planned to be 9% for this period.

[104] The current budget allocation formula for education and training is not based on the number of enrollments but on the school-age population quotas in the different provinces (see also World Bank and the Government of Vietnam 2017).

[105] The state funding allocation to TVET institutions under ministries is largely determined based on four criteria: (i) income–expense situation of previous year; (ii) duty assigned by the ministry for the following year (expected school's admission quota); (iii) number of staff, teachers, and officers, approved by authority; and (iv) current regime of spending. (See also MDRI and NEXIA STT 2017).

enterprises and/or revenues from production and business operation services are also sources of funds for public TVET institutions.[106] So far, these sources have been seen as an important means to offset the increasing gap between state budgets and actual costs of training delivery and shall successively replace the traditional system of input-based state funding for those institutions achieving full autonomy status after 2020. The regulated maximum margins of these fees are specified for different broad areas of disciplines (Figure 2.25) and have increased considerably during the last decades. In the future, the spread between tuition fees to be charged by financially autonomous public TVET institutions and those, which are not eligible to attain this status, though remaining significant, shall be gradually diminished (Figure 2.25). However, TVET colleges piloting the autonomy status have already voiced some concerns that applying full tuition fee margins to offset revenue and expenditure gaps has led to discrimination against students in the selection of educational institutions.[107]

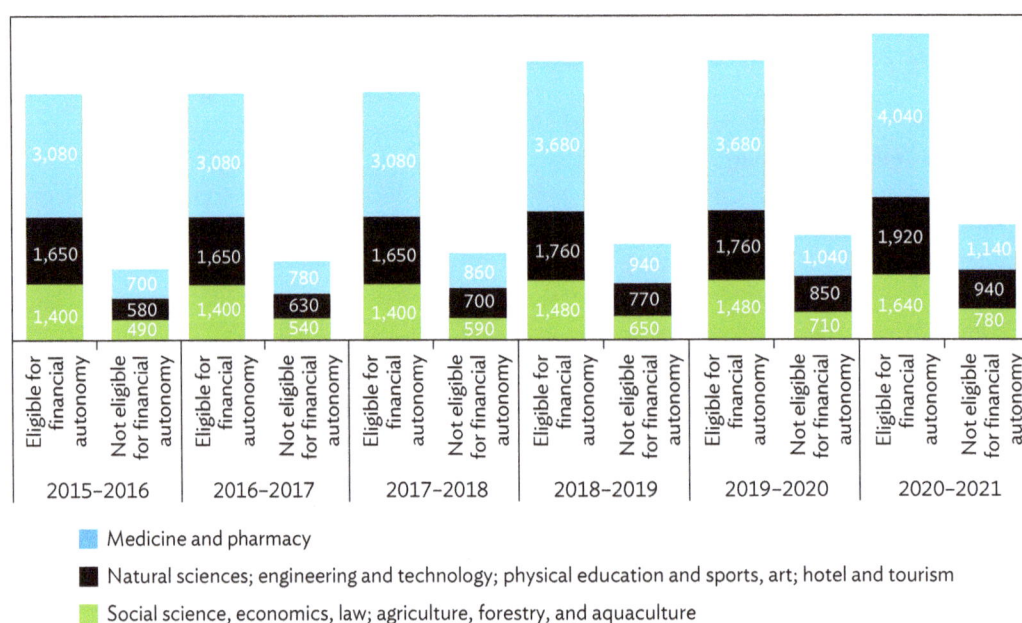

Figure 2.25: Maximum Amount of Monthly Tuition Fees to Be Charged by Vocational Colleges from Their Students in Academic Years, 2015–2021, by Areas of Disciplines
(D thousand)

Source: Government of Viet Nam. Decree No. 86/2015/ND-CP dated October 2015 on Mechanism for Collection and Management of Tuition Fees. Ha Noi.

113. There is still no common perception as to what extent public TVET institutions are actually capable (or ready) to recover their recurrent and nonrecurrent expenditures by such revenues. While MOLISA has calculated the average rate of income from tuition in public TVET institutions by about

---

[106]　Sample surveys among TVET institutes show high variances in some institutes' strategies and accomplishments to increase their revenues through business and production services to local industry partners and communities, as a key means toward full autonomy.

[107]　Presentations of three TVET colleges on experiences with piloting autonomy in Viet Nam at GIZ Workshop on 2 November 2017 in Ha Noi.

33% (NIVT 2015), recent surveys suggest huge differences among these institutions (even among those offering similar majors) ranging from 5.6% to 25.5% (MDRI and NEXIA STT 2017). Higher rates but similar variances have been found in the proposals of TVET colleges applying for support through a potential ADB-funded TVET development program.[108]

114. Nevertheless, the government has intensified its ambition to convert public TVET institutions into autonomously operating business units that are self-responsible for their service portfolios, staff appointment, structural organization, student recruitment, revenue generation, budget allocation, and even infrastructure investments. Since 2006, this approach has been one of the key strategic government visions to tackle the problems of demand orientation in Viet Nam's largely deficient skills supply system, align state funding more effectively to performance, and make the state management function more efficient. It finds a prominent reference also in the list of tasks and solutions to be tackled in MOLISA's draft plan for its project of TVET reform up to the years 2020/2030 (see chapters III and IV).

115. After 10 years of reforms, however, public TVET institutions achieving autonomy status are still an exception.[109] This contrasts with the meanwhile considerable amount of privately run TVET institutes, which have this status already by law. These are not subject to state regulations for maximum fee levels and accordingly cover their operating expenses up to almost 100% from tuition fees. However, surveys show that the proportion of income from tuition in private schools largely depends also on their business model which is closely linked to their status level and their concentration on relatively lower investment-intensive disciplines and majors. Colleges eligible to offer high-level formal qualifications in such majors seem to achieve relatively higher revenue than schools forced to generate their main income from elementary or intermediate training and short-term courses in technical disciplines that require high investments in training facilities and technical equipment. In public TVET institutions, this has led to a trend for requesting upgrades of their status levels (many TVET colleges strive to become universities) and shifting their enrollment focus on higher level qualifications, which seems to yield higher revenues rather than being induced by actual labor market demands. Another trend emerging in some of Viet Nam's advanced colleges is to get support through government-secured loan arrangements to finance facilities and technical equipment for state-of-the art production units, the obvious main purpose of which is to recover a higher share of institutional costs (including its own depreciation costs) by productive income-generating activities. It remains questionable whether there are already appropriate control mechanisms in place to ensure that such business activities, though not necessarily affecting degradation of training quality, will create unfair competition to private businesses and, hence, could provoke adverse distortions of local economies and labor markets in the vicinity of these institutions.

---

[108] Between July and November 2017, a total of 30 TVET colleges, most of them selected by the government to become "high-quality schools," submitted detailed proposals on their past and future financial capacity. However, such sample figures can provide only a temporary spotlight on funding conditions of public TVET institutes. The MDRI/NEXIA STT (2017) study mentions that revenue rates from tuition are often fluctuating dramatically, when enrollment targets of schools cannot be met. To further support the government's strategy toward school autonomy, it is highly recommended to conduct representative surveys among TVET institutions at all levels and of all forms on a nationwide scale. The study provides valuable criteria and indicators that could be used for such surveys.

[109] So far, only three MOLISA colleges have received autonomy status on a pilot basis starting in 2016 (HCMC Vocational College of Technology, LILAMA2, and Quy Nhon College). All of them reported that they have been facing serious challenges during the initial phases, ranging from building up management capacities to costly investments, streamlining of staffing structures and the recruitment of students who are willing to pay considerably higher tuition fees. So far, the latter could be achieved only for such courses the government has ordered and whose participants are supported through tuition fee exemptions paid from central government budgets.

116. With the new TVET law and subsequent regulations, the government is trying to spur and better manage the "the Mechanism for Exercising the Autonomy of Public Administrative Units" through a phased approach.[110] It envisions the gradual withdrawal of external institute management functions (direct state management) including different state means of financial support from public colleges and schools. These shall be accredited and approved for their capacity and capability to stay viable under government-regulated market conditions.[111] For this, the legal framework defines different status levels depending on an institution's prospective ability to recover its recurrent expenditures and investments by own revenues (basically from tuition fees but also from contributions of enterprises and revenues from business activities and bank loans) either both or partly or not at all, and provides detailed criteria on modality and administrative implications of future state funding schemes.

Box 2.2: Road Map for Pricing Public Administrative Services Funded by the State Budget

By 2016: Calculating a full amount of salary costs, direct expenses (managerial and fixed asset depreciation costs have not been included yet);

By 2018: Calculating a full amount of salary costs, direct expenses, and managerial costs (fixed asset depreciation costs have not been included yet);

By 2020: Calculating a full amount of salary costs, direct expenses, and managerial and fixed asset depreciation costs.

Source: Government of Viet Nam. Decree No. 16/2015/NĐ-CP Stipulating the Mechanism for Exercising the Autonomy of Public Administrative Units, Article 10.

---

117. Obviously, these regulations try to counterbalance existential threats of the reform to many yet competitively unviable TVET institutions and seem to guarantee their survival, at least in the medium term. However, an empirical study on the current situation of TVET financing in Viet Nam has revealed that the envisaged model might not work well under such intricate conditions for state fund allocation through orders and competitive bidding, as long as it does not provide also enough incentives (or sanctions) to improve financial management efficiency that focuses on better performance and, hence, will not necessarily promote the elimination of ineffective factors in the current expenditure structures of public TVET institutions (see section II.3.C School Facilities and Training Equipment). The study warns that the envisaged financing mechanism will not dissolve quality-adverse low-price positioning of public TVET institutions for recruiting students because of the sustained option to further receive the traditional input-oriented state budget support when failing to break even. Yet, this support has shown to be highly opaque, unequal, and proved to be limited in covering necessary expenses for quality training as well as concerning crucial investment needs of most TVET institutes. There is much evidence that the vicious circle caused by limited state budgets can only be broken by basing also central and local state financing schemes on transparent common output criteria. Such

---

110 Government Decree No. 16/2015/NĐ-CP dated 14 February 2015 Stipulating the Mechanism for Exercising the Autonomy of Public Administrative Units.

111 The government provides tax incentives to (public and private) educational institutions and will place annual orders on type and numbers of graduates to be trained in specified occupational areas. To get contracted for such orders TVET institutions have to participate in bidding procedures.

criteria should not only relate to the performance of all TVET institutions to produce occupation-specific graduates but also be determined by calculating the difference between reasonable cost that reflect minimum expenditure standards and maximum tuition of every student in same field of training.[112]

118. Indeed, the government regulation stipulating the future mechanism for exercising the autonomy of public administrative units specifies that the price of public administrative services funded by the state budget "shall be determined on the basis of economic-technical cost norms adopted by competent authorities and the road map for calculating the full amount of expenses" (Box 2.2). However, applied to TVET institutions, MOLISA's recent regulation confines this solely to the task of schools for calculating their revenues through tuition fees.[113] Basing also future state budget support schemes on such norms seems, at least currently, not intended and there is also no clear reference in MOLISA's draft plan for its project on TVET reform up to 2020/2030 on this issue.[114]

119. Promoting the principle that consistent state funding of public TVET institutions will also be an indispensable requirement in the future, the MDRI and NEXIA-STT (2017) study presents an approach on how corresponding unit cost standards can be developed based on realistic expenditure structures of nonpublic schools. It provides detailed recommendations on how future state funding modalities for TVET can be adjusted to performance-based output parameters on a nationwide scale. These recommendations ascribe to MOLISA a leading role in conducting the following stepwise approach:

(i) Develop an information management system of unit cost norms and financial information to identify (actual) vocational training cost for each occupation.

(ii) Determine reasonable training costs based on actual costs essential for quality training.

(iii) Develop a data collection system on school performance comparing actual enrollment data with fund allocations.

(iv) Identify appropriate pathways for performance-based budget allocations based on measurable training outcomes.

(v) Pilot the performance-based budget allocation model in a representative scope, and

(vi) Increase funding for vocational training via a training levy and human development fund (MDRI and NEXIA STT 2017).

---

[112] Decree No. 86/2015/ND-CP specifies different maximum fee levels applicable to public colleges and vocational secondary schools that exercise financial autonomy and (considerably lower ones) for those that do not. The margins are not specific to different occupational majors but reflect just three broad fields of educational disciplines (see Figure 2.24a-c).

[113] Decree No. 86/2015/ND-CP stipulates that only "educational institutions that exercise financial autonomy in terms of recurrent expenditures and investment" adjust their fees to such future norms. All others "shall determine tuition fees according to the State's grant and learners' contribution according to the decline in State's subsidies."

[114] The draft plan rather uncleanly envisages a "shift from regular budget allocations to TVET institutions to the mode of bidding and orders, assigning public service delivery tasks on the basis of competition in terms of quality, efficiency and outputs, giving priority to TVET institutions meeting TVET quality accreditation standards."

III. Human Resources Development and TVET Policies and Strategies

1. Human Resources Development Policy Framework

120. In 2011, Viet Nam's political leaders reviewed their Socio-Economic Development Strategy (SEDS) for the first millennium decade and critically concluded that, despite some basic achievements, the economy had not developed as envisaged, in particular "the quality of growth, productivity, effectiveness and competitiveness of the economy" was rated as low.[115]

121. A revised strategy, providing overall guidance, key target areas, and policy objectives[116] for the following sequence of two 5-year Socio-Economic Development Plans (2011–2015 and 2016–2020), virtually kept the state apparatus responsible for further substantial system improvements[117] by focusing on three "strategic breakthrough" components: (i) improved socialist-oriented market economy regulations and respective administrative reforms; (ii) rapid development of high-quality human resources through comprehensive renovation of the national education system; and (iii) development of a synchronous and modern (traffic and urban) infrastructure system.

122. In parallel, the Viet Nam government launched a new Human Resources Development Strategy[118] and a respective master plan for the period 2011–2020, which specified priority areas for training interventions and provided quantitative targets for the number of workers to be trained in different institutions and levels of the technical and vocational education and training (TVET) system as well as the estimated number of qualified teachers and trainers required for this (Tables 3.1–3.4).

---

[115] Government of Viet Nam. Vietnam's Socio-Economic Development Strategy (SEDS) for the Period of 2011–2020. Ha Noi. http://www.economica.vn/Portals/0/Documents/1d3f7ee0400e42152bdcaa439bf62686.pdf.

[116] The SEDS envisions that the country will become "a modern industrialized nation" and sets that "education and training, and science and technology are to meet the requirements of the country's industrialization and modernization" as one of the main objectives. It also specifies economic and social development indicators to be achieved by 2020, such as an average annual GDP growth rate of 7%–8% and the percentage of trained workforce over total labor force to be increased to 55%.

[117] Basically, through intensified legal and administrative reforms promoting a stepwise increase of decentralized responsibility and autonomy of public administrative units to become more efficient and demand oriented.

[118] The Human Resources Development Strategy 2011–2020 identifies Viet Nam's human resources as a foundation and the most advantageous factor for the country's sustainable development, international integration, and social stability and stipulates that their competitiveness be raised to a level similar to that in advanced countries. In this context, the strategy also identifies strategic challenges and bottlenecks and proposes remedial actions along with ambitious qualitative and quantitative targets for higher education, TVET, and the health sector to be achieved by a set of different means (30 action programs).

Figure 3.1: Policy Framework for Human Resources Development in Viet Nam

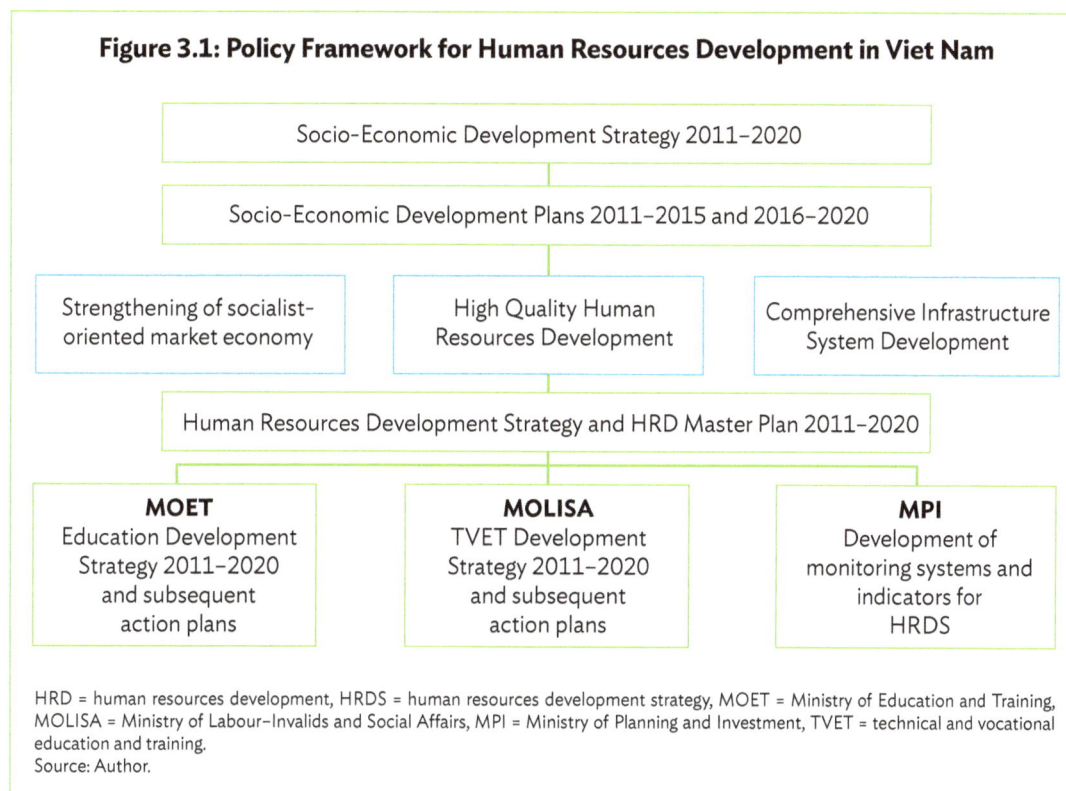

Socio-Economic Development Strategy 2011–2020

Socio-Economic Development Plans 2011–2015 and 2016–2020

| Strengthening of socialist-oriented market economy | High Quality Human Resources Development | Comprehensive Infrastructure System Development |

Human Resources Development Strategy and HRD Master Plan 2011–2020

| **MOET** Education Development Strategy 2011–2020 and subsequent action plans | **MOLISA** TVET Development Strategy 2011–2020 and subsequent action plans | **MPI** Development of monitoring systems and indicators for HRDS |

HRD = human resources development, HRDS = human resources development strategy, MOET = Ministry of Education and Training, MOLISA = Ministry of Labour–Invalids and Social Affairs, MPI = Ministry of Planning and Investment, TVET = technical and vocational education and training.
Source: Author.

Table 3.1: Specific Targets in the Government's Human Resources Development Strategy, 2011–2020

Targets	2010	2015	2020
I. Raising of intellectual power and working skills			
1. Rate of trained laborers (%)	40.0	55.0	70.0
2. Rate of vocationally trained laborers (%)	25.0	40.0	55.0
3. Number of university and college students per 10,000 people (number of students)	200	300	400
4. Number of international standard vocational schools (number of schools)	–	5	> 10
5. Number of international standard excellent universities (number of universities)	–	–	> 4
6. Highly qualified human resources in breakthrough fields (number of persons)			
State management, policy making, and international law	15,000	18,000	20,000
University and college lecturers	77,500	100,000	160,000
Science and technology	40,000	60,000	100,000
Medicine, health care	60,000	70,000	80,000
Finance/Banking	70,000	100,000	120,000
Information technology	180,000	350,000	550,000
II. Raising of physical strength of human resources			
1. Average life expectancy (years)	73	74	75
2. Young people's average height (meters)	> 1.61	> 1.63	> 1.63
3. Malnutrition rate among children under 5 (%)	17.5	< 10.0	< 5

– = not applicable.
Source: Government of Viet Nam. Human Resources Development Strategy 2011–2020. Ha Noi.

Table 3.2: Estimated Needs of Laborers by Training Providers, 2015 and 2020

Training Level		2015	2020
Number of laborers	(Million people)	55.0	63.0
Trained laborers	(Million people)	30.5	44.0
	Percentage over total laborers (%)	55.0	70.0
Laborers receiving vocational training	(Million people)	23.5	34.4
	Percentage over total laborers (%)	77.0	78.5
Laborers receiving training through education and training system	(Million people)	7.0	9.4
	Percentage over total trained laborers (%)	23.0	21.5

Source: Government of Viet Nam. Human Resources Development Master Plan 2011–2020. Ha Noi.

Table 3.3: Estimated Needs of Trained Laborers by Training Level, 2015 and 2020

Training Level	2015		2020	
	Number of Laborers (million)	Percentage over Trained Laborers (%)	Number of Laborers (million)	Percentage over Trained Laborers (%)
Elementary vocational training	18	59.0	24	54.0
Intermediate vocational training	7	23.0	12	27.0
College level vocational training	2	6.0	3	7.0
Tertiary vocational training	3.3	11.0	5	11.0
Postgraduate vocational training	0.2	0.7	0.3	0.7

Source: Government of Viet Nam. Human Resources Development Master Plan 2011–2020. Ha Noi.

Table 3.4: Estimated Number of Jobs as Teachers and Trainers, 2015 and 2020

Training Level	2015	2020
College level (person)	13,000	28,000
Intermediate level (person)	24,000	31,000
Elementary level (person)	14,000	28,000

Source: Government of Viet Nam. Human Resources Development Master Plan 2011–2020. Ha Noi.

2. TVET Reform Strategy of the Ministry of Labour–Invalids and Social Affairs

123. Based on this broad policy framework and the 2006 Law on Vocational Training, the Ministry of Labour–Invalids and Social Affairs (MOLISA) developed its Vocational Training Development Strategy 2011–2020, which was approved by the Prime Minister in May 2012.[119]

---

[119]   Government of Viet Nam. Decision No. 630/QD-TTg of the Prime Minister Approving the Vocational Training Development Strategy for the 2011–2020 Period. Ha Noi. Adopted 29 May 2012.

124. Addressing a range of sector-specific tasks, this strategy set out a list of ambitious objectives and specified a broad array of respective "solutions" to be implemented under nine systemic reform components: (i) renovated state management of vocational education and training (TVET); (ii) development of vocational teachers and managerial staff; (iii) development of occupational standards and the national vocational qualifications framework; (iv) development of respective training curriculum and instructional materials; (v) strengthening of standards for TVET facilities and equipment; (vi) enhancement of quality assurance; (vii) enhancement of linkage between TVET institutions, labor market, and enterprises; (viii) improved awareness about TVET development; and (ix) promotion of international cooperation.

125. Among these nine solutions, the first two have been prioritized as "breakthrough solutions" affecting the quality of the whole vocational training system, while the third (focusing on occupational standards and the national vocational qualifications framework) was seen as the key for a comprehensive TVET system reform. Table 3.5 provides a summary of the contents of actions envisaged for accomplishing these three solutions until the year 2020.

Table 3.5: Breakthrough and Key Solutions in the TVET Development Strategy, 2011–2020

Solution	Envisaged Actions
1. Innovated state management of vocational training	• Improve the legal system of vocational training by amending the Law on Vocational Training and regulations related to vocational training in the Labor Law. • Improve mechanisms and policies on vocational training by (i) improving policies to attract vocational teachers, (ii) innovating financial policies on vocational training (tuition fees and order mechanism), (iii) making the training policies of foreign language consistent with the level of training, and (iv) improving policies for trained employees. • Improve the mechanism and capacity of state management on vocational training toward clearly defined functions, tasks, and competence combined with responsibility and increasing inspection and examination activities and assuring supervision by state agencies, sociopolitical organizations, and people. • Introduce mechanisms for vocational training institutions to operate independently and autonomously. • Promote information technology application in vocational training and vocational management; set up database for vocational training. • Implement transferable training qualifications and enhance channeling into vocational training. • Establish a vocational training assistance fund toward socialization with initial capital from the state budget, contributions of enterprises, and other sources to develop vocational training. • Plan a network of vocational training institutions by region and locality; priority is given to newly established nonpublic vocational training institutions; cooperation and establishment of vocational training institutions invested by foreign capital is encouraged. There are specialized vocational training institutions for the disabled and the ethnic minorities. • Promote socialization and diversification of resources for development of vocational training, including government, enterprises, students, and national and international investors, for which the state budget is important (to raise the rate of expenditure on vocational training from the state budget for education to 12%–13%). The government has assistance policies on capital, land, and tax for nonpublic vocational training institutions.

continued on next page

Table 3.5 continued

2. Development of vocational teachers and managerial staff	• Standardize qualification of teachers in national, regional, and international key occupations in terms of vocational skills and vocational pedagogy; 100% of these teachers shall meet the standards in 2014. • Ensure the training and retraining for vocational teachers toward standardization, securing sufficient number of teachers; an appropriate structure by profession and training levels. Mobilize scientists, technicians, artisans, skilled workers, and excellent farmers participating in vocational training for rural workers. • Arrange and reorganize training and innovating activities, retraining institutes for vocational teachers to train and retrain vocational pedagogy and improve vocational skills for vocational teachers. • Standardize the vocational management staff. Set up the training and retraining content and program for vocational management staff; develop the professional vocational management staff. • Establish vocational training institute with the training and retraining function for new technology; training and retraining teachers and vocational management staff; research vocational training science based on the merger and upgrade of the National Institute for Vocational Training.
3. Development of occupational standards and the national vocational qualifications framework	• Build a national vocational qualifications framework compatible with national education framework. • Complete the national occupational skills framework. • Promulgate national occupational skills standards for popular occupations. • Receive and transfer sets of occupational skills standards of regionally and internationally prioritized occupations. • Develop a framework for training curriculum.

Source: Government of Viet Nam. Decision No. 630/QD-TTg of the Prime Minister Approving the Vocational Training Development Strategy for the 2011–2020 Period. Ha Noi. Adopted 29 May 2012.

126. As shown in Table 3.6, MOLISA's TVET strategy comprises a comprehensive list of quantitative targets regarding the number of graduates to be trained at different levels, schools, and training centers to be additionally established, teachers and staff to be qualified, and new training resources to be developed. However, it does not contain any cost calculations and budgets.[120] Rather, the strategy notes that financing shall be defined in coordination with the Ministry of Planning and Investment and the Ministry of Finance and channeled through specific annual and medium-term projects and programs.[121]

---

[120] ADB's 2014 TVET Assessment (ADB 2014) already evaluated these targets as overambitious and "possibly unrealistic" to implement. In addition, the study criticizes that the strategy "tends to be unclear about specific means to achieve objectives" and "is presented without resource constraints."

[121] In fact, substantial financial means for some of the strategy's systemic reform components have been included in the National Target Program on Jobs and Vocational Training 2012–2015, which the Prime Minister approved through Decision No. 1201/QD-TTg in August 2012 and (inter alia) specifies budgets also for the Rural Vocational Training Program during this period. The decision specifies the total expenditure for a project named "Renewal and Development of Vocational Training," which, except for "investments in training facilities and equipment for key trades (...) in high-quality schools," mainly covers five soft components of TVET quality reform (MIS, staff training, curricula, quality assessment, and certification) and designates an estimated aggregate budget of VND18,946 billion for its implementation.

Table 3.6: Performance Targets in the TVET Development Strategy, 2011–2020

Performance Indicator	Performance Targets	
	2011–2015	2016–2020
The rate of trained employees will increase.	40%, equivalent to 23.5 million people (20% of which include collegial vocational and intermediate vocational training)	55%, equivalent to 34.4 million people (23% of collegial and intermediate vocational training)
The new training programs will be applied for collegial and intermediate vocational trainings.	• About 2.1 million people receiving new program at collegial and intermediate vocational training • About 7.5 million people receiving new programs at elementary level and vocational training under 3 months	• About 2.9 million people receiving new program at collegial and intermediate vocational training • About 10 million people receiving new programs at elementary level and vocational training under 3 months
The network of vocational institutions will be expanded.	VCs: 190 (60 nonpublic, 26 high quality) VSSs: 300 (100 nonpublic) VTCs: 920 (320 nonpublic) *(at least 1 VC + 1 VTC per province/city and 1 VTC + 1 VSS per district/town)*	VCs: 230 (80 nonpublic, 40 high quality) VSCs: 310 (120 nonpublic) VTCs: 1,050 (350 nonpublic)
The number of vocational teachers will increase.	VCs: 13,000 VSSs: 24,000 VTCs: 14,000	VCs: 28,000 VSSs: 31,000 VTCs: 18,000
TVET programs and curricula will be upgraded or newly developed at each level.	International level: 26 Regional level: 49 National level: 130 Elementary level: 300	International level: 35 Regional level: 70 National level: 150 Elementary level: 200
Quality of TVET institutions and programs for focal occupations will be accredited.	High-quality schools and model VTC will be accredited. All key national, regional, and international occupations will be accredited. 3 public (and a number of nonpublic) quality accreditation centers will be established.	
The framework of national vocational qualification will be developed.	• 250 standards of national vocational skills issued. • 2 million people receiving certificate.	• 400 standards of national vocational skills issued. • 6 million people receiving certificate.
Improving the labor market system connecting vocational training with employment.	N/A	N/A

N/A = not applicable, TVET = technical and vocational education and training, VC = vocational college, VSS = vocational secondary schools, VTC = vocational training center.
Source: Government of Viet Nam. Decision No. 630/QD-TTg of the Prime Minister Approving the Vocational Training Development Strategy for the 2011–2020 Period. Ha Noi. Adopted 29 May 2012.

3. Achievements and Prospects

127. Despite some limitations in realism, clarity, and precision of implementation arrangements, Viet Nam's comprehensive framework of strategies and policies on human resources development (HRD) and TVET has been rated as an extensive, strong, and forward-looking basis for systemic reforms and development (ADB 2014).

128. Yet, a high-level government assessment of achievements made after the implementation of the first 5 years of the Socio-Economic Development Program in early 2016 had to announce rather disillusioning results. Though incremental achievements of socioeconomic reforms could be identified, the implementation of the three ambitious SEDS breakthrough components was rated as sluggish. Overall, "the creation of a foundation to basically transform (the) country into a modern industrialized nation did not meet the requirements." Regarding HRD in particular, the assessment concludes that the quality of human resources appears to improve only slowly, hence, perpetuating the country's shortage of high-quality laborers. Moreover, "science and technology have yet to become the drive to increase productivity, competitiveness and to promote socio-economic development" (Government of Viet Nam 2016).

129. Based on a synopsis of lessons learned and a prognosis of challenging economic context conditions for further policy interventions, the government's perspective for the next Socio-Economic Development Plan (2016–2020) is emphatically guided by the impetus to intensify substantial reform efforts and accelerate fundamental structural innovations as laid out in the overarching SEDS for the running period.[122] Compared with the previous program, the target areas and objectives of the new plan do not undergo substantial diversifications. They are, however, formulated with a stronger emphasis on the need for more effectiveness and efficiency and stipulate rapid and vigorous implementation. While generally a comprehensive reform of the education system is regarded further on as "a top national policy," there are now more comprehensive and qualitative specifications on tasks and solutions for each subsector including TVET. The plan inter alia demands to "push forward the training of human resources with knowledge and skills toward practical application" and to "strengthen the education of work style and professional responsibility to help students meet the needs of technical and technological human resources in domestic and international labor markets" (Government of Viet Nam 2016).

130. **New TVET law.** With this, the Socio-Economic Development Plan 2016–2020 implicitly refers to the new Law on Vocational Education and Training, which took effect on 1 July 2015 and provides an augmented legal basis for some fundamental enhancements of Viet Nam's complex (since largely fragmented) TVET system.

131. In its preliminary policy section (Article 6), the new law prioritizes government investment in this subsector and puts more emphasis on developing high-quality TVET institutions for national, regional, and international focal occupations while maintaining a parallel focus on equity of access for socially,

---

[122] On a political level, this impetus has been spurred by a Resolution of the 12th National Congress of Viet Nam's Communist Party stipulating that a focal task in the next 5 years is to radically, comprehensively reform education and training, improve human resources quality to meet labor market demands and to develop education, training in attachment with socioeconomic development requirements, and scientific–technological progresses.

ethnically, and geographically disadvantaged student populations. Chapters 2 and 5 comprise revised specifications on key input factors of TVET, such as responsibilities and qualification requirements of institution managers as well as minimum quality standards for teachers and trainers. There is a comprehensive chapter on principles and procedures of quality accreditation of TVET institutions and programs (Chapter 6) and a special chapter now outlines rights <u>and</u> obligations of enterprises in TVET, including obligatory participation in syllabus and curriculum development, provision of (paid) internships based on bilateral agreements, assessment of learning outcomes, and even a directive to "only employ trained workers or workers possessing vocational certificates for occupations listed by the MOLISA"[123] (Chapter 6).

132. In addition, the law provides a new basis for subsequent regulations supporting high-quality public TVET institutes to become fully autonomous (and, hence, more accountable) regarding organizational management, staff recruitment, financial planning, effective training delivery, and internal quality assurance modalities in developing framework of standards to be further pursued and gradually implemented by a central state management agency.[124]

133. Resolving confusing system governance arrangements in the previous laws, the legislator has eventually streamlined the overall responsibility for Viet Nam's TVET sector by shifting the central state management function for all TVET institutions on elementary, intermediate, and college levels, including the considerable number of technical schools and colleges formerly supervised by the MOET, to MOLISA. This fundamental structural change took effect on 1 January 2017.[125]

134. So far, the most visible impact of reinforced policy directions and legal amendments appears in a virtually overwhelming torrent of government regulations, decrees, and top-down circulars dealing with a broad spectrum of system governance rearrangements and detailed functional reorientations (Appendix 7). Beyond that, MOLISA has been drafting a comprehensive new plan for implementing a national Project for TVET Reform and Quality Improvement until 2020 with an Orientation to 2030 (MOLISA 2017).

135. **MOLISA's new project plan for TVET reform until 2020/2030.** Based on a detailed analysis of performance and accomplishments regarding TVET reform, the draft plan identifies the urgent need for a new road map, readjusting perspectives, objectives, and tasks for the upcoming years. This should take into account key lessons learned and provide feasible solutions not only to overcome a range of persistent reform shortcomings and weaknesses but also to tackle a broad array of new challenges (increasing global competitiveness, rapid technological change, limited financial means) for the country's socioeconomic development.

136. The basic tenor in a comprehensive list of accomplishments prefacing the plan (Table 3.7) is that, indeed, many of the reform strategy's quantitative targets (e.g., regarding the network expansion of TVET institutions, the total number of teachers, the adoption of new training curricula, the number of quality-accredited schools as well as the number of occupational skills standards and skills assessment centers) could be achieved. However, regarding the impact of these accomplishments on qualitative improvements and the relevance of the TVET system, so far only slight initial and gradual

---

[123]   Government of Viet Nam. Law No. 74/2014/QH13 on Vocational Education and Training, Chapter IV, Article 52.

[124]   Government of Viet Nam. Law No. 74/2014/QH13 on Vocational Education and Training, Articles 25 ff.

[125]   Government of Viet Nam. Law No. 74/2014/QH13 on Vocational Education and Training, Chapter VII.

movements could be observed. Inter alia, the list of reform limitations and weaknesses comprises the following issues:

(i)   Scale and structure of TVET enrollments has not met the strategy's objectives and consistently declined over the years. Enrollment rates at the lowest level account for 88%, and at intermediate and college level only for 12%. Enrollments in courses for heavy, hazardous, and talented occupations are very low.

(ii)   The implementation of high-quality vocational training (developing key occupations, high-quality vocational schools, and piloting vocational training at international and ASEAN level) is still slow.

(iii) There are still imbalances in the structure of training occupations and disciplines and between regions, resulting into inadequate supply of human resources for the labor market.

(iv)   Quality and effectiveness of training of many TVET institutions have been improved but still have not met the requirements regarding the demand of human resources of sectors and localities; there are many shortcomings in the management of quality assurance and the external control of TVET quality.

(v)   Relationships between TVET institutions and enterprises are lax and informal; graduates do not have strong enough foreign language skills and soft skills; unemployment rate of graduates at intermediate and college level is high;

(vi)   In some places training for rural laborers is not really effective; the number of unemployed graduates is still high (about 30%) and tends to increase.

(vii) TVET institutions fulfilling international standards have not been established and developed.

MOLISA has identified the following main causes for missing its strategic targets:

(i)   All stakeholders including students and parents, employers, and public authorities still perceive the role and importance of TVET to be inadequate for society and the economy. Its reputation compared with other subsectors providing general and higher education qualifications is still low.

(ii)   TVET is not sufficiently linked to systems that forecast the demand of the labor market, particularly with regard to the economic process of regional and international integration.

(iii) The unique (but legally fixed) three-level structure of Viet Nam's TVET system has limitations in responding to labor market requirements and resists a smooth integration in the national qualification framework incorporating also levels of the higher education sector.

(iv)   Operational mechanisms of the TVET reform are sophisticated and lack effectiveness, particularly regarding the process toward school autonomy, which not only requires feasible and synchronous solutions but also a high motivation at the operational management level to overcome severe systemic challenges (student recruitment, financing schemes, organizational constraints, etc.).

(v)   The capacity of state management agencies at all levels is limited; the contingent of state management officials in charge of vocational education is inadequate, unprofessional, and partially unqualified, especially at the local level. The application of information technology in TVET management and training has not met the requirements. Scientific research activities in vocational education have not paid due attention to investment needs.

(vi) Quality assurance conditions at TVET institutions are weak and do not effectively contribute to the improvement of training quality (training programs are not matching practical conditions of production, business, and services; the number of teachers is inadequate and most teachers are short of professional and pedagogical skills; universities have trained teachers only in some occupations/disciplines; the capacity of vocational teacher training facilities in some colleges have not met the requirements for improving pedagogical and professional skills; training facilities and equipment have not met the requirements of training programs and are often outdated compared with the technology applied in the industry).

(vii) So far, independent TVET quality accreditation centers have not been established. National vocational skills standards have been promulgated late; many key occupations do not have national vocational skills standards. The organization for assessing and granting vocational skills certificates is still in a pilot period and not yet widely implemented.

(viii) Cooperation at international level with potential partnering countries is not deep enough. The recognition of diplomas and certificates between Viet Nam and ASEAN countries and internationally is still in the process of agreement and testing; some government regulations on training cooperation with other countries are not reasonable.

(ix) The mobilization of investment resources for TVET has not met the development requirements. The state investment budget for TVET has increased in recent years but has neither met the demand nor was compatible with the reform objectives; many localities have not prioritized investment resources for TVET development.

137. To address and tackle prevalent TVET reform shortcomings and clearing their causes, the draft plan comes up with a comprehensive list of tasks and "solutions," which are grouped into eight major areas (Table 3.7).

138. Interestingly, some of the nine systemic reform components of the long-term TVET strategy have been significantly rearranged in this plan: two of the highly system-relevant breakthrough components addressing the development of vocational teachers and managerial staff (component ii) and the development of occupational standards (component iii). Together with other components of the overarching TVET reform strategy, e.g., those concerning the development of curricula, learning materials, and standards for training facilities and equipment, these reform components now appear more subordinated in the plan's activity lists for tasks 2 and 4 that put the key focus on school autonomy and quality assurance conditions. From a logic-analytical perspective such structural rearrangements indicate a remarkable shift in MOLISA's focal points for its own GDVT operations, which now seem to concentrate more on regulative standardization rather than on solutions shaping the concrete requirements, objectives, and implementation processes of teacher development, management capacity building, curriculum design, and financing schemes.

139. Unfortunately, many of these activities are characterized only by an accumulative structure rather than a systematic elaboration of problems, causes, means, and effects. The vast majority of proposed "solutions" is still formulated unclear in terms of ideas or intentions. Many propositions such as, for instance, "applying information technology to build a management information system" and "promoting the role of enterprises, employers and professional associations" (in taking up their responsibilities for a range of highly system-relevant tasks), lack a designation of agents, rationally sequenced modes of joint interventions, and significant indicators qualifying tangible approaches for different agents to achieve the objectives. Though identified as crucial shortcoming in reform attempts during the previous period, all envisaged "solutions" in the list continue to appear without budget constraints.

Table 3.7: Synopsis of Tasks and Solutions Proposed in MOLISA's Draft Project Plan on Renovation and Improvement of the Quality of TVET until 2020 with an Orientation to 2030

Tasks	Envisaged Solutions and Activities
1. Renovate and improve the effectiveness and efficiency of state management of TVET	• Core administrative activities shall focus on (i) the unification of legal documents and further development of strategies, programs, and projects for TVET development; (ii) further decentralization of the state management for TVET and capacity development of state management agencies; (iii) consolidation of policies toward teachers, students, post-training of workers/employees, and enterprises and employers; and (iv) building national TVET information management systems. • Activities regarding TVET financing reforms include (i) the renovation of funding and state budget investment structures and methods for the TVET sector through order and bidding procedures and performance-based funding criteria*; and (ii) renovation and improvement of policies on land, tax, and credit to promote involvement of industry in TVET development. * including a demand for TVET funding "at a rate of 20%–22% for education and training in total state budget expenditure" and a list of priority areas and beneficiaries to be funded.
2. Grant full autonomy to TVET institutions in association with measures that ensure enhanced accountability, independent assessment mechanisms, state control, social monitoring mechanisms, and improved administration capacity of TVET institutions	• TVET institutions shall be entitled to autonomy in performing tasks, organizing structures, personnel, and finance in accordance with road maps depending on capacity, sector, occupation, and locality. • Independent assessments shall ensure the quality and effectiveness of training. • To enhance their accountability, TVET institutions shall periodically publish their quality-ensuring conditions, results of quality accreditation as well as their outcomes regarding employment rates of their graduates. For this, the role of school boards also shall be strengthened. • Advanced internal quality control and management systems shall be established by applying information technology to build a management information system and by improving the capacity of administrators and teachers in charge of management and quality assurance through training (*ambitious quantitative targets for training are specified*).
3. Improve TVET institution network planning	• The network of TVET institutions shall be reviewed and rearranged in the direction of standardization, reduction of contact points, increase of enrollment scales, and improvement of the quality and efficiency of operations. • For a number of specific occupations, economic sectors, and subjects (e.g., health care, culture and arts, service for people with disabilities) special TVET sectors and key institutions shall be established.
4. Standardize vocational training quality assurance conditions	• National quality assurance standards including (i) output standards for occupational majors; (ii) standards for TVET facilities and equipment; (iii) qualification, work, and employment standards for teachers and administrators; (iv) economic–technical norms for cost calculation of training courses; and (v) adequate quality accreditation criteria and process standards shall be developed and promulgated in cooperation with employers and professional associations. • Standardization of core quality assurance factors such as (i) the development of outcome-oriented and modularized training curricula, reform of corresponding training delivery modes as well as relevant assessment forms, procedures, and methods; (ii) the development of appropriate contingents of qualified teachers and school managers*; and (iii) the enhancement and standardization of TVET facilities and equipment. • * For activity (ii) ambitious quantitative targets are specified (see section 4 of Appendix 8).

continued on next page

Table 3.7 continued

5. Strengthen vocational training quality accreditation	• A number of quality accreditation organizations (20/30) shall be set up and state orders for quality inspection of TVET institutions shall be issued. *(Personnel composition of these organizations is roughly outlined and ambitious quantitative targets for TVET institutions to be accredited are specified, see section 5 of Appendix 8.)*
6. Link TVET with labor markets, decent work, and social security	• Forecast systems for human resources needs shall be improved. • A career orientation and consultancy system at TVET institutions utilizing job placement centers, job exchanges, job fairs, and promote startup business models shall be established. • Special emphasis shall be put on "green training," gender equality issues, and the movement of skill competitions. • The role of enterprises, employers, and professional associations shall be enforced in (i) TVET policy formulation, (ii) standards development, (iii) international skill competitions, (iv) part-time collaboration with state management agencies, (v) participation in sectoral skills councils, and (vi) public–private partnership models.
7. Develop the system of national occupational skills assessment and certification	• Alignment of the current system to regional and international standards; recognition of occupational skills shall be negotiated on regional and subregional levels. • Further development and quantitative expansion of the current certification system (including ambitious quantitative targets for establishing new skills assessment centers). • Stronger promotion of enterprises to raise professional skills of their workers and participate in skills assessments.
8. Strengthen communication, scientific research, and international cooperation	• Communication work in TVET promotion shall be intensified in three directions: (i) to enterprises and employers regarding their interests, rights, and obligations; (ii) for management agencies at all levels regarding the importance of TVET for socioeconomic development and international integration; and (ii) for learners, families, and the society regarding career opportunities through vocational training at all levels. • Scientific research in TVET shall be promoted by building capacity and upgrading the National Institute for Vocational Training (NIVT) into an academy of vocational training to conduct strategic and applied research. *(Future tasks of such an academy are specified in some detail, see section 8 of Appendix 8).* • International cooperation in TVET shall be strengthened in four directions: (i) by attracting official development assistance funds for innovating and improving TVET quality; (ii) by participating in international organizations focusing on professional standards, TVET quality assurance, and accreditation; (iii) by strengthening cooperative training with foreign countries, especially in particular occupations for the service sector and industry 4.0; and (iv) by developing the capacity of bodies and staff in charge of international cooperation at TVET state management agencies and TVET institutions.

MOLISA = Ministry of Labour–Invalids and Social Affairs, TVET = technical and vocational education and training.
Note: Appendix 8 provides a more detailed synopsis including also quantitative targets.
Source: Ministry of Labour–Invalids and Social Affairs. 2017. Project on Renovation and Improvement of the Quality of Technical and Vocational Education and Training – Up to 2020, with Orientation to 2030 (Draft October 2017). Ha Noi.

140. A general peculiarity of the plan appears in the loose relation between proposed solutions and explicit objectives provided by a rather short statement in a preceding section. While the overall objective basically recapitulates challenging but largely generic aspects of Viet Nam's socioeconomic development needs, specific project-relevant objectives for the two periods marked by the years 2020 and 2030 are expressed only by broad sets of quantitative targets that do not reflect also the qualitative challenges associated with them (Table 3.8).

Table 3.8: Objectives of MOLISA's Project on Renovation and Improvement of the Quality of TVET until 2020 with an Orientation to 2030

Overall objective	Create drastic change in quality and efficiency of vocational training; meet trained workforce demand for sectors, fields of the economy, including high-quality human resources, approach to levels of advanced countries in the world; and contribute to higher labor productivity, improved growth quality and competitiveness of the economy in the context of international integration.
Specific objectives to be achieved by 2020	• The proportion of training at the intermediate level or higher in the total enrollment scale of vocational education will be about 30%, of which at least 10% will be trained in key occupations. • At least 75% of TVET graduates will have jobs or higher productivity or income. • Develop 70 high-quality institutions, of which 3 will reach the levels of developed countries in the G20 group, 40 will reach the levels of ASEAN-4 countries; there will be about 150 national key occupations and 50 occupations targeted for levels approaching the levels of ASEAN-4 countries or G20 countries.
Specific objectives to be achieved by 2030	• The proportion of training at the intermediate level or higher in the total enrollment scale of vocational education will be about 40%, of which at least 20% will be trained in key occupations. • At least 85% of TVET graduates will have jobs or higher productivity or income. • Develop 120 high-quality institutions, of which 10 will reach the levels of developed countries in the G20 group, 70 will reach the levels of ASEAN-4 countries; there will be about 200 national key occupations and 90 occupations targeted for levels approaching the levels of ASEAN-4 countries or G20 countries. • TVET of Viet Nam will reach levels equivalent to those of developed countries in the ASEAN region.

ASEAN = Association of Southeast Asian Nations, MOLISA = Ministry of Labour–Invalids and Social Affairs, TVET = technical and vocational education and training.
Source: MOLISA. 2017. Project on Renovation and Improvement of the Quality of Technical and Vocational Education and Training – Up to 2020, with Orientation to 2030 (Draft October 2017). Ha Noi.

141. In its appendix, however, the draft plan backs up some of its overall targets[126] by more detailed sets of quantitative norms to be annually achieved until 2020. Yet, some of these norms still appear to be ambitious compared with what has been implemented in the respective fields during the previous 5 years.[127] A considerable number of target areas, except those on the total number of training centers, schools, and colleges, had not been addressed so far but would require effort in terms of organizational capacity, personnel resources, and budgets to achieve the respective quantitative norms.

---

[126] Basically those that are related to envisaged enrollment targets, teacher and staff training, curriculum and textbook development, training facilities and equipment standardization, quality management and accreditation, occupational skills standards and evaluation, and the promotion and application of information and communication technology (ICT). The selected norms seem to refer exclusively to quantitative targets already set out in MOLISA's long-term TVET reform strategy 2011–2020 approved in 2012.

[127] For instance, the target to "further train teachers in occupational skills and evaluate occupational practice skills" covers a total number of 20,000 teachers to be trained during the next 4 years. This is almost five times the number that has been achieved between 2011 and 2015. Similar disproportionate figures apply to training for school managers (27,000/3,180) and skill evaluators (8,000/1,924) as well as to the accreditation of high-quality training programs for national focal occupations (1,500/44).

142. Unfortunately, the plan forgoes the chance to disaggregate and map the quantitative targets of student enrollments at the different TVET levels to estimated labor demands of Vietnamese enterprises by specific subsectors and type of occupational qualifications and provides no indication how its target figures respond to the employment forecasts for specific economic sectors as shown in its annex.[128]

143. One of the challenges of better planning at central level seems to relate to the weak education management information system [EMIS]) for collecting, processing, analyzing, and reporting labor market and supply system-relevant information across the wide range of TVET institutions including occupation-specific faculty enrollment and performance data.

---

[128] The plan's annex displays tables with recent data of national labor market surveys on enterprises and employment structure disaggregated by level 1 industry sectors. However, in its analytical section, the plan deals only with aggregate figures for macro economic sectors (agriculture/forestry/fishery, manufacturing/construction industry, services). These figures are then broadly mapped to the three levels of Viet Nam's TVET system (elementary, intermediate, college).

IV. Assessment of Viet Nam's TVET Reform Strategy

144. Since 2012, the National Institute for Vocational Training (NIVT) of the Ministry of Labour–Invalids and Social Affairs (MOLISA) has published four annual technical and vocational education and training (TVET) reports.[129] The reports not only show in-depth the key directions and gradual accomplishments in Viet Nam's ongoing process to reform and improve its vocational education and training system by following a comprehensive socioeconomic development strategy and an ambitious human resources development (HRD) master plan, but also have critically revealed in some detail the limitations and weaknesses of many reform initiatives during this process.

145. In its most recent review prefacing its new Plan for a Project on Reform and Quality Improvement of Technical and Vocational Education and Training until 2020 with an Orientation to 2030, MOLISA has compiled a comprehensive list of successful achievements making the country's institutional settings for TVET more capable and ready to move into an advanced and flexible skills supply system that meets the requirements of a dynamically developing labor market and associates its performance with the needs of rapid socioeconomic development and technological progress.

146. These achievements cover a range of successful government interventions—from the enactment of a new TVET Law, which adopted some "breakthrough contents compatible with TVET in developed countries" and has fostered a series of subsequent regulations, to streamlining the overall TVET system governance structures and an expansion and diversification of the network of vocational education and training (TVET) institutions with regard to training forms, training levels, and operational models. The latter was accompanied by a higher number of TVET enrollments, particularly in short-term courses for rural workers, and a rapid increase in the number of teachers and management staff at different school levels. The focus on standards, quality assurance, and accreditation of TVET institutions and programs has been intensified and for some other components at least basic or initial accomplishments could be reported (Table 4.1).

---

[129] For the years 2011, 2012, 2013/14, and 2015. Each of the last three reports took about 2 years to publish (2014, 2016, and 2017).

Table 4.1: Summary of Achievements Stated by MOLISA on Its Past Efforts to Reform Viet Nam's TVET System

Category	Achievements
TVET governance and management	• The new TVET Law 2014 provides a significantly augmented legal basis for fundamental enhancements of Viet Nam's complex TVET system, such as a new focus on high-quality TVET institutions for national, regional, and international focal occupations, revised specifications on key input factors of TVET (teacher and manager qualifications), principles and procedures of mandatory quality accreditation, rights and obligations for enterprise participation in TVET, and basic regulations for implementing school autonomy. • Two tracks of TVET (MOET and MOLISA) are now streamlined under one central government agency (MOLISA/DVET) from 2017 onward. A national qualification framework has been enacted providing the basis for aligning training programs to occupational competencies and skills standards at different levels. • 38 legal documents (decrees, decisions, and circulars) issued, guiding the implementation of the new TVET law including mechanisms and policies for groups of learners, teachers, and managers; autonomy and accountability of vocational education institutions; quality standards and accreditation; tuition exemptions for disadvantaged groups and others (see corresponding list in Appendix 7). • Increased number of officers in charge of state management from the central to local levels and managers at vocational education institutions.
Number of TVET institutions, staffing, and enrollments	• National network of TVET institutions developed (between 2011 and 2016, total number of TVET institutions increased by about 16%) and diversified in training forms, training levels, and operational models. All provinces and centrally run cities now have vocational schools and colleges; network of high-quality vocational schools and key disciplines/professions at national, regional, and international levels are planned for each region, locality, and level of training; a number of specialized vocational schools for people with disabilities and ethnic minority people, schools for gifted and talented disciplines (culture, arts, physical education, and sports), and political schools have been established and developed. • About 9.17 million people were enrolled for vocational training in the period 2011–2015 (almost half of them under the TVET program for rural laborers); enrollment at elementary, intermediate, and college levels has been adjusted flexibly according to the demands of society. • Number of teachers and management staff increased rapidly and shifted considerably in their distribution among the three training levels (see Chapter II); formal qualifications of teachers and school managers have improved and almost fully match basic standard requirements. • New training programs on pedagogical skills have been piloted; 45 vocational training divisions at universities and colleges have been established; approximately 45% of managers of TVET institutions have been trained in management skills.
TVET Curricula	• Training program development has been piloted under the Developing a Curriculum (DACUM) model which shall ensure the relevance of training with job requirements among different training levels. • 8 curricula from Malaysia, 12 curricula from Australia, and some programs from Germany were transferred, partly piloted, and tested at some colleges; national-level key vocational training programs have been issued; a number of pilot courses based on international standards (e.g., dual TVET) have been implemented at selected TVET institutions in Viet Nam with support of international partner organizations. • Training at different levels has been organized in different forms (academic year or modularized by credit accumulation); teaching methods have been gradually renovated to promote activeness and independence through self-learning and group work; enterprises and employers participated in assessments and examinations.

continued on next page

Table 4.1 continued

Facilities and equipment	• Facilities and equipment of (some) vocational education institutions have been invested to meet the training requirements (between 2011 and 2015, 212 sets of equipment for institutes at intermediate and college levels were issued). • 400 managers at vocational education institutions have been trained in the management work and efficient use of facilities and equipment.
Quality accreditation and assurance of TVET institutions and programs	• 25% of vocational colleges, 10% of vocational schools, and 3.5% of vocational training centers have successfully achieved quality accreditation based on the 2010 quality criteria and standards; the number of vocational education institutions conducting self-accreditation increases annually. • With technical support from international organizations, such as GIZ and the British Council, a quality management system has been piloted in a number of colleges, which were invested to become high-quality colleges. Some TVET institutes have set up specialized units for quality assurance. • In 2017, MOLISA issued comprehensive sets of new accreditation and assessment criteria and standards for different levels of TVET institutions; in addition, quality accreditation criteria and standards for training programs have been introduced and a special set of quality accreditation criteria for high-quality TVET institutions has been developed and piloted. • The new TVET law also regulates TVET inspection; independent quality monitoring institutions acting on behalf of state orders shall be introduced in the future.
Occupational skills standards (NOSS)	• NOSS have been developed for 191 and promulgated for 189 occupations; 36 assessment centers have been granted certificates and a team of assessors has been formed and trained on their tasks. • A pilot assessment of occupational skills has been conducted for workers in 22 occupations and 4 Japanese-standard occupations.
Financing schemes	• Investment resources for TVET have been increased and developed in line with the trend toward alternative sources of revenues for TVET institutions ("socialization") such as tuition fees, revenues from nonbusiness services of TVET institutions, investment, and donation of organizations and individuals. • Three public vocational colleges have been assigned by the government to be autonomous on a pilot basis from 2016 to 2019. • A network of nonpublic vocational education institutions has been established and further expanded with a variety of organization forms and training methods.
Information about TVET and information management system	Diverse research activities on TVET, labor market, and employment as well as four annual TVET reports (2011, 2012, 2013/14, 2015) have been published. Management and information systems have been piloted in some colleges; digital versions of electronic lectures and software simulations (2D/3D) have been piloted; the application of information technology in teaching has improved.
International cooperation	International cooperation in TVET has been promoted in scale, effectiveness, form and content diversification, especially in scientific research and transfer of management tools; vocational quality and skills standards are developed toward internationalization. Bilateral cooperation activities with agencies and organizations of other countries have been implemented.

DVET = Directorate of Vocational Education and Training, MOET = Ministry of Education and Training, MOLISA = Ministry of Labour–Invalids and Social Affairs, NOSS = national occupational skills standards, TVET = technical and vocational education and training.
Source: Ministry of Labour–Invalids and Social Affairs. 2017. Project on Renovation and Improvement of the Quality of Technical and Vocational Education and Training – Up to 2020, with Orientation to 2030 (Draft October 2017). Ha Noi (partly complemented by findings elaborated during the preparation mission for this report).

147. **Limitations and weaknesses.** Compared with these largely basic or yet embryonic achievements, the long list of limitations and weaknesses, which have been highlighted in some detail in the previous chapter, has been considerably restraining the progress of MOLISA's efforts toward a systemic renovation of the country's TVET system and, so far, prevented it from achieving breakthrough as envisaged in the overall reform strategy paper. Reflecting the findings on structure, quality, and performance of Viet Nam's current skills supply system, which are presented in Chapter II, the core sector problem can be largely condensed to this general statement:

> Although there are a number of promising exceptions, still most of the TVET institutions in Viet Nam do not provide graduates with sufficiently appropriate skills to increase productivity and competitiveness of companies and, hence, boost the country's economy through higher labor productivity and value production (see Appendix 1 for the problem tree).

A continuing mismatch between supply and demand along with limited attractiveness, quality, and relevance of TVET programs at different levels can be traced back to a broad range of prevailing (partly deep-seated and interrelated) issues, both at the system level as well as at the institutional level.

148. **Key issues at the TVET system level**. Governance structures, though having become more streamlined through a new legal framework that eventually assigns MOLISA's DVET the exclusive central state management function of the entire TVET sector, continue to be highly fragmented in crucial direct management tasks (including financing) that largely determine the actual operations of the almost 2,000 TVET institutes but scattered among 13 line ministries, 63 provincial People's Committees, diverse social–political organizations, and private owners.

149. A tardy process of coordinating TVET provision across the different agencies not only affects the persistence of insufficient, inefficient, and opaque state funding schemes of TVET institutions but also appears as a key constraint for a sector-wide implementation of stringent procedures for standard compliance, output assessment, and quality validation of programs. The government's approach to gradually withdrawing external management functions including different state means of financial support from public TVET institutions by granting them an autonomy status for collecting (capped) tuition fees has not shown to be viable yet for the vast majority of TVET institutions. It seems to be also a risky endeavor, as it may further lead to inequalities in access opportunities for high-quality programs and place incentives on increasing enrollments, particularly at higher-level programs, regardless of the job market. Experts suggest that consistent state funding of public TVET institutions based on uniform, transparent, and major specific cost norms and maximum course enrollment margins will be an indispensable requirement for TVET funding in the future.

150. Recurrent failures to establish an institutionalized involvement of employer representatives and sector associations in TVET policy development <u>and</u> implementation, in conjunction with incomplete information on system performance resulting from the persistent lack of a sector-wide information management system, do not only hamper the impact and relevance of many well-intended reform activities but also have contributed already to rather unclear objectives and insufficiently operationalized "solutions" that cover essential parts of MOLISA's previous and current reform strategy papers and plans.

151. Altogether (and complementing each other), these system-immanent issues are also responsible for a range of unfavorable effects that can be associated with the sustained limited reputation of TVET in Viet Nam's society (partly expressed by decreasing enrollment rates). Crucial factors for this are in particular the following: (i) its limited performance in retraining adult workers and farmers, (ii) limited opportunities for high-quality training in remote regions, (iii) the lack of an inclusive professional development system for teachers and managers, and, most decisive, (iv) a deployment system that still favors academic qualifications of teachers more than work-relevant practical skills and expertise to be gained only by mandatory professional work experience in the occupations taught, particularly at elementary and intermediate levels.

152. **Key issues at institutional level.** As mentioned in Chapter II, a wide range of complementary issues prevent training programs from matching practical conditions of production, business, and services.

153. The key issues are as follows: (i) the lack of entrepreneurial capacities to manage TVET institutions, as managers are almost exclusively recruited from teachers and receive insufficient support in their long-term professional development (e.g., by confidence-building advisory services, individual coaching, and networking activities);[130] (ii) a weak integration of theory lessons with practical training, which is not only caused by insufficient pedagogical qualifications of teachers and lecturers (cf. systemic issues); but also by (iii) inadequate and obsolete training facilities and equipment as well as a lack of sufficient materials and consumables for hands-on training in many TVET institutes because of limited budgets (cf. systemic issues).

154. Persistent constraints at institutional level are further that (iv) TVET curricula are not sufficiently aligned to the world of work, which is often caused and complemented by inadequate learning outcome and assessment standards. As the process of developing and promulgating national occupational skills standards is tardy, still covers only a small range of occupations and is also not yet aligned to the national qualification framework, recent regulations require TVET institutions to cooperate with companies in their vicinities to adapt their curricula and training designs to local industries' particular needs. However, although some best practice models for such collaborations have been successfully piloted at few advanced colleges with external support, (v) the vast majority of Viet Nam's TVET institutions still struggle to achieve binding commitments and active support from companies in their curriculum design and training delivery, which, beyond a noncommittal provision of undetermined internships, integrates practical work experiences of students with basic skills and relevant knowledge to be gained at the school and vice versa (Dual TVET). Yet, as long as the government does not underpin its recent legal amendments on rights and obligations of enterprises in TVET also by more effective incentives (or sanctions), such well-intended propositions, may not really induce a tangible shift in the latent disposition of employers to avoid collaboration with TVET institutions that do not yet perform well enough in the demand orientation of their training delivery because of various organizational and financial constraints. MOLISA's new quality accreditation models seem to emphasize unilateral obligations for TVET institutions to solve this chicken-and-egg-problem. However, unless public TVET suppliers gain the basic capacity (including appropriate training facilities and equipment as well as competent staff) to make themselves more attractive, the demand side will likely remain skeptic and reluctant with regard to active contributions.

---

[130]   MOLISA's current supply-driven approach to offer just some ad hoc one-off training courses does not appear to be a very effective strategy in this field.

155. The ADB (2014) TVET assessment report condensed its findings on the key issues that characterized the overall development status of Viet Nam's TVET system at that time into a set of five essential problems: (i) insufficient enterprise-based training, (ii) wrong skills taught, (iii) skills not properly taught, (iv) inequitable access, and (v) less-than-effective organization and management of skills development. Previous chapters of this report have updated these findings by a range of new information to show the current status of the government's ambitious process to reform and improve Viet Nam's vocational education and training system. A positive aspect that has been emerging and consolidating in most recent policy directions and extensive regulative attempts is that the government, MOLISA through its DVET, has become fully aware of these problems, critically analyzes the limitations and weaknesses of respective previous solutions, and tries to counterbalance them by sharpening the focus of future reform activities on crucial system-relevant but interdependent components that complementarily address substantial quality improvements in key areas rather than just single supply-driven quantitative targets (see Table 3.7).

156. Since most issues elaborated in the final problem scenario of the ADB 2014 TVET assessment report have been more or less explicitly addressed in Viet Nam's current policy framework for its ongoing TVET reform, they shall not be replicated here in full detail, though they appear to be still valid in most of their aspects and parts. Instead, the five key problems will guide the recommendations on how to improve the strategic forward actions toward quality improvement of Viet Nam's TVET system in the upcoming years.

V. Recommendations

1. Reform TVET Governance Structure, Organization, and Management

157. Reform of TVET governance and management structures has been high on the agenda of MOLISA's TVET Development Strategy since 2012. However, despite remarkable achievements in streamlining the central state management functions from a dual structure under MOLISA and MOET to one central government agency (DVET under MOLISA) as well as the issuance of respective legal prescriptions in the new TVET law and subsequent regulations, the system still suffers from a broad range of severe shortcomings and limitations. MOLISA has identified core constraints of TVET governance and management, inter alia, in the limited capacity of state management agencies at all levels, in sophisticated operational mechanisms of the TVET reform, and in an inadequate mobilization of investment resources. In its most recent alignment of propositions that shall address and alleviate these and other issues through upcoming reform activities it has not yet become very clear how the proposed solutions will actually contribute to a fundamental change in the prevailing shortcomings. Though single solutions focus more or less verbosely on measures that should be part of the reform, the accumulative structure of such propositions does not seem to be guided by a rationally sequenced mode of (thoroughly budgeted) interventions that take into account the actual problems, their causes, means, and envisaged effects.

158. Uniform legal documents and the dissemination of a consolidated policy are essential in simplifying MOLISA's disposition toward extensive regulations pertaining to TVET-related operations and delivery. However, it is not clear whether the concrete implications of such interventions are fully reflected in their design and to what extent these are sufficiently informed by the actual conditions, capacity, and performance potential of the people to whom they are addressed. This appears true for "solutions" addressing both areas, the highly diverse network of almost 2,000 TVET institutions, and the not less inhomogeneous structure of institution owners and management agencies. This applies also to the wide range of policy propositions addressing other crucial stakeholders (such as students and employers) of the TVET system.

159. A key constraint, the lack of a comprehensive national TVET management information system (both labor market and education management information system), affects all single reform propositions and potential solutions regarding TVET governance and management and, hence, should become more prominent and more detailed in the government's reform ambitions.[131] Reliable

---

[131] Currently, MOLISA's draft plan only takes up and nonspecifically prolongs the rather unclear vision to "build national TVET information management systems ensuring the connectivity between state management agencies in charge of vocational education at all levels and vocational education institutions; build systems of linkages between supply and demand of training in vocational education." In the annex of its draft plan, target specifications suggest that single TVET institutes will be made responsible and shall become the agents for establishing such systems, which is not an appropriate approach to solve this key system-relevant issue.

and consistent data are needed on enrollment, training outputs and outcomes, training capacity and quality, financial needs, and performance as well as on labor market orientation of TVET institutions. These should be challenging circumstances and respective support structures, periodically collected in a central database, professionally processed and shared among different agents and agencies through a multidirectional web portal, and urgently become an indispensable basis for designing, monitoring, and evaluating tangible policy interventions because only these can drive sound operative innovations and verify respective measurable improvements in system performance. It would also crucially facilitate MOLISA's considerable but, with regard to technology, weakly supported efforts to collect data on 522 TVET institutions formerly supervised by MOET.[132]

160. Such data, processed and utilized through state-of-the-art information and communication technology (ICT), could also provide the backbone of more effective and efficient capacity-building measures for staff of state management agencies and TVET institute managers, which will be a prerequisite for further decentralization of management tasks. Moreover, they can shape the basis for an organizational shift from the prevailing, widely inflexible and, hence, inefficient, top-down mode of policy implementation (management by order/decree and input-based training) to a more participatory processual approach (management by achievable objectives, agreed targets, and networking). There are good reasons for the assumption that this would also promote the affinity of industry representatives and employers and their commitment to more actively participate in TVET policy development, implementation, and funding, as they may be better convinced on this by realistic data and good practice showing how such contributions will pay off in the long term through targeted investments and systemic collaboration (see recommendation 3).

161. Utilization of a powerful education management information system (EMIS) would also contribute considerably to more feasible and viable options in solving MOLISA's second most important problem addressed by the task to reform the TVET financing system, which currently follows a difficult direction in promoting financial autonomy of TVET institutions and gradually withdrawing direct state budget support from them. While, principally, the renovation of state budget investment structures and funding methods for the TVET sector through order-and-bidding procedures and performance-based funding criteria is a step in the right direction, pilot implementations of the envisaged model indicate that this might be likely not viable for the vast majority of public TVET institutions to achieve such autonomy status if based only on discipline and/or major unspecific regulations of maximum tuition fee margins. Complementary to this approach, experts have suggested aligning sound revenue and expenditure structures of TVET institutes with consistent and transparent state budget schemes through nationally uniform discipline or major specific cost norms. Section 4 of Chapter II has already outlined the following recommendations for a stepwise approach:

1) Develop an information management system of unit cost norms and financial information to identify (actual) vocational training cost for each occupation.

2) Determine reasonable training costs based on actual costs essential for quality training.

3) Develop a data collection system on school performance comparing actual enrollment data with fund allocations.

4) Identify appropriate pathways for performance-based budget allocations based on measurable training outcomes.

---

[132] Currently this information is being delivered by e-mail in form of Word or Excel files from school to designated personnel in the DVET and vice versa with guidelines of DVET, or by using traditional communication tools such as phones.

5) Pilot the performance-based budget allocation model in a representative scope.

6) Increase funding for vocational training via a training levy and human development fund.[133]

162. For undertaking enhanced efforts toward establishing an appropriate system for information management, MOLISA could draw on valuable lessons learned from an extensive spectrum of projects in developing countries focusing on the implementation of EMIS around the world, including respective previous (though failed) projects conducted under the Ministry of Education in Viet Nam.[134] However, since the development of management information systems for educational purposes usually has not only a country-specific but also often a narrow project-specific focus (ranging from a simple tool for strengthening teaching and learning to a comprehensive platform for data collection and information sharing), it is not possible to merely adopt a model designed for a particular context.[135]

163. More important and valuable for a context-specific approach is a generic set of challenges that had to be tackled across all types of EMIS projects but often could not be managed because of a range of organizational rather than technical constraints. These lessons have been summarized in a recent World Bank report and compiled in Box 5.1.

164. Based on its Systems Approach for Better Education Results, the World Bank has complemented the synopsis of EMIS challenges with a list of possible solutions, which operationalize EMIS implementation activities into a five-stage approach and offer also some key takeaways for EMIS project teams.[136] Detailed information and highly valuable recommendations on implementing a sustainable TVET reporting system in Viet Nam, including basic requirements for a respective indicator system, have already been developed through a GIZ-supported trilateral partnership program for MOLISA's National Institute for Vocational Training (NIVT) (GIZ and NIVT 2014). Lessons learned during the development of MOLISA's TVET reports from 2010 onward have been recently elaborated into a comprehensive guideline (Horn 2015), which should be thoroughly reflected in the initial stages of a systematic EMIS approach.

---

[133] MDRI and NEXIA STT (2017) provide more detailed information on what should be considered for implementing each of the six steps.

[134] See e.g., Bernbaum and Moses (2011). In the World Bank-supported Second Higher Education Development Project (2007–12) the development of the Higher Education Management and Policy Information System proved to be more difficult than anticipated and was eventually canceled. Among the factors that contributed to its failed implementation was the lack of a clear definition regarding its overall objective. A successfully established EMIS in the Primary Education for Disadvantaged Children Project (2003–11) was eventually abandoned because of large implementation costs and no source of funding was available for its maintenance. The system has been replaced by a new EMIS designed, at no cost, by a state-owned telecommunication corporation. This system covers all general education levels (Husein, Saraogi, and Mintz 2017).

[135] This applies also to an increasing amount of global OpenEMIS initiatives launched in the early 2000s under the aegis of UNESCO and implemented (mostly in African countries) in partnership with a nonprofit organization since 2012 (OpenEMIS. https://www.openemis.org).

[136] World Bank. SABER. http://saber.worldbank.org/.

Box 5.1: Key Lessons Learned on Education Management Information System Challenges

- **Unclear vision and limited buy-in:** Many projects remained unsuccessful because of the lack of shared vision on the functionalities of the education management information system (EMIS) as well as because of limited government support and buy-in. To overcome these challenges, the project teams need to focus on developing a legal framework to support EMIS operations. This would lay the groundwork for establishing the EMIS. Moreover, conversations should be made with various education stakeholders across the education system to make them understand the importance of data for decision-making. Building a "data-driven" culture in many countries is at least a 20-year process, which should be factored in at the planning stage. Training of top decision makers would also be a useful step at this point to avoid conflicts and bring everyone to a common consensus.

- **Absence of institutionalization:** Regular changes in senior management of the government is a common characteristic in many countries. Changes in leadership result in project delays because of varied interests and priorities. Again, having a written legal mandate would be helpful in pushing for reforms. A clearly defined organization structure with a mission statement, structured workflow, and defined roles and responsibilities would be helpful. A legal policy with a dedicated EMIS budget for its operations would avoid funding issues and dependence on donors for EMIS sustainability.

- **Unreliable and poor quality of data:** A common problem related to an EMIS in many countries is the collection of inconsistent, incomplete, and unreliable education data. A starting point to solve this issue is to have a well-defined infrastructure in place that supports data collection, analysis, processing, and dissemination. In addition, discussions should be held with various stakeholders on the type of policy questions they want the data to be able to answer to ensure that data collected are not limited to a small number of indicators such as enrollments and class size. Moreover, sound validation mechanisms (internal and external) must be in place to verify data accuracy and reliability. A code of conduct should be developed for EMIS staff to ensure professionalism in task performance.

- **Untimely production and dissemination of data:** Regular production and dissemination of data are another area of concern. There are often delays in the production and dissemination of a final statistics yearbook to the public. A strategic data dissemination strategy should be in place for publishing data via websites, the annual statistics handbook, and other communication channels. User-friendly platforms should be made available to access data. The dissemination strategy should be bolstered by the policies to support the capacity to disseminate the data.

- **Limited use of data for decision-making:** Often because of weak data quality issues, the potential for an EMIS as a tool for making data-driven decisions is not realized. In other cases, even when the EMIS is functioning well, stakeholders do not understand how to use the data. To solve these issues, it is important to create a data-driven culture in the country via workshops and focus group discussions. Charts and graphs should be used to help people understand what the data are trying to reveal. Producing statistics that are easily understandable and accessible would be helpful for using the data.

- **Integration issues:** Technological issues are common in many countries and relate to lack of integration of various information systems, weak internet access, and availability of computers. Ensuring a sound data architecture with a clearly defined structure of databases, hardware, and software is essential. Moving away from paper-based to information technology-based surveys in the form of tablets and phones might simplify the data entry work for schools and ease the process of management and transfer to subnational and national levels.

- **Capacity and coordination issues:** Operational issues revolve around inadequate funding, procurement issues, and lack of coordination between various donors and government as well as weak capacity issues. To overcome these problems, it is important to ensure that the institutionalized processes are sound with clearly outlined mission and duties. Investments should be channeled toward improving the local capacity of the EMIS staff so that dependence on outside support is reduced. A dedicated budget should be allocated toward EMIS operations so that the system continues to work even after the project comes to an end.

Source: A. H. Husein, N. Saraogi, and S. Mintz. 2017. Lessons Learned from World Bank EMIS Operations 2009–2014. Washington, DC: World Bank.

2. Provide the Right Skills and Teach Skills More Effectively

165. Targets, objectives, and solutions that can be associated with MOLISA's strong commitment to overcome prevailing shortcomings of the country's TVET system and accelerate its progress, both (i) in producing graduates with the skills required by industry and demanded on the labor market, and (ii) in enabling students to acquire such skills through effective training programs and methods, are manifold and addressed in several components of its Project Plan on Renovation and Improvement of the Quality of TVET until 2020 with an Orientation to 2030.

166. Key areas of interventions focus on upholding, updating, and refining considerable accomplishments achieved during recent years with regard to the National Qualification Framework, developing occupational skills and training quality standards and rigorously standardizing core input factors for an advanced skills supply system such as qualifications of TVET teachers and school managers, competency-based curriculum design and practice-oriented training delivery methods, as well as work regimes specifying teacher duties, minimum workloads, and maximum class sizes. These and other standards, norms, and regulations largely comply with recommendations of the ADB 2014 TVET assessment and other expert reports and have built a good and necessary basis for further activities focusing on a nationwide implementation of this innovative but complex reform process framework.

167. Though several key tasks—such as standardizing the conditions for vocational training quality assurance, strengthening vocational training quality accreditation, linking TVET with labor markets, and further developing the system for occupational skills assessment and certification—address different aspects of MOLISA's comprehensive initiative toward a fundamental TVET quality reform, these culminate in the envisaged solution to "grant full autonomy to TVET institutions in association with measures that ensure enhanced accountability, independent assessment mechanisms, state control, social monitoring mechanisms, and improved administration capacity of TVET institutions" (MOLISA 2017).

168. A weakness of these policy propositions, particularly of those "solutions" that focus on implementing fundamental changes in accountability structure and operational settings of TVET institutions toward autonomy, is (apart from a missing reflection on budget constraints) their unclear and indefinite character as they are largely formulated only in ideas or intentions and lack a clear designation of agents, modes of interventions, and indicators qualifying tangible approaches for different agents to achieve the envisaged objectives. What is strongly missing are conceptual specifications on the change management model, its strategy and leadership aspects, as well as on the design and setup of sustained support structures and effective means. As international experience with attempts of fundamental systemic change processes in education have shown, they are likely to fail when they are based only on high-level government visions and implemented by top-down orders that do not sufficiently integrate operational conditions and motivations of all stakeholders and clients involved.

169. According to advanced theories on organizational development (e.g., Fullan 1993, 2001), such change will not happen unless (i) people are interacting; (ii) new knowledge is being produced in the heads of people; (iii) new solutions are being discovered; (iv) agents involved actually own these solutions, are passionately committed, and energetic about pursuing them; and (v) critical voices prevent locking into weak solutions and allow for continually seeking potentially better ideas. Apart from these, change processes need time and the availability of sufficient resources. Fullan's eight lessons about change (Box 5.2) provide some additional basic but valuable advice.

Box 5.2: Fullan's Eight Lessons about Change (1993)

You can't mandate what matters	This is a lesson about being able to force through preconceived ideas of what is important. If it really is important, then forcing it will harm the quality of the implementation.
Change is a journey not a blueprint	This lesson tells you that your plans will at some point (usually sooner, rather than later) become overtaken by events; that you need to learn how to travel well on your journey with your colleagues; that it is the journey of change management, and not the arrival point, that is important. This doesn't mean that the change never happens, only that when you get to where you thought you were going, things will have moved on again.
Problems are our friends	Here, problems are not seen as evidence of an incompetent person making a mistake; instead they are seen as an inevitable part of what happens when you change anything important enough to be worth changing. Solving these problems is seen as the way we learn how to manage change more effectively and, therefore, they are to be welcomed as friends.
Vision and strategic planning come later	This may sound strange, given the emphasis on prior vision and development planning, but it is a reminder that if you stick rigidly to your preconceived ideas you can become blinded to unexpected solutions to problems and new ways forward.
Individualism and collectivism must have equal power	The best ideas might come as well from an insightful or well-informed individual as from a discussion group involving those most directly involved in the problems of change management. Don't be prejudiced about where an idea comes from.
Neither centralization nor decentralization works	This lesson addresses the assumption that there is only one source of appropriate influence in a change process. Sometimes it is appropriate to tell people what is to be achieved and give guidance; at other times it is appropriate for managers in the hierarchy to listen to those responsible for implementing change.
Connection with the wider environment is critical for success	This lesson highlights the assumption that other stakeholders outside of the organization will have an interest in the change process and a role to play in its successful implementation.
Every person is a change agent	This is a reminder of two things. First, that no one can sit back, relax, and see the responsibility for making changes as "somebody else's," and second, that each person's ideas for managing change are as valid as anyone else's.

Source: UK Department for Education, National College for Teaching and Leadership. Diploma of School Business Management, Phase 4 Module 2. https://www.nationalcollege.org.uk/?q=node/237 (accessed January 2018).

170. Putting those basic lessons and principles into practice requires, apart from a fundamental mind shift of government agents toward participatory change management processes, more efforts in extending the envisaged unidirectional traditional training for teachers and managers by persistent advisory services and coaching opportunities for individual schools and through panels and platforms (including modern ICT-based social-media applications) that support sustained networking between and among practitioners and experts and, hence, can facilitate the stepwise evolution of communities of practice sharing innovative knowledge and practical experience.

171. If, as envisaged, ICT shall become an important lever of change in administrative effectiveness and efficiency in school management as well as in raising the quality and flexibility of training processes (by e-learning tools), not only clear technical and usability specifications need to be elaborated carefully in advance by appropriate experts but also key lessons learned about implementing ICT in education in other countries should be taken into account. Beyond that, proven international models can guide this process of technical innovation by a systematic stepwise approach from "entry" and "adoption" of technologies over "adaptation" and "appropriation" to the final phase of creative "invention." Ely (1990) gives eight conditions that facilitate the implementation of educational technology innovations, which are highly valuable for developing strategies and plans in this area. These conditions range from dissatisfaction with the current way of doing things, to appropriate assistance to acquire new knowledge and skills, availability of necessary infrastructure, sufficient time and capacity, clear incentives for change, participation and commitment of all stakeholders involved, and, last but not least, the leaders' role in making responsibility evident in all innovation-related activities.

172. Regarding overall effectiveness of teaching, MOLISA's reform plan clearly includes all three essential factors that are crucial and interdependent elements for quality improvements: standards, instructor qualifications, and assessment of learning outcomes. However, beyond comprehensive descriptions and regulations demanding sophisticated procedures of quality assurance and accreditation, not enough has been done yet in establishing effective support structures that guide and help teachers to adopt the new concepts also under difficult conditions of lacking appropriate facilities and equipment.[137] While school managers and teachers could also learn a lot from their colleagues in private TVET institutions (e.g., in outsourcing practical training sessions to industry partners), the need for more independent training outcome assessments is largely dependent on mandatory involvement of industry representatives or professional associations. MOLISA's new quality accreditation model includes unilateral obligations for TVET institutions to solve this problem. However, as mentioned, unless public TVET institutions gain the basic capacity (including appropriate training facilities and equipment as well as competent staff) to make themselves more attractive, the demand side will likely remain skeptic and reluctant with regard to such contributions. Hence, it is strongly recommended to put more effort on institutionalizing active stakeholder participation also at the operative level of the skills supply system, for instance, by demanding more commitment on this from the Viet Nam Chamber of Commerce and Industry (VCCI) and providing better targeted incentives (see also next recommendation).

173. Similar applies to legal prescriptions demanding teachers to upgrade occupational skills and work experience through periodic placements and internships in companies. As long as these generic prescriptions are watered down by regulations that position such activities at the same level as conventional training or self-study and assign work experience in industry the same status as experiences gained in TVET institutions, this might not promote fundamental changes in this regard. Currently, compliance with desired qualification norms does not seem to sufficiently pay off for teachers in public TVET institutions since, despite recent decrees, this is also not promoted enough by appropriate incentives that attract candidates with proven occupational skills and work experience into the teaching profession and, beyond that, would also motivate those teachers already employed to continuously upgrade their occupational skills and qualifications. Taking into account rather low base salary levels of young teachers employed in Viet Nam's public TVET institutions, it is highly recommended to significantly increase respective financial incentives and make them commensurable with actual career development efforts TVET teachers need to invest on to qualify for this.

---

[137] Literally, the new quality accreditation standards assign solely the TVET institutes to ensure that their facilities, equipment, and training materials comply with new curriculum standards.

174. In addition, the current preservice training system does not effectively enough link theoretical knowledge, pedagogical skills, and practical occupational experience in its program design. This could be gradually enhanced by piloting and experimenting with international models of dual study programs where workers in industry get the opportunity to study part-time at a university to become a certified instructor while practicing the knowledge gained in parallel at their work environment. Particular attention should also be given to the recently presented Association of Southeast Asian Nations (ASEAN) TVET Teacher Standards (Paryono and Bock 2017), which was developed jointly by SEAMEO VOCTECH and the GIZ-RECOTVET Initiative. The standards aim to establish a common understanding of the competencies of a TVET teacher. When developing or updating national standards, the described competencies could be utilized as a reference to national standards or for mapping and benchmarking them to ensure that Viet Nam, as an ASEAN member country, is supplied with comparable and high-quality TVET teachers.

3. Stimulate Greater Enterprise-Based Training and Financial Support

175. Greater involvement of enterprises in TVET reform and delivery has become more prominent in the new legal framework for TVET as well as in MOLISA's latest approaches and substantial undertaking toward enhancing quality assurance and quality accreditation of TVET institutions. However, MOLISA still focuses on making individual schools as the key agents for organizing the enduring commitment of companies to participate in the schools' operational duties and actively cooperate in training delivery.

176. While pilot initiatives supported by external partners have successfully experimented with advanced models of cooperative training (Dual TVET) and tripartite partnerships at the microlevel and an increasing number of high-level TVET colleges have been managing to establish productive relationships with enterprises in their vicinities, the government admits that relationships between most of its TVET institutions and enterprises are still lax and informal. Recent surveys among employers indicate that the reputation of the public TVET system in general has not yet improved as expected and unless public TVET suppliers gain more capacity to make themselves more attractive, the demand side will likely remain skeptic and reluctant with regard to active contributions. Larger enterprises (mainly foreign direct investment [FDI] companies and state-owned enterprises that invest in new technologies) prefer to establish their own training centers to train their employees on a set of specific (often narrow) job-relevant skills. This is also explicitly promoted by the new TVET law and supported by the option to deduct expenses for vocational training activities from income taxes.[138] However, in order to ensure the quality of enterprise-based training, a standard and training program for the Enterprise- based trainers need to be developed, master trainers need to be trained, and a system to organize these trainings, for example coordinated by VCCI, needs to be established. Box 5.3 provides examples of private sector engagement in TVET in the Asian countries.

177. With regard to initial formal TVET, the TVET law grants enterprises also the right to register for delivering TVET at elementary level but receive state funding for this only through subsidies for people with disabilities. Particularly among FDI companies this option has not yet been widely used. For this and all other levels of formal and nonformal TVET, enterprises are encouraged to cooperate with officially registered TVET institutions and are now obliged to employ only trained workers or workers possessing vocational certificates for specific occupations listed by MOLISA. What is still

---

[138] Article 51 of the TVET Law 2014.

Box 5.3: Approaches of Asian Countries in Shaping Framework Conditions for Private Sector Engagement in TVET

In most developing countries, private stakeholders are still rarely involved in shaping framework conditions for skills development and technical and vocational education and training (TVET). A joint conference of the Southeast Asia Regional Policy Network of the Organisation for Economic Co-operation and Development (OECD), GIZ RECOTVET, and the Asian Development Bank recently elaborated (inter alia) opportunities and challenges for public authorities to create such conditions for private sector engagement in TVET delivery, specifically looking at opportunities to institutionalize the cooperation between private and public stakeholders in the integration of learning and working at the workplace. During the conference, some countries reported about their current approaches and accomplishments:

The Philippines reported on its framework conditions for work-based training. The Republic Act 7796 stipulated the creation of the Technical Education and Skills Development Authority (TESDA) to manage TVET in the country. To improve the responsiveness and relevance of training, TESDA has implemented strategies to pursue public–private partnership in TVET, expand enterprise-based training, and strengthen the links between public and private employers when hiring TVET graduates. TESDA also provides incentives and rewards to generate wider industry support and commitment for training, expanding, and purposively directing scholarships and other assistance to fund the development of critical and hard-to-find skills, higher technologies, and incentivize the vocational education and training institutions. To increase the private actor's importance in occupational standards, governments should capitalize on and extend technical assistance, incentivize, recognize good practices, and communicate effectively with media.

Malaysia shared its experience in involving the private sector in the development of its national occupational skills standard (NOSS). The NOSS provides opportunities to community and industry to access services offered by the Department of Skills Development (DSD) and other related agencies. Likewise, the DSD provides assistance and guidance to ensure that all companies and enterprises participate in the National Dual Training System, which is an industry-oriented training program that combines workplace and institutional training. The National Development Planning Committee also established the Industry Skills Council (ISC), which enhances quality and delivery of TVET programs to improve graduate employability by enabling industry-led programs to reduce skills mismatch. The ISC, in collaboration with industry players, identifies relevant competencies for each sector and subsector. The industry working group also recommends to the ISC policies, strategies, and action plans for developing skilled and competent human resources for industry.

The Republic of Korea shared an example of a TVET program called the Work-Based Learning System (Dual System), which is a new TVET program led by companies with programs based on national competency standards (NCS). In-company trainers train workers in a company instead of in a school or vocational training institute and provide certifications issued by the government and the industry. To implement this program, the Republic of Korea established a legal framework and sustainable government incentives for companies. It also strengthened the roles of the industry sector councils and the regional councils and increased the flexibility of the program's development. It has linked its training, certificates, jobs, and competency-based compensation, with the industry sector councils and companies participating in the program development. Its high schools, colleges, universities, and vocational institutes are utilized as training facilities. The Republic of Korea also has an accreditation of the NCS drafted by the private sector and an assessment of learning workers in collaboration between public and private sectors.

Source: OECD Southeast Asia Regional Policy Network on Education and Skills and GIZ Regional Cooperation Programme to Improve the Training of TVET Personnel. Bridging the Gap: The Private Sector's Role in Skills Development and Employment. Summary Report on the 2016 SEARPN Education and Skills Network meeting and RECOTVET's 4th Regional Policy Dialogue on TVET. 11–12 October 2016. Cebu City, Philippines. https://www.oecd.org/employment/leed/Summary-Report-2016-SouthEast-Asia-%20FINAL.pdf.Ectatem fuga. Bitam quatqui aecaeceprat liquo qui tem fugiam quiscimagnis eum quas debis et fugit eossedic te peles abo.

missing, however, are reasonable strategies and incentives for employers to support and collaborate with TVET institutions that do not yet perform well in the demand orientation of their training delivery because of various organizational and financial constraints.

178. Unfortunately, the TVET law only marginally covers the establishment of an enduring institutional framework for private sector involvement. Recent initiatives that should promote the interest of industry and employers to invest more in enterprise-based training have been confined to a 2014 GIZ-supported NIVT study on costs and benefits for enterprises in internship programs, which came up with rather detailed, though not representative, results showing that such investments may actually pay off in the long-term perspective of a company's HRD strategy (NIVT 2015). However, apart from positive reactions of enterprises involved in this study, no further impact on tangible solutions concerned with institutionalizing such employer contributions could be identified yet. Thus, this report resumes the recommendation of its predecessor: stimulating enterprise training should be given a higher priority in Viet Nam's TVET system by some crucial systemic amendments.

179. **A possible option to establish a tripartite national TVET agency.** A widely used indicator to measure the stage of a country's HRD reform initiatives is the degree by which such agencies are becoming institutionalized and how they are actually performing their strategic and operational duties with regard to a wide range of multilevel TVET governance tasks including the promotion of industry stakeholders to increase their commitment and actively contribute also financially to the national TVET system (e.g., ETF, ILO, and UNESCO Inter-Agency Working Group on TVET Indicators [2012] and World Bank [2013]). In general, it can be assumed that a newly established agency representing the state, the industry (employers and workers), and the TVET suppliers would compete with authorities, and its acceptance by all stakeholders involved will only gradually grow, not least depending on a joint acknowledgment to achieve feasible outcomes. Main challenges are to exceed the status of only a formal arrangement and actually achieve effective and efficient capacity to be able to influence policy design, actively participate in its implementation, and monitor its concrete impacts. Some lessons learned from similar endeavors in other developing countries, which could be supportive, include the following:[139]

(i) Tripartite national TVET agencies will be able to become the central institution for collaborative efforts among stakeholders rather than a government-driven forum for directives. In so far, they serve as a platform for a sustained involvement of stakeholders and develop forms of productive dialogue. Initially establishing sectoral, more professionally structured, and competent organizations may likely increase their acceptance by actors.

(ii) The mandate and objectives of the new agency have to be integrated in the TVET law and delineated with responsibilities for vocational training, which, at the same time, fall under the authority of other state institutions (e.g., MOET, MOLISA, Ministry of Industry and Trade, and other sectoral ministries). In addition to national authorities, regional or municipal authorities will be affected as these bodies have been active much longer in the training field. To avoid inefficient friction, responsibilities should be clearly aligned, legally determined, and well-coordinated. This process is rather challenging, hence, initially a narrow yet realistic allocation of responsibilities could help this facility become effective over the long term.

---

[139] These and some of the following recommendations were initially developed by the author for a background paper on TVET governance for the GIZ Regional TVET Conference Supporting AEC Integration through Inclusive and Labor Market-Oriented TVET in Vientiane, Lao People's Democratic Republic on 14–15 December 2015 (Russell 2015). The text has been revised and adapted to the Viet Nam context.

(iii) If possible, the distribution of tasks and responsibilities should largely follow the principle of subsidiarity[140] to make decisions and implementation steps closer to practical relevance. Delegating TVET implementation and control responsibilities to the private sector increases its willingness to contribute to TVET improvement persistently also by financial means.

(iv) The willingness of companies to participate in industry sector-wide vocational training programs can be promoted by dual training arrangements or by trade-specific vocational training centers operated by respective trade associations. In particular, where the development of broad occupational profiles of trainees cannot be fully covered by on-the-job training in individual companies because of their highly specialized production processes and workflows, such composite approaches can systematically provide institutional support to generate (also future) labor-market-relevant qualifications. This requires, however, school curricula and on-the-job training activities to be constantly aligned with each other.

(v) Approaches to quality improvements through enterprise involvement should build on existing structures. Since the institutional and regulatory framework for TVET in Viet Nam (occupational standards, curricula, graduate certificates, provider accreditation and quality assurance standards, teacher qualifications, etc.) has already reached an advanced (though not yet sufficiently operational) stage, this should be enhanced and further developed by expanding ownership and, hence, compliance to base cooperative forms of training on these standards and increase the demand on respective training outputs also among industry partners. This should not be left to single TVET institutions alone.

(vi) Initial expectations on the efficiency of a multi-stakeholder TVET agency must not be exaggerated. Its options to function well will essentially depend on the acceptance of this institution in the national vocational education and training context. Its prospect to eventually succeed will depend on its ability to address multiple stakeholders' needs and thus promote their active and sustained participation. Box 5.4 provides a summary of procedural topics that can be taken into account to successfully establish a tripartite national TVET agency.

180. **Intensify effort to involve enterprises in financing TVET.** Regarding TVET as a decisive factor for sustained and inclusive economic growth implies that its costs, both in investments and operating expenses, should be equitably shared among those who directly and indirectly benefit. This includes governments, individuals, enterprises, and the community. Unlike for basic compulsory and higher education, which is traditionally financed through state budgets and (sometimes in combination with) tuition fees, the appropriateness of this model for funding TVET has become widely questioned. It makes the system supply driven, it is not strong and flexible enough to fulfill the demand for a varying amount of costly equipment and resources required for specific training areas, and it does not encourage enterprises as the key clients of skilled human resources to pay for training. Previous sections of this report have shown that the Viet Nam government's vision to solve these problems by granting TVET institutions full autonomy, which allows them to act as market-oriented business units though having to cope with discipline/major unspecific tuition fee margins, may become a risky endeavor.

---

[140] Subsidiarity is a principle of social organization that is often associated with the idea of political and administrative decentralization (e.g., in the European Union). In its most basic formulation, it means that social problems should be dealt with at the most immediate functional level consistent with their solution. A central authority has a subsidiary (that is, a supporting, rather than a superordinate) function, when it performs only those tasks, which cannot be performed effectively at a more immediate or local level. By this, subsidiary structures vary significantly from the neoliberal paradigm of deregulation.

Box 5.4: Topics Relevant for Establishing a Tripartite National TVET Agency

- Identify interests in TVET with regard to local and regional needs, investigate expectations of stakeholders in vocational education and training, and combine them with policy-relevant aspirations.
- Check who could systematically present and represent such interests based on institutionally legitimized lobbies (e.g., employer and workers associations, chambers of trade and commerce, etc.). Avoid the establishment of pseudo committees and political bodies that have no real backing of the actual actors responsible for making binding decisions.
- Wherever possible, focus on options of subsidiary structures for decision-making, implementation, and controlling. Beneficial are regional and local satellite institutions ("competent bodies") that are able to communicate local needs and can be made accountable for implementing locally appropriate measures.
- Take care that the central national agency has the capacity to negotiate multiple stakeholder interests, coordinate multiple TVET approaches, and support respective regional and local activities. This will require appropriate data gathering, information processing, and adequate public relations and research capabilities.
- Do not underestimate the need for continuous information events, staff training, and networking between central actors and multiplier bodies. Any new idea needs first to be understood for its relevance and implications before it becomes broadly socialized and potentially make an impact.
- Be careful in standardizing occupational profiles and professional qualifications by merely adopting international models. Highly sophisticated drawing board constructs without clear orientation to the actual skills and knowledge required and created with limited consideration of actual training conditions will be perceived as obstructive regulations rather than as constructive means to improve human resources development and labor market performance.
- Avoid subordination of a TVET agency to a single ministry. Since a key task of this institution is to balance and coordinate educational, economic, and social interests, it should be able to act autonomously, notwithstanding the need of having close linkages to the competency of different ministries and government departments.
- Take into account that it is smarter to start with a vision of becoming a well-accepted service provider rather than a competitor to existing regulators and polity bodies. Proving itself in practice may provide a good basis for a stepwise expansion of purview and responsibilities.

Source: Russell (2015).

181. Yet, the private sector, governments, and civil society have conflicting interests and perspectives on focus and benefit of public funding. Industries tend to lobby for resources to be spent on demand-driven formal sector training and skills upgrading of employees through trade-specific short-term training. Government mandates extend beyond these specific requirements and include skills development addressing (often) huge informal economic sectors and disadvantaged target groups like the pre-employed, unemployed, and ethnic minorities. As in many other developing countries, formal TVET in Viet Nam also competes with general secondary education as a preferred path to higher education and for becoming employed directly after graduation.

182. Given the limited revenues available for sustained financing, many governments have developed policies that focus on diversifying TVET funding sources by stimulating more private investments from both private households as well as employers, improving the targeting of public spending, and increasing the income of training institutions through productive activities. Liberalizing the training market shall trigger a structural transformation of a supply-driven system into a demand-driven one. However, reports evaluating progress and impact of such reform projects show that crucial governance issues are associated with effective implementation. Often these reforms have to struggle with systemic imperfections and failures, both in the labor market and in the training market (Almeida et al. 2012).

183. Imperfections in labor markets prevent employers from investing in training their future workers since they may be poached by others. Workers, on the other hand, are less likely to invest in initial training if employers have market power and keep wages down. Another common type of vicious cycle is that employers do not create high-productivity jobs because there are no skilled workers, while workers do not invest in advanced skills because there are no corresponding jobs.

184. Imperfections in training markets result from adverse effects on training quality caused by a situation in which training providers, who rely on uniform tuition fee margins as their main source of funding, are forced to follow economies of scale (i.e., lowering unit costs per trainee and/or increasing enrollment numbers per course) to stay profitable. These effects will be worse the less information is provided to students about career prospects and the quality of training offers and the less choice (and financial means) students have to select alternative options.

185. There is a huge amount of literature describing advanced TVET financing models and instruments (Figure 5.1 and Table 5.1) and highlighting their respective strengths and weaknesses (e.g., Dohmen 2001, Johanson 2009, Dunbar 2013).[141] Yet, case studies investigating how they have been proving themselves in practice often report rather mixed results. Inefficiencies and failures seem to occur because of a lack of consistent and conducive strategic, regulatory, and administrative frameworks. Above all, it often seems not to be sufficiently appreciated that private financing in TVET "is intrinsically linked to the expected return in that investment and to greater involvement by those financers in its development" (Dunbar 2013, 34).

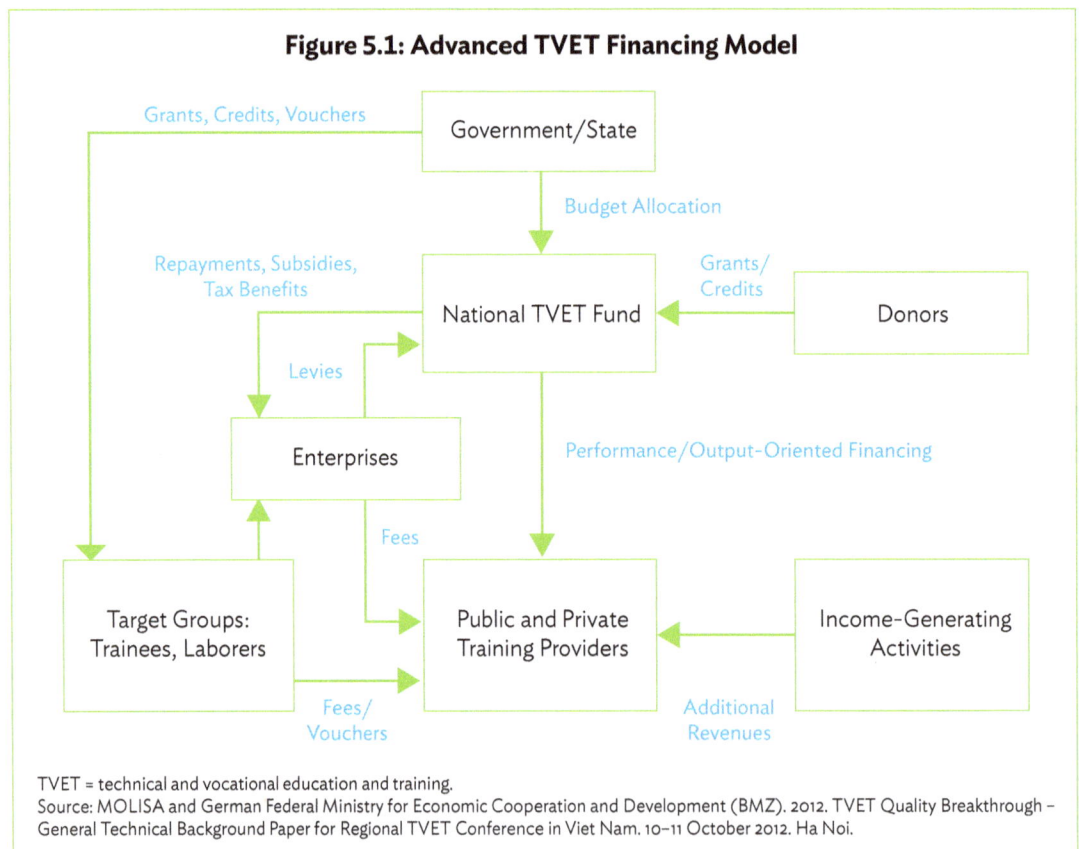

Figure 5.1: Advanced TVET Financing Model

TVET = technical and vocational education and training.
Source: MOLISA and German Federal Ministry for Economic Cooperation and Development (BMZ). 2012. TVET Quality Breakthrough – General Technical Background Paper for Regional TVET Conference in Viet Nam. 10–11 October 2012. Ha Noi.

---

[141]   ADB (2014) also refers in its recommendations to skills development funds successfully established in Singapore and Malaysia and outlines in some detail advantages and limitations of a training-levy system.

186. Experiences from countries with well-functioning TVET systems indicate that advanced collaborative financing schemes require some basic framework conditions, which are indispensable for reconciling the networked complexity of planning processes and other governance areas with the need for efficiency and accountability (Ziderman 2016):

(i) To attract private financing to TVET, especially through a levy system, the private sector needs to be actively involved in creating a better system. This includes a central role in sourcing and determining the allocation of funds to be raised from private sector contributions as well as involvement in its governance.

(ii) TVET and labor market information systems need to be strong enough so that both policy makers <u>and</u> stakeholders can understand where the training market (in supply and demand) is not working well, where there are private underinvestments or public overinvestments and why. In addition, such systems need to be accessible, informative on actual training costs and qualification benefits, and easy to use also for students and parents to spur demands and acceptance of vocational training.

(iii) Verifying potential returns on investments in vocational training requires a comprehensive, integrated, and fully costed financial blueprint for each subsector including differentiated unit cost patterns, credible cost–benefit analyses as well as realistic cost projections for resource generation and funding of recurrent expenditures. Cost transparency provides a promising starting point for mutual appreciation of and the disposition to financial contributions, particularly in cases where sharing of costs allows an existing system to become more efficient (e.g., in reforms toward a formal dual system approach).

(iv) Any change in the financial framework with a view to create incentives for training providers to deliver quality training (e.g., through performance-based budgeting schemes) will only be effective if TVET quality is defined also in relevance and outcomes are impartially measured and monitored. Effective sanctions must be in place to punish noncompliance and also supportive means assisting institutions to improve quality (see previous recommendations).

(v) Subsidies, loans, funds, and training voucher systems can be highly effective means for financing, respectively finetuning demand orientation of TVET and spurring its quality. However, effective implementation requires sophisticated and elaborate concepts that take into account locally specific framework conditions, market forces, and social constraints to avoid misuse and unintended effects. On the other hand, complex requirements regarding administrative tasks can lead to highly bureaucratic governance structures that may subvert their efficiency and prevent their acceptance. Establishing principles of subsidiary can help mitigate such risks.

(vi) Financing regulations for both public and nonpublic TVET activities should be closely combined with mandatory accreditation procedures prompting training providers not only to comply to a standard set of minimum input, process, and output criteria but preferably giving them impetus to continuously improve their quality and strive to achieve excellence in their training delivery through a multistep certification approach. While this will stimulate competition among TVET institutions to become eligible, respectively attractive for public and private funding, it also has proven itself as an effective governance measure for clearing the market.

(vii) Recovering a share of institutional costs by productive income-generating activities of public training providers is a common TVET policy approach in many developing countries including Viet Nam. This requires administrative reforms giving training institutes substantial autonomy and operational freedom (including the right to hire competent staff). Yet, issues that need to be addressed are business management capacities of principals and concerns that income-generating activities may create unfair competition to private businesses and distort local markets. In addition, control mechanisms should be in place to ensure that business activities will not be conducted at the expense of training quality.

Table 5.1: Enterprise-Financed Training Funds by Country and Type
(East Asia and Pacific Region)

Category	Organization	Type	Sources for Information
People's Republic of China	Training Funds (provincial level)	Exemption-based scheme: Enterprises are required to spend 1.5%–2.5% of their payroll toward in-service training, or else to pay an equivalent amount to the government.	P. Yang and Z. Tian. 2016. Skill/TVET Financing. China's Experience in a Nutshell. Unpublished PowerPoint for the Second ASEAN+3 Forum on Dual Learning System and TVET Financing. Seoul, Republic of Korea. 23–24 May.
Republic of Korea	VTPF (1967–1997 government administered) Employment Insurance Fund (1997–today)	Exemption-based scheme: Employers above a certain size are required to conduct training or pay a levy.	E. Song. 2016. Skills Development Funds: Country Experiences and Implications for South Asia. ADB Initial Internship Report.
Malaysia	Human Resource Development Fund administered by tripartite agency (PSMB)	Levy-reimbursement scheme	E. Song. 2016. Skills Development Funds: Country Experiences and Implications for South Asia. ADB Initial Internship Report.
Mongolia	Ministry of Labor: Employment Promotion Fund – TVET Promotion Fund	Shared funding (state and local budgets, official development assistance, enterprises); Employers basically contribute through foreign worker levy.	S. Meyanathan.. 2016. Ministry of Labor Mongolia VETPCD: TVET Financing in Mongolia.
Papua New Guinea	Training Assistance Fund operated by National Training Council	Training levy (hybrid: exemption-based, levy-grant), used as a general source of funds for TVET	R. Horne. 2014. Marshalling Private Resources for TVET. Draft Thematic Paper. 18. Research Project into the Financing of Technical and Vocational Education and Training in the Pacific. Melbourne: ACER.
Singapore	Skills Development Fund administrated by the Skills Future Singapore Agency	Levy is imposed on lower-wageworkers. Levy rate is 1% of the monthly remuneration.	Skills Future SG. Skills Development Levy (SDL) System. https://sdl.ssg.gov.sg/Default.aspx.
Thailand	Skills Development Fund (TSDF)	Levy-reimbursement scheme for training expenses through tax deduction	International Labour Organization (ILO). 2016. Compilation of Assessment Studies on Technical Vocational Education and Training.
ASEAN Countries that Have Plans or Proposals to Set Up an Enterprise-Financed Training Fund			
Indonesia	A Skills Development Fund has been proposed to encourage enterprises to train their workers and as a way to raise additional funding for training institutions. It is expected to be resourced through a training levy on foreign workers.		E. Allen. 2016. Analysis of Trends and Challenges in the Indonesian Labor Market. ADB Papers on Indonesia. No. 16. Manila: ADB.
Lao People's Democratic Republic	A proposed national training fund is to be set up and shall be resourced through a 1% levy on annual salary or wages. Firms will be liable to this levy if they don't conduct a sufficient amount of training for their own employees.		ILO. 2016. Compilation of Assessment Studies on Technical Vocational Education and Training.
Myanmar	Like in Viet Nam the government has considered to set up a training fund, which could be resourced through enterprise payroll levies.		R. P. Wright. 2017. Financing TVET in the East Asia and Pacific Region.

ASEAN = Association of Southeast Asian Nations, TVET = technical and vocational education and training.
Source: Adopted and updated from Wright, R. P. 2017. *Financing TVET in the East Asia and Pacific Region*. Washington, DC: World Bank.

4. Increase Equal Access to High-Quality Training

187. Promoting access to TVET continues to play a prominent role in Viet Nam's current HRD policy framework and is supported extensively by several policy propositions on TVET system development in the new TVET law and subsequent regulations. By stipulating exemptions from or reductions of tuition fees and granting other allowances for students from ethnic minorities that live in remote ("disadvantaged or severely disadvantaged") areas and/or are from poor households and for other disadvantaged groups (including disabled persons), the government stays committed to facilitate broad participation in TVET. Prevailing issues are unclear or insufficient data about effectiveness and efficiency of these programs, a lack of information on socioeconomic background and needs of these target groups and, so far, limited effectiveness of efforts to channel enrollments from lower secondary schools also into formal, especially higher levels of TVET.

188. While the latter depends on a persistently low reputation of TVET among parents and students compared with higher general education and on a significantly lower share of lower secondary graduates among disadvantaged groups in rural areas, there are some indications that more needs to be done in improving the linkage between nonformal short-term courses and the formal TVET system by creating pathways (certificates) that facilitate the progression into higher levels of vocational education and training. The approval of the National Qualification Framework provides a good basis for reinforced activities in this direction.

189. **Gender equality.** ADB has identified three key strategic focal points to ensure that TVET becomes more inclusive for women and contributes better to decent work for women and girls (Butler unpublished). Using this framework as a reference allows the identification of a set of important elements and activities with this regard. ADB (2017b) also provides more detailed recommendations for each of the following items.

(i) Embed gender equity in all formal TVET institutions and key instruments including the regulatory system and measures for TVET compliance:

- Develop, implement, and maintain national TVET gender strategies with systems deliverables and supported by action plans and communication strategies.

- Collect, analyze, and use sex-disaggregated data relating to TVET activities and outcomes to progress gender equity for women and girls.

- Strengthen the coordination mechanisms between TVET and other education sectors, labor and employment sectors, industry, and national organizations promoting women's education and employment.

- Invest in gender mainstreaming in all TVET activities through adequate resourcing, targeted needs-based funding, and monitoring and evaluation.

- Invest in the design and delivery of gender-inclusive and gender-sensitive curricula, resource materials, learning environments, delivery modes and assessment, supported with sexual harassment and gender-awareness training.

- Establish gender-responsive support systems and services for individuals, organizations, and industry, from infrastructure requirements to incentive schemes, scholarships, and awards.

(ii) Leverage the capacity of TVET to challenge gendered social norms that impact the socioeconomic status of women and girls:

- Encourage the participation of industry champions, role models, and mentors to attract, inform, and support women and girls in TVET.

- Ensure that TVET training programs for women and girls articulate with a variety of learning pathways and include multiple entry and exit points with documentation to record successful completion/s.

- Support women's access to quality training in marketable skills and employment by embedding a range of jobs supported by on- and off-the-job training in employment schemes and large infrastructure projects.

- Negotiate partnerships with industry and industry sectors to provide placements, jobs, and work-related training for women and girls.

- Recognize, validate, and document both prior learning and skills achieved when women and girls participate in TVET courses.

- Develop and utilize marketing campaigns and social media to provide training and employment information to widen training choices and participation for women and girls.

(iii) Utilize the capacity of TVET to increase opportunities and pathways to decent work for women and girls:

- Engage women as decision makers and key stakeholders at all levels (government, system, industry, community, and delivery) of TVET.

- Establish and implement realistic quotas and targets to increase and maintain enrollments for job-related training for women and girls, especially in emergent and nontraditional jobs, occupations, and industries.

- Provide career and employment information and advice for women and girls that is gender sensitive and informed by labor market opportunities and trends to expand their training choices.

- Provide integrated multicomponent education and skills training for women and girls to enhance employability.

- Scale up employment and training programs and pilots with proven positive outcomes for women and girls.

190. **Community-based training.** In addition, this report reiterates the recommendations of ADB (2014) that Viet Nam could benefit from the experience of other countries in rural training by employing community-based training methodologies that have proven successful in delivering employment-oriented skills-training programs closely linked to the local economy.

191. In the early 1980s, governments, nongovernment organizations, and international organizations developed such methodologies specifically to promote income generation in rural areas. The TVET program in rural India, the International Labour Organization's Training for Rural Gainful Activities program in Nepal, and the Swedish International Development Cooperation Agency-supported Regional Project on Skill Development for Self-Reliance in East and Southern Africa all utilized community-based training approaches to generating local employment in rural areas. More recently, community-based training methods have been adopted in many developed countries to address the training and employment needs of special target groups such as out-of-school youth,

redundant workers, and the disabled. The Ontario Network of Employment Skills Training Projects and Association of Service Providers for Employability and Career Training programs in Canada are community-based training approaches run by nongovernment organizations, and they provide skills training for employment in local communities. Community-based training has also been used as a tool for strengthening vulnerable groups in rural areas. For example, the national Training for Rural Employment and Empowerment Program in Pakistan is a community-based training methodology linking skills training to the economic empowerment of rural women. A similar approach has been in use by the national training authority in the Philippines, the Technical Education and Skills Development Authority, since the early 1990s (Box 5.5).

192. Community-based training has evolved into a generic community-based training methodology, which is based on the following principles:

(i) the identification and analysis of potential employment and income-generating activities in the local economy;

(ii) the determination of appropriate training needs before deciding on training content and objectives;

(iii) the collection of detailed information on the training target group;

(iv) the participation of the local community in the training planning process;

(v) the selection of an appropriate, flexible delivery system; and

(vi) the provision of post-training support services—including access to credit and technical support services—to facilitate the successful application of training to income-earning activities.

Box 5.5: Community-Based Training in the Philippines

Community-based training (CBT) in the Philippines draws its basic target from an enterprise development program. It is primarily addressed to the poor and marginal groups who cannot access or are not accessible by formal training provisions.

The majority of these people have low skills, limited management abilities, and few economic options. They also have no access to capital, as most of them are unqualified for formal credit programs. Hence, the program goes further than just mere skills training provision.

CBTED in the Philippines is based on a methodology, which is purposively designed to catalyze the creation of livelihood enterprises. These will be implemented by the trainees immediately after the training.

Correspondingly, there are guidelines, tools, and financial means provided by the national technical and vocational education and training agency, Technical Education and Skills Development Authority, to assist partner agencies such as local government units, nongovernment organizations, people organizations, and other agencies with missions to help the poor get into productive undertakings to help themselves and their communities.

Local chief executives are encouraged to establish so called technical education and skills development committees, which serve as advisory boards to local mayors and human resources generation units for planning and implementing needs-oriented training and local enterprise development programs.

Source: Technical Education and Skills Development Authority. http://www.tesda.gov.ph.

References

(Note: This list does not include a considerable number of decisions, decrees, and circulars of the Government of Viet Nam, particularly those of the Ministry of Labour–Invalids and Social Affairs. Appendix 7 provides a reference to these documents.)

Asian Development Bank (ADB). 2014. *Technical and Vocational Education and Training in the Socialist Republic of Viet Nam: An Assessment.* Manila.

_____. 2016a. *Asian Development Outlook 2016: Asia's Potential Growth.* Manila.

_____. 2016b. *Country Partnership Strategy Viet Nam, 2016–2020: Fostering More Inclusive and Environmentally Sustainable Growth.* Manila.

_____. 2016c. Inclusive and Sustainable Growth Assessment: Viet Nam, 2016–2020. Draft as of 22 August 2016. https://www.adb.org/sites/default/files/linked-documents/cps-vie-2016-2020-ld-01.pdf (accessed January 2018).

_____. 2017a. *Key Indicators for Asia and the Pacific 2016: Viet Nam.* www.adb.org/statistics (accessed September 2017).

_____. 2017b. Draft Final Report: Gender Assessment of Technical and Vocational Education and Training (TVET) and School-to-Work Transition in Viet Nam. June.

Almeida, R. et al. eds. 2012. *The Right Skills for the Job? Rethinking Training Policies for Workers.* Washington, DC: World Bank. http://documents.worldbank.org/curated/en/535251468156871924/The-right-skills-for-the-job-Rethinking-training-policies-for-workers (accessed January 2018).

Bernbaum, M. and K. Moses. 2011. *EQUIP2 Lessons Learned in Education: Education Management Information Systems.* Washington, DC: USAID. https://www.fhi360.org/resource/equip2-lessons-learned-education-education-management-information-systems (accessed January 2018).

Bodewig, C., R. Badiani-Magnusson, K. Macdonald, D. Newhouse, and J. Rutkowski. 2014. *Skilling Up Vietnam: Preparing the Workforce for a Modern Market Economy – Directions in Development.* Washington, DC: World Bank.

Butler, E. Gender and Technical and Vocational Education and Training (TVET) Framework. Unpublished. Quoted in ADB. 2017. Gender Assessment of Technical and Vocational Education and Training (TVET) and School-to-Work Transition in Viet Nam (Draft). Consultant's Report. Manila.

Communist Party of Viet Nam and Central Steering Committee. Resolution No. 29-NQ/TW on Fundamental and Comprehensive Innovation in Education, Serving Industrialization and Modernization in a Socialist-Oriented Market Economy during International Integration. Ha Noi. Ratified in the 8th Session on 4 November 2013. Ha Noi.

Directorate of Vocational Education and Training (DVET) and National Institute for Vocational Education and Training (NIVET). 2017. *Viet Nam Vocational Education and Training Report 2015.* Ha Noi. http://www.tvet-vietnam.org/en/article/1321.viet-nam-vocational-education-and-training-report-2015.html (accessed January 2018).

Dohmen, D. 2001. Enhancing the Sustainability of VET Funding in Developing Countries. *Social Science Open Access Repository.* http://www.ssoar.info/ssoar/handle/document/21858 (accessed January 2018).

Dunbar, M. 2013. Assignment Report: Engaging the Private Sector in Skills Development. Health and Education Advice and Resource Team (HEART). Oxford: Oxford Policy Management. http://r4d.dfid.gov.uk/Output/193702/ (accessed January 2018).

Ely, D. 1990. Conditions that Facilitate the Implementation of Educational Technology Innovations. *Journal of Research on Computing in Education*. 23 (2). pp. 298–305.

_____. 2001. Leading in a Culture of Change. San Francisco: Jossey-Bass.

European Training Foundation (ETF), ILO, and UNESCO Inter-Agency Working Group on TVET Indicators. 2012. Proposed Indicators for Assessing Technical and Vocational Education and Training. http://apskills.ilo.org/resources/proposed-indicators-for-assessing-technical-and-vocational-education-and-training (accessed January 2018).

Fullan, M. 1993. *Change Forces: Probing the Depths of Educational Reform.* London: Falmer Press.

_____2001. *The New Meaning of Educational Change.* Third Edition. New York: Teachers College. Press.

General Department of Vocational and Training and National Institute for Vocational Training (NIVT). 2015. *Vocational Training Report – Vietnam 2013–2014.* Ha Noi. http://www.tvet-vietnam.org/en/article/1065.vocational-training-report-viet-nam-2014-2014.html (accessed November 2017).

General Statistics Office of Viet Nam (GSO). 2014. *Result of the Viet Nam Household Living Standards Survey 2014.* Ha Noi. http://www.gso.gov.vn/default_en.aspx?tabid=515&idmid=5&ItemID=18411.

_____. 2016a. *Major Findings – The 1/4/2015 Time-Point Population Change and Family Planning Survey.* Ha Noi. https://www.gso.gov.vn/Default_en.aspx?tabid=515 (accessed November 2017).

_____. 2016b. *Report on Labour Force Survey (Quarter 1, 2016).* Ha Noi.

_____. 2016c. *Result of Viet Nam Household Living Standards Survey 2014.* Ha Noi. https://www.gso.gov.vn/Default_en.aspx?tabid=515 (accessed December 2017).

_____. 2017. *Report on Labor Force Survey (Quarter 1, 2017).* Ha Noi.

_____. 2016-2017, GSO Quarterly reports on Labor Force Survey.

GIZ and National Institute for Vocational Training (NIVT). 2014b. *Report on Cost and Benefit Analysis of TVET Internship Programmes in Enterprises.* Ha Noi. http://www.tvet-vietnam.org/kontext/controllers/document.php/609.7/5/29dbca.pdf.

Government of Viet Nam. Decision No. 579/QD-TTg of the Prime Minister Approving the Strategy on Development of Vietnamese Human Resources during 2011–2020. Ha Noi. Adopted on 14 April 2011.

_____. Decision No. 1216/QD-TTg of the Prime Minister Approving the Master Plan on Development of Vietnam's Human Resources during 2011–2020. Ha Noi. Adopted on 22 July 2011.

_____. 2012a. Education Development Strategy, 2011–2020. Ha Noi.

_____. 2012b. Vocational Training Development Strategy, 2011–2020. Ha Noi.

_____. Decision No. 1201/QĐ-TTg of the Prime Minister dated 31 August 2012 Approving National Target Program on Jobs and Vocational Training in the Period of 2012–2015. Ha Noi.

Government of Viet Nam. Resolution No. 44/NQ-CP dated 9 June 2014 on Promulgation of Action Programme of the Government in Furtherance of the Resolution No. 29-NQ/TW dated 4 November 2013 at the 8th Conference of the 11th Central Executive Committee on Radical Changes in Education and Training to Meet Requirements of Industrialization and Modernization in a Socialist-Oriented Market Economy in Course of International Integration. Ha Noi.

_____. 2016. Report No. 77/BC-CP on Five-Year Socio-Economic Development Plan 2016–2020 to the 13th National Assembly Delegates. 16 March. Ha Noi.

Ho, T. H. T. and A. Reich. 2014. Historical Influences on Vocational Education and Training in Viet Nam. Paper presented to the Australian Vocational Education and Training Research Association. Brisbane, Australia. 22–24 April.

Horn, S. 2015. *Guideline for Sustainable Development of TVET Reporting in Viet Nam.* Ha Noi. http://www.tvet-vietnam.org/en/article/1327.guideline-for-sustainable-development-of-tvet-report-in-viet-nam.html.

Husein, A. H., N. Saraogi, and S. Mintz. 2017. *Lessons Learned from World Bank Education Management Information System Operations.* Washington, DC: World Bank. http://documents.worldbank.org/curated/en/607441491551866327/Lessons-learned-from-World-Bank-education-management-information-system-operations-portfolio-review-1998-2014 (accessed January 2018).

International Monetary Fund. International Financial Statistics. http://data.imf.org/?sk=4C514D48-B6BA-49ED-8AB9-52B0C1A0179B (accessed December 2017).

Japan International Cooperation Agency (JICA). 2014. Promoting Tripartite Partnerships to Tackle Skills Mismatch: Innovative Skills Development Strategies to Accelerate Vietnam's Industrialization. Policy Paper. https://www.jica.go.jp/vietnam/english/office/others/c8h0vm00008ze15n-att/policy_paper.pdf (accessed November 2017).

Johanson, R. 2009. A Review of National Training Funds. SP Discussion Paper No. 0922. Washington, DC: World Bank.

Ministry of Industry and Trade (MOIT). Advisory Report: Moving Toward ERP/EPM/E-Learning Systems for Vietnam's Higher Education System. May 2015 report supported by the World Bank. Unpublished.

Ministry of Labour–Invalids and Social Affairs (MOLISA). 2016. Report on Vocational Training in the Northern Midland and Mountainous Region. 23 September.

_____. 2017. Project on Renovation and Improvement of the Quality of Technical and Vocational Education and Training – Up to 2020, with Orientation to 2030 (Draft October 2017). Ha Noi.

MOLISA and German Federal Ministry for Economic Cooperation and Development (BMZ). 2012. TVET Quality Breakthrough – General Technical Background Paper for Regional TVET Conference in Viet Nam. 10–11 October 2012. Ha Noi.

Mekong Development Research Institute (MDRI) and NEXIA STT. 2017. *Recommendation for an Effective Financial Model: Program's Cost Norms Study – Final Report.* http://mdri.org.vn/publication/recommendation-for-an-effective-financial-model-programs-cost-norms-study/.

National Assembly of the Socialist Republic of Viet Nam. Law No. 38/2005/QH11 on Education. Ha Noi. Adopted on 14 June 2005.

National Assembly of the Socialist Republic of Viet Nam. Law No. 76/2006/QH11 on Vocational Training. Ha Noi. Adopted on 29 November 2006.

National Assembly of the Socialist Republic of Viet Nam. Law No. 74/2014/QH13 on Vocational Education. Ha Noi. Adopted on 27 November 2014.

National Assembly of the Socialist Republic of Viet Nam. Resolution No. 142/2016/QH13 on the Five-Year Socio-Economic Development Plan of 2016–2020. Ha Noi.

Nguyen, N. A., T. T. Nguyen, T. H. Nguyen, T. T. N. Trinh, and V. T. Nguyen. 2015. Labour Market Transitions of Young Women and Men in Viet Nam. Youth Employment Programme – Work4Youth Publication Series No. 27. Geneva: International Labour Organization (ILO).

Paryono, Dr. and C. Bock. 2017. Regional Standards for TVET Personnel. Presentation. 23 May. http://files.seameo.org/18_3rd%20HOM%20on%20SEA-TVET%2C%2023-25%20May%202017%2C%20Kuala%20Lumpur%2C%20Malaysia/12_Session%202_Regional%20Initiatives%20%2823%20May%29/3_GIZ-RECOTVET_PPT_Regional%20Standards%20for%20TVET%20Personnel%20%28Rev%29.pdf (accessed January 2018).

Peeraer, J. and P. Van Petegem. 2011. How to Address Integration of ICT in Teaching Practice? Research on Factors Influencing the Use of ICT in Education. https://www.researchgate.net/publication/258312739_How_to_address_Integration_of_ICT_in_Teaching_Practice_Research_on_Factors_influencing_the_use_of_ICT_in_Education (accessed August 2018).

Russell, T. 2015. TVET Governance. Background Paper for GIZ Regional TVET Conference. Vientiane, Lao People's Democratic Republic. 14–15 December 2015. http://www.regional-tvet-conference-laos.org/kontext/controllers/document.php/57.7/9/8308f0.pdf (accessed January 2018).

Tan, S. 2012. Reconsidering the Vietnamese Development Vision of "Industrialisation and Modernisation by 2020." *ZEF Working Paper 102*. Center for Development Research, University of Bonn. https://www.econstor.eu/handle/10419/88325 (accessed August 2017).

United Nations Development Programme (UNDP). 2017. Human Development Report 2016 – Viet Nam. Briefing Note for Countries on the 2016 Human Development Report. http://hdr.undp.org/sites/all/themes/hdr_theme/country-notes/VNM.pdf (accessed September 2017).

Viet Nam Chamber of Commerce and Industry (VCCI) and International Labour Organization (ILO) Bureau for Employers' Activities. 2016. VCCI Labour Market Report: Trends in the Workplace – Skills and Labour Productivity. Ha Noi.

World Bank and CIEM. 2012. *Skills for Productivity: An Analysis of Employer Skills Survey 2011*. http://microdata.worldbank.org/index.php/catalog/2569/ (accessed December 2017).

World Bank. 2013. What Matters for Workforce Development: A Framework and Tool for Analysis. *Systems Approach for Better Education Results (SABER) Working Paper Series*. No. 6. Washington, DC. http://documents.worldbank.org/curated/en/2013/04/18070138/matters-workforce-development-framework-tool-analysis (accessed January 2018).

World Bank Group. Enterprise Surveys: Viet Nam 2015 Country Profile. www.enterprisesurveys.org (accessed December 2017).

World Bank and the Ministry of Planning and Investment of Viet Nam (MPI). 2016. *Vietnam 2035: Toward Prosperity, Creativity, Equity, and Democracy*. Washington, DC: World Bank.

World Bank and the Government of Viet Nam. 2017. *Viet Nam Public Expenditure Review, Fiscal Policies towards Sustainability, Efficiency, and Equity*. Washington, DC: World Bank.

World Economic Forum. 2016. *Global Competitiveness Report 2016–2017*. Geneva.

Wright, R. P. 2017. Financing TVET in the East Asia and Pacific Region: Current Status, Challenges and Opportunities. Vol. 2. Washington, DC: World Bank. http://documents.worldbank.org/curated/en/494921508752195355/Financing-TVET-in-the-East-Asia-and-Pacific-Region-current-status-challenges-and-opportunities (accessed January 2018).

Ziderman, A. 2016. Funding Mechanisms for Financing Vocational Training: An Analytical Framework. IZA Policy Paper No. 110. Bonn: IZA. http://ftp.iza.org/pp110.pdf (accessed January 2018).

Appendixes

Appendix 1. Problem Tree for TVET Development

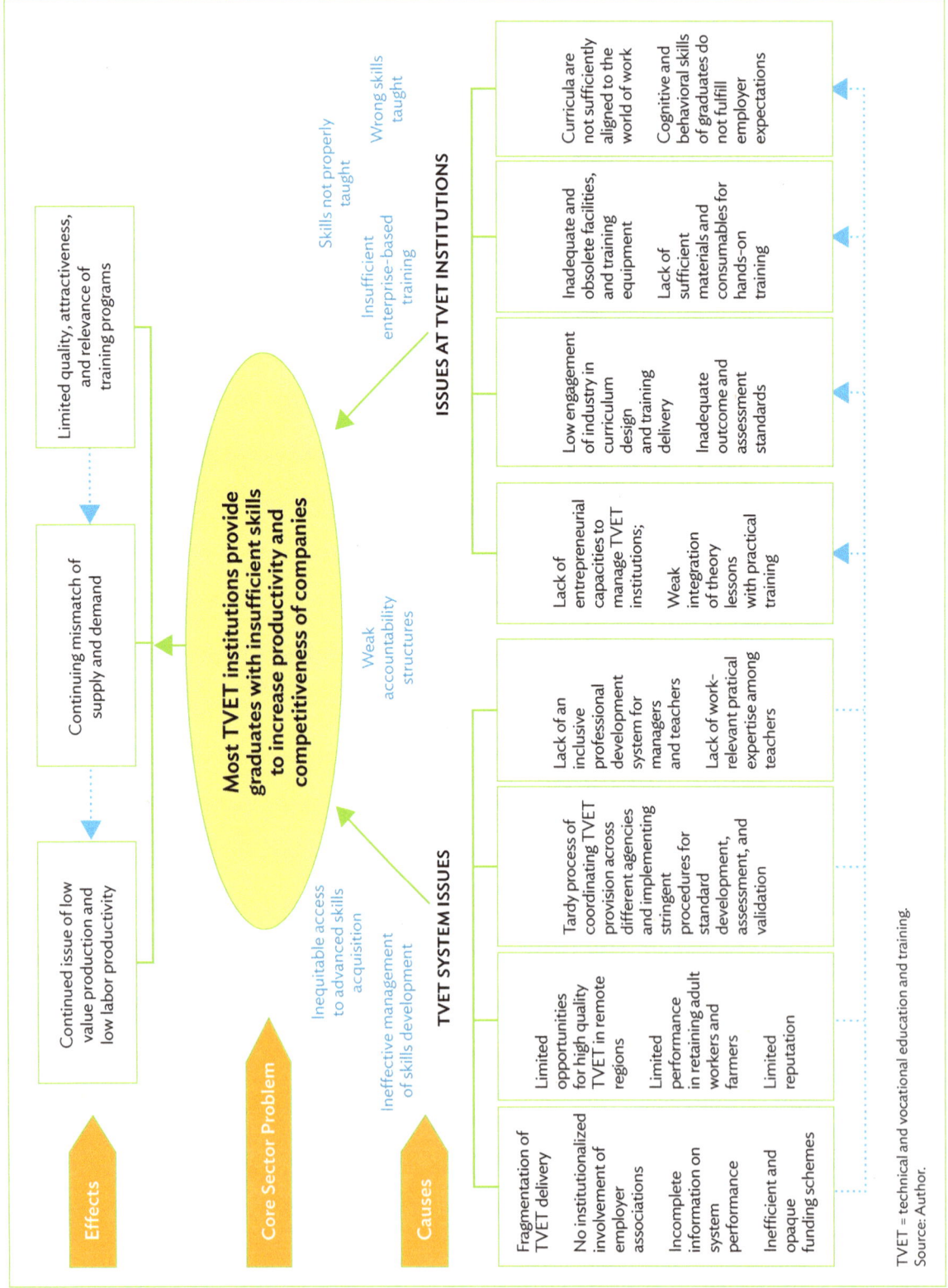

Effects

- Continued issue of low value production and low labor productivity
- Continuing mismatch of supply and demand
- Limited quality, attractiveness, and relevance of training programs

Core Sector Problem

Most TVET institutions provide graduates with insufficient skills to increase productivity and competitiveness of companies

- Inequitable access to advanced skills acquisition
- Ineffective management of skills development
- Weak accountability structures
- Insufficient enterprise-based training
- Skills not properly taught
- Wrong skills taught

Causes

TVET SYSTEM ISSUES

- Fragmentation of TVET delivery
- No institutionalized involvement of employer associations
- Incomplete information on system performance
- Inefficient and opaque funding schemes

- Limited opportunities for high quality TVET in remote regions
- Limited performance in retaining adult workers and farmers
- Limited reputation

- Tardy process of coordinating TVET provision across different agencies and implementing stringent procedures for standard development, assessment, and validation

- Lack of an inclusive professional development system for managers and teachers
- Lack of work-relevant pratical expertise among teachers

ISSUES AT TVET INSTITUTIONS

- Lack of entrepreneurial capacities to manage TVET institutions;
- Weak integration of theory lessons with practical training

- Low engagement of industry in curriculum design and training delivery
- Inadequate outcome and assessment standards

- Inadequate and obsolete facilities, and training equipment
- Lack of sufficient materials and consumables for hands-on training

- Curricula are not sufficiently aligned to the world of work
- Cognitive and behavioral skills of graduates do not fulfill employer expectations

TVET = technical and vocational education and training.
Source: Author.

Appendix 2. Organizational Structure of the Former Directorate of Vocational Education and Training

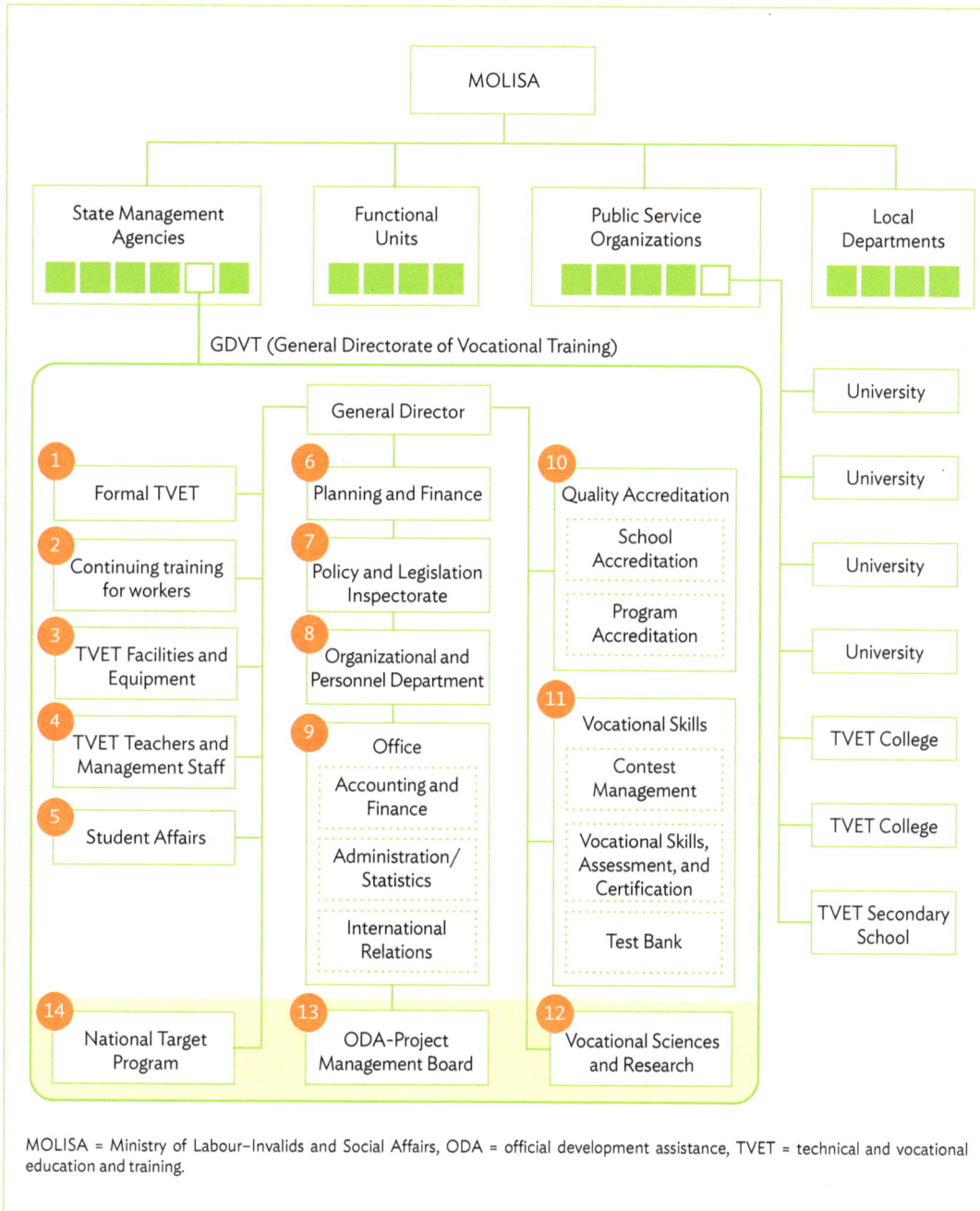

```
                              ┌─────────────┐
                              │   MOLISA    │
                              └─────────────┘
        ┌────────────────┬──────────────┴──────────────┬──────────────────┐
┌──────────────┐  ┌──────────────┐  ┌──────────────┐  ┌──────────────┐
│ State        │  │ Functional   │  │ Public Service│  │ Local        │
│ Management   │  │ Units        │  │ Organizations │  │ Departments  │
│ Agencies     │  │              │  │              │  │              │
│ ▮▮▮▮□▮        │  │ ▮▮▮▮          │  │ ▮▮▮▮□         │  │ ▮▮▮▮          │
└──────────────┘  └──────────────┘  └──────────────┘  └──────────────┘
```

GDVT (General Directorate of Vocational Training)

General Director

#	State Management	#	Functional Units	#	Public Service Organizations	Local Departments
1	Formal TVET	6	Planning and Finance	10	Quality Accreditation	University
2	Continuing training for workers	7	Policy and Legislation Inspectorate		School Accreditation	University
3	TVET Facilities and Equipment	8	Organizational and Personnel Department		Program Accreditation	University
4	TVET Teachers and Management Staff	9	Office	11	Vocational Skills	University
5	Student Affairs		Accounting and Finance		Contest Management	TVET College
			Administration/ Statistics		Vocational Skills, Assessment, and Certification	TVET College
			International Relations		Test Bank	TVET Secondary School
14	National Target Program	13	ODA-Project Management Board	12	Vocational Sciences and Research	

MOLISA = Ministry of Labour–Invalids and Social Affairs, ODA = official development assistance, TVET = technical and vocational education and training.

	Office or Department	Functions, Tasks, and Authority	Number of Staff
1	Formal Training Department	1. Elaborate and submit to competent authorities for promulgation legal documents directly related to the contents of regular vocational training according to different levels, including (a) regulations on the list of occupations; (b) curricula and syllabuses; (c) the enrollment regulation; (d) regulations on examination and consideration of graduation; (e) provision of samples of certificates; (f) regulation and certification management; and (g) regulations on joint training and transfer among training levels. 2. Assume the prime responsibility for, and coordinate with concerned agencies and units in, organizing the formulation, adjustment, and supplementation of lists of training occupations; guide and inspect the use of the list of trained vocations at different levels. 3. Assume the prime responsibility for, and coordinate with concerned agencies and units in, organizing the formulation, adjustment, and appraisal of framework programs on collegial and intermediate vocational training for each profession and general curricula for college and vocational colleges; guide and inspect the organization of program formulation and compilation of vocational training curricula of vocational training institutions. 4. Guide and inspect vocational training institutions in the enrollment of primary, vocational, and intermediate vocational schools nationwide. 5. Guide and inspect the process of organizing training, examination, and recognition of graduates according to training levels; the granting of certificates of primary vocational training, intermediate vocational training diplomas, and vocational training diplomas; examine the granting of diplomas and certificates of foreign vocational training institutions operating in Viet Nam. 6. Guide and supervise the joint training in vocational training. 7. Guide and supervise the regular vocational training cooperation of vocational training establishments. 8. Direct and guide the transfer of programs, curricula, and learning materials of the Association of Southeast Asian Nations (ASEAN) and international levels and organize training courses on national, regional, and international key occupations. **Relationship with other units outside the General Directorate of Vocational Training (GDVT) (institutes, ministries, industry associations)** Establish and maintain relations with ministries, branches, localities, vocational training institutions, enterprises, and professional associations, but mainly with ministries, industries, and business associations.	12

continued on next page

Appendix 2 continued

	Office or Department	Functions, Tasks, and Authority	Number of Staff
2	Department of Training for Workers	1. Elaborate and submit to competent authorities for promulgation legal documents on regular vocational training and vocational training for rural laborers. 2. Guide and inspect the implementation of legal documents on regular vocational training and vocational training for rural laborers. 3. Conduct regular vocational training including the following tasks: (a) formulate and submit to competent authorities medium-term, long-term, and annual plans; (b) provide guidance on specific conditions and procedures for opening training courses, on the subject and form of enrollment; curriculum, syllabus, learning materials; link; and organizing the training, examination, evaluation, and recognition of graduation and granting of diplomas and certificates; (c) coordinating with the office to guide the building and management of the database on vocational training; (d) guide, inspect, and sum up reports on the implementation of plans and policies on regular vocational training. 4. Conduct vocational training for rural laborers, including the following tasks: (a) formulate and submit to competent authorities medium-term, long-term, and annual plans; (b) guide and inspect propaganda, and provide counsel on vocational training and employment; survey and forecast the demand for vocational training, the need to employ laborers, and build the list of occupations and training programs; and implement models, vocational training orders, and vocational training activities according to regulations; (c) coordinate with the office to guide the building and management of the database on vocational training; (d) guide, inspect, supervise, and synthesize implementation reports for plans and policies on vocational training for rural laborers. 5. Perform the permanent task of the working group in assisting the Central Steering Committee in implementing the vocational training scheme for rural laborers, which include the following functions: (a) formulating operation plans, inspection, and supervision; (b) organizing regular and extraordinary meetings to serve inspection and supervision; (c) synthesize the biannual and annual reports on the implementation and results of activities of the working groups and the Central Steering Committee; (d) organizing preliminary conferences and summation conferences of the steering committee; (e) organizing regular meetings with news agencies and between the Standing Board of the Central Steering Committee and the Standing Steering Committee of 1,956 provinces and cities. 6. Coordinate with the Department for Teachers and Vocational Training Managers in elaborating and organizing the implementation of programs, contents, and plans for fostering teaching skills for vocational trainers. 7. Coordinate with the Organization and Personnel Department in elaborating and organizing the implementation of programs, contents, and plans for fostering permanent employment and vocational training managers for rural laborers. **Relationship with other units outside the GDVT (institutes, ministries, industry associations)** Establish and maintain relations with ministries, branches, localities, vocational training institutions, enterprises, and professional associations, but mainly with the Ministry of Agriculture and Rural Development, Farmers' Association, and localities.	11

continued on next page

Appendix 2 continued

	Office or Department	Functions, Tasks, and Authority	Number of Staff
3	Department of Facilities and Equipment	1. Elaborate and submit to competent authorities for promulgation planning, long-term, five-year, and annual plans, schemes, and projects on development of material foundations and vocational training equipment. 2. Elaborate and submit to competent authorities for promulgation legal documents on material foundations and vocational training equipment, including (a) criteria of material foundations of vocational training institutions; (b) standards of vocational training equipment for each job; (c) regulations on management of material foundations and vocational training equipment in vocational training institutions and the norms of material consumption in vocational training; (d) documents guiding the material facilities, equipment, and learning materials in vocational training institutions; and policies and regimes related to material foundations and vocational training equipment. 3. Direct, guide, inspect, supervise, evaluate, and organize the implementation of legal documents and planning of schemes and projects on material foundations and vocational training equipment, once approved. 4. Guide and inspect the implementation of standards on material foundations and vocational training equipment of vocational training institutions according to regulations. 5. Guide the management of material foundations and vocational training equipment. 6. Guide and direct the competition of self-teaching vocational training equipment at all levels; organize the implementation of the national competition of self-made vocational training equipment. 7. Guide the reception and application of criteria on material foundations and the list of foreign-based vocational training equipment. 8. Professionally foster the contingent of managers of material foundations and vocational training equipment of vocational training institutions; collaborate with the office to organize statistical and information work and build a database on material facilities and vocational training equipment. 9. Organize and conduct scientific research on material foundations and vocational training equipment. **Relationship with other units outside the GDVT (institutes, ministries, industry associations)** Establish and maintain relations with ministries, branches, localities, vocational training institutions, enterprises, and professional associations.	11
4	Teachers Department	1. Formulate and submit to competent authorities for promulgation regulations pertaining to teachers such as the following: (a) Long-term, five-year, and annual strategies; planning for training and fostering the development and use of teachers; (b) Training-related schemes and projects that foster the raising of a contingent of quality teachers, build their capacity, and ensure their quality; (c) Professional standards and professional qualifications of teachers, the statute of assessment of civil servants, and regulations on the contents and form of recruitment of vocational training officials; (d) Teacher's work regime; emulation and reward work for teachers; (e) Vocational training programs and vocational training; providing professional training and fostering of vocational training officials; and forms of vocational training pedagogic	10

continued on next page

Appendix 2 continued

	Office or Department	Functions, Tasks, and Authority	Number of Staff
4	Teachers Department	certificates, forms of professional fostering certificates, and regulations on management and granting of vocational training skills certificates to vocational training officials. 2. Direct, guide, inspect, supervise, evaluate, and organize the implementation of legal documents, strategies, master plans, schemes, and projects after these are approved. 3. Guide the establishment, organization, and operation of the Vocational Training Faculty of the college. 4. Guide and supervise the formulation and implementation of teachers' training and retraining programs and curricula; implement policies and regimes for teachers; implement professional standards and professional teachers; and inspect the implementation of the regulation on evaluation of vocational training officials. 5. Manage the professional training for teachers. 6. Direct the organization of the examination for promoting job titles and vocational training professions and the awarding of honorary titles for teachers according to the provisions of law. 7. Organize the assessment for the granting of professional practice certificates to teachers. 8. Coordinate with the office to organize the implementation of statistics and information and build a database on the quantity, quality, and structure of the contingent of teachers; synthesize and report on matters related to training, fostering, recruitment, and use of teachers. 9. Guide and direct vocational training teachers at all levels; organize national seminars and other professional teacher-related activities. 10. Participate in scientific research on vocational training pedagogy, renewal of contents, methods of vocational training, mode of training and fostering; apply scientific research results to the building and development of the contingent of teachers and build the system of training and foster establishments for vocational training teachers. **Relationship with other units outside the GDVT (institutes, ministries, industry associations)** Establish and maintain relations with ministries, branches, localities, vocational training institutions, enterprises, and professional associations, but mainly with the Ministry of Education and Training and the Ministry of Home Affairs.	10
5	Department of Student Affairs	1. Elaborate and submit to competent authorities for promulgation legal documents on student work, such as the following: (a) regulations on the rules for pupils' and students' work in main-level vocational training institutions; (b) regulations on evaluation of training results of regular students and pupils in vocational training institutions; (c) regulations on emulation and commendation work for pupils and students; and (d) regulations on physical training, sports, culture, and arts activities for pupils and students in vocational training institutions 2. Elaborate and submit to competent authorities for promulgation legal documents on policies toward pupils and students in vocational training institutions. 3. Assume the prime responsibility for, and coordinate with concerned agencies and units in, organizing, directing, guiding, and inspecting the implementation of the promulgated documents on (a) the regulation	9

continued on next page

Appendix 2 continued

	Office or Department	Functions, Tasks, and Authority	Number of Staff
5	Department of Student Affairs	on management of pupils and students; the regulation on evaluation of training results of pupils and students; regulations on emulation and commendation work and regulations on organization of physical training, sports, culture, and arts activities for pupils and students in vocational training institutions; (b) educating the political, moral, lifestyle, cultural, and aesthetic values of pupils and students; (c) preventing and combating crimes and social evils and building a healthy educational environment in vocational training institutions; (d) physical education, security and national defense, and health care at vocational training institutions; (e) the cultural, art, physical training, and sport movements of students and trainees; (e) the policy on scholarships, scholarships from the state budget, and credit policies for pupils and students to learn vocations; and (g) career guidance, vocational training, and job placement for pupils and students. 4. Coordinate the inspection, examination, and settlement of complaints and denunciations and handle violations related to trainees and students according to regulations. 5. Coordinate with the Legal Department – the Inspectorate in organizing the law dissemination, propagation, and education for pupils and students. 6. Assume the prime responsibility for organizing and directing professional fostering for the contingent of cadres, civil servants, and employees engaged in the management of pupils and students in vocational training; coordinate with the Department of Vocational Training in directing the organization of students and ensuring the excellence of students at national, ASEAN, and international levels. 7. Act as the principal body assisting the general director in (a) directing and organizing the implementation of vocational guidance, vocational training, employment, and psychological counseling for pupils and students; (b) coordinating with ministries, branches, social organizations, and localities in directing and guiding the implementation of school health and physical education in vocational training institutions; (c) coordinate with the Central Committee of the Ho Chi Minh Communist Youth Union, the Viet Nam Student Association, other sociopolitical organizations, branches, localities, and job-teaching establishments in organizing and monitoring student activities; (d) cooperate with other countries in the region and internationally on student work. 8. Examine and monitor the implementation of support policies for pupils, apprentices, recruitment, and job creation. 9. Monitor and synthesize the work of developing the Party and mass organizations among pupils and students at vocational training institutions; coordinate with the office to regularly show the statistics of pupils and students of vocational training periodically and annually. **Relationship with other units outside the GDVT (institutes, ministries, industry associations)** Establish and maintain relations with ministries, branches, localities, vocational training institutions, enterprises, and professional associations, but mainly with social organizations (such as the youth union and others) and local and vocational training institutions.	9

continued on next page

Appendix 2 continued

	Office or Department	Functions, Tasks, and Authority	Number of Staff
6	Department of Financial Planning	1. Elaborate and submit to the general director the following: (a) strategy, long-term, five-year, and annual plans; projects on development of vocational training; (b) planning on the network of vocational training colleges, intermediate vocational schools, and vocational training centers; and (c) mechanisms, policies, criteria, and financial norms in vocational training. 2. Elaborate and submit to the general director for promulgation, professional guidance documents on planning of and finance for vocational training. 3. Assist the general director in managing financial resources in vocational training, including state budget and other lawful sources as prescribed by law and decentralized by the Ministry of Labour, War Invalids and Social Affairs. 4. Propose, allocate, guide, inspect, synthesize, and report funding sources in vocational training according to the provisions of law, particularly that the funding source for vocational training projects funded under the National Target Program shall comply with Decision No. 937/QD-LDTBXH of the Minister of Labour, War Invalids and Social Affairs on 24 June 2013. 5. Direct, guide, inspect, supervise, evaluate, and organize the implementation of legal documents, strategies, planning, plans, projects, and schemes; manage and use vocational training financial resources according to the provisions of law. 6. Coordinate with the office to organize the implementation of statistics and information and build a database on the field of planning and finance. 7. Perform the tasks of grade-2 budget-estimating units and decentralization of the Minister of Labour–War Invalids and Social Affairs as follows: (a) guide, evaluate, and sum up plans, norms, and estimates of funding sources which the GDVT submits annually to the minister for approval; (b) submit to the director general of the General Department for approval the plan for allocating annual budget estimates to the departments and units under the GDVT; (c) appraise and submit to the general director the detailed estimates of the irregular funding sources, non-allocation of financial autonomy, and annual national target programs of the departments and units under the GDVT; (d) assist the general director in evaluating and making reports on evaluation of documents related to the bidding process according to law provisions and submit them to the general director for decision; (e) organize the finance-related functions of the level-2 estimating unit; guide, examine, consider and approve, and synthesize the final settlement reports and notify the result of ratification and settlement of accounts to the units under the general department; and (f) manage public assets in accordance with regulations. 8. Coordinate with departments and units under the general department to implement the public finance reform program in vocational training. **Relationship with other units outside the GDVT (institutes, ministries, industry associations)** Establish and maintain relationship with ministries, sectors, localities, vocational training institutions, enterprises, and professional associations, but mainly with the Ministry of Finance, the Ministry of Planning and Investment, and the Ministry of Labour–Invalids and Social Affairs.	10

continued on next page

Appendix 2 continued

	Office or Department	Functions, Tasks, and Authority	Number of Staff
7	Legal Department Inspectorate	1. Regarding the legal work, perform the following functions: (a) For legislative development, (i) lead or participate in drafting laws, ordinances, and resolutions of the National Assembly, the National Assembly Standing Committee on vocational training; (ii) preside over and coordinate with relevant units in submitting to the director general the proposed long-term and annual legislative programs on vocational training, and organize their implementation after their approval; (iii) develop the model charter of vocational training institutions; (iv) lead or participate in drafting regulations on registration of vocational training; (v) lead or participate in drafting other legal documents as assigned by the director general; (vi) conduct the judicial review of draft legal normative documents by other units under the General Department before these are submitted to the ministry; coordinate with concerned units in preparing dossiers, draft legal documents on vocational training, and submit them to the ministry for proposing agencies and organizations to the Ministry of Justice for appraisal and submission to the government or Prime Minister; (vii) act as focal point to assist the director general in preparing legal documents drafted by units inside and outside the General Department. (b) Review and systematize legal documents and legal texts on vocational training: (i) Preside over and coordinate with units to monitor and review and submit to the director general the amendments and supplements to the Law on Vocational Training; (ii) Lead and coordinate with relevant units to regularly review and systemize legal documents on vocational training and submit proposals for the director general to submit to the ministry the plan for handling legal normative documents regarding inconsistencies, overlapping, unlawful issues; (iii) Lead the implementation of the legal system of vocational training in accordance with regulations. (c) Examine and handle legal documents on job training: (i) Assume the prime responsibility for, and coordinate with concerned units in, inspecting legal documents according to regulations; (ii) Report on the examination results of legal documents to the general director for submission to the competent state agency to suspend the implementation of, or amend, or supplement to, legal documents, and when authorities have promulgated conflicting, overlapping, or inconsistent legal documents on vocational training. (d) Disseminate information on the law on vocational training: (i) Submit to the general director of the program the dissemination and education of the law on vocational training; (ii) Lead and coordinate with the concerned units in organizing the program implementation for disseminating and providing education pertaining to the law on vocational training after it is approved. (e) Examine the observance of the law on job training to monitor the implementation of law, coordinate with concerned units in inspecting the law observance; and summarize and review the practical implementation of the law on vocational training. (f) Build and develop a database on legal documents on vocational training, registration of vocational training, and rehabilitation in vocational training; inspect, examine, and settle complaints and denunciations about vocational training.	10

continued on next page

Appendix 2 continued

	Office or Department	Functions, Tasks, and Authority	Number of Staff
7	Legal Department Inspectorate	(g) Regarding the administrative reform: (i) Study and submit to the general director plans and solutions to renovate and improve the effectiveness of institutional reform in vocational training; coordinate with concerned departments and units to implement the administrative reform program according to the objectives and contents of the program after these are approved. 2. Regarding the inspection, examination, and settlement of complaints and denunciations, perform the following tasks: (a) Work out annual plans on vocational training inspection and supervision, then submit them to the director of general education for approval. (b) Perform the task of specialized inspection of vocational training; inspect and implement policies, laws and tasks of agencies, organizations, and individuals under the direct management of GDVT. (c) Assume the prime responsibility for developing professional training material on vocational training, proposing competent authorities to suspend or cancel illegal provisions detected through inspection. (d) Inspect and urge agencies, organizations, and individuals to implement the conclusions and proposals of vocational training inspectors, and the decision on sanctioning administrative violations in the vocational training field of the general director of GDVT. (e) Guide the provincial/municipal Labor, War Invalids, and Social Affairs departments, the provincial/municipal Labor, War Invalids, and Social Affairs divisions to inspect and examine occupations; conduct professional training on inspectors and managers of vocational training of the Department of Labor, Invalids, and Social Affairs at district level; foster and manage activities for vocational inspectorate collaborators. (f) Guide the implementation of self-inspection activities in vocational training establishments throughout the country. (g) Perform the task of settling complaints and denunciations falling within the scope of state management of GDVT according to regulations. (h) Monitor anticorruption work under the state management of job training according to the provisions of law. 3. Submit to the general director the approval of the charter of private vocational training colleges. 4. Assume the prime responsibility for, and coordinate with the regular vocational training department, the material and vocational training equipment department, the teacher education department, and the vocational training management staff in inspecting the conditions for granting vocational training registration certificates according to regulations.	10

continued on next page
continued on next page

Appendix 2 continued

	Office or Department	Functions, Tasks, and Authority	Number of Staff
8	Staff Development	1. Elaborate and submit to competent authorities for promulgation the personnel strategy, the scheme on consolidation of functions, tasks, powers, and organizational structure; long-term, five-year, and annual plans on organization and personnel; and training and retraining of the contingent of cadres, civil servants, and officials under the management of the General Department. 2. Elaborate and submit to competent authorities for promulgation legal documents on the work of the organization and personnel, including the following: (a) Prescribe the functions, tasks, powers, and organizational structure of the GDVT; (b) Prescribe the functions, tasks, powers, and organizational structure of vocational training management agencies under ministries, branches, and localities; (c) Regulations on assignment and decentralization of state management of vocational training from the central to local levels; (d) Set conditions for establishment, permission for the establishment, division, separation, merger or dissolution of vocational training establishments, and the establishment of foreign-based vocational training representative offices in Viet Nam; (e) Regulations on classification of vocational training establishments; (f) Regulations on appointment, reappointment, recognition, and recognition of leaders of vocational training institutions; (g) Regulations on standards of heads of vocational training institutions; and (h) Regulations on payroll norms of public vocational training centers. 3. Direct, guide, inspect, supervise, evaluate, and organize the implementation of legal documents, strategies, planning, plans, and schemes on organization and personnel; create and foster the contingent of cadres, civil servants, and employees under the management of the General Department after they are approved. 4. Regarding the organization and payroll, study and submit to the general director and organize the implementation of the following tasks: (a) guide and inspect the establishment, permission for establishment, division, separation, merger, and dissolution of vocational training establishments, and foreign trade representative offices in Viet Nam; rating of public vocational training institutions; payroll norms of district-level public vocational training centers; and assist the director general in organizing the appraisal and submission for approval of the establishment plan, the establishment, division, separation, merger, dissolution, and reorganization of the units under the General Department; and vocational colleges in the whole country; (b) define the functions, tasks, powers, and organizational structure of the units under and attached to the General Department; (c) work out plans and allocate administrative payroll norms for units of the General Department; evaluate and submit to the competent agencies the payroll plans of the nonbusiness units under the General Department.	9

continued on next page

Appendix 2 continued

	Office or Department	Functions, Tasks, and Authority	Number of Staff
8	Staff Development	5. On personnel work, study and submit to the General Director and organize the following tasks: (a) build the ranks of civil servants and professional standards of public servants and employees of units under or attached to the General Department; (b) develop the standards of leaders of units under the General Department; plan on rotation of officials, public employees, leading officials in management and plans on the change of working positions for officials, public employees, and professional staff; (c) guide the appointment, recognition, reappointment, and re-recognition of leaders of vocational training establishments; submit to competent authorities for recognition of the managing board and principals of private vocational training colleges nationwide; (d) decide on the receipt, transfer, rotation, appointment, dismissal, recruitment examinations, and rank promotion, wage raise, emulation, commendation, and disciplining of officials and employees of attached units of the General Department; coordinate with the office to stipulate and organize the work of emulating and commending managers of vocational training; (e) guide and conduct the annual evaluation of cadres, civil servants, and public employees of units under the General Department according to regulations; (f) propose the sending of cadres, civil servants, and employees to work abroad in accordance with the authority of the General Department; (g) make statistics on officials and employees of units under the General Department; manage the dossiers of public employees and employees according to the decentralization; (h) formulate programs and measures to organize the implementation of administrative reforms in the administrative apparatus, and renovate and improve the quality of the contingent of cadres and civil servants belonging to and under the General Department. 6. Regarding the protection of internal politics, study and submit to the general director and organize the implementation of the following: (a) regulations on protection of internal politics in units under and attached to the General Department; (b) lists of confidential documents of the branch according to the state's regulations as assigned; (c) follow up delegations of Vietnamese vocational training managers and teachers to foreign countries and foreign delegations entering Viet Nam for work in vocational training. 7. Regarding training, study and submit to the General Director and (a) organize the implementation of the regulation on sending Vietnamese abroad for vocational training and foreigners entering Viet Nam for vocational training; (b) guide the elaboration and synthesis of planning and plans on training and retraining of the contingent of cadres, civil servants, and managers engaged in vocational training management in the ministries, branches, localities, and vocational training establishments; (c) guide, examine, formulate, and implement training programs and materials for vocational training managers; organize professional training and fostering of state management officials in charge of vocational training in ministries, branches, localities, and vocational training establishments; (d) select and nominate officials and employees of units under the General Department to train and foster their qualifications at home and abroad; (e) inspect and supervise the units under the General Department in implementing the regulations on sending cadres and employees to study and improve their professional skills at home and abroad.	9

continued on next page

Appendix 2 continued

	Office or Department	Functions, Tasks, and Authority	Number of Staff
8	Staff Development	8. Develop plans and inspect the organization, personnel, and training activities of units under the General Department. 9. Guide the formulation and inspection of the organization and implementation of operation regulations of the units under the General Department. 10. Guide and examine the regulations on sending Vietnamese abroad for vocational training and foreigners to Viet Nam for vocational training. 11. Coordinate with the office to organize statistical and information work and build a database on job-training establishments; the quantity, quality, and structure of the state management cadres in charge of vocational training and vocational training establishments; and synthesize and report on issues related to the training, retraining, and use of vocational training managers. 12. Participate in the propagation, dissemination, and education of the law for cadres, civil servants, and employees as assigned by the General Department. **Relationship with other units outside the GDVT (institutes, ministries, industry associations)** Establish and maintain relationship with ministries, sectors, localities, vocational training institutions, enterprises, and professional associations.	9
9	Office	1. Synthesize and elaborate the program and plan of the General Department; supervise and urge units and organizations under the General Department to implement programs and plans after they are approved; make periodic and irregular reports on the performance of tasks by the General Department; examine the formalities and procedures for the issuance of administrative documents of the General Department; formulate and organize the implementation of the internal rules and regulations, ensuring discipline and discipline of labor and order in activities of the General Department. 2. Work out the working schedule of the General Department leaders and synthesize the working schedules of the leaders of departments and units; prepare contents, minutes, and draft notices and conclusions of the briefings with leaders of departments and units to be presided over by the leaders of the General Department. 3. Work out plans on information, propagation, and provision of information to communication agencies, agencies, organizations, and individuals according to regulations; assume the prime responsibility for and coordinate with the departments and units of the General Department in maintaining the operation of the website. 4. Act as the main body in relations with ministries, branches, localities, agencies, and organizations related to vocational training; assume the prime responsibility for mobilizing project funding, formulating detailed outlines of programs and projects calling for official development assistance (ODA) capital support and foreign preferential loans. 5. Organize, manage, and guide the implementation and implementation of administrative, clerical, and archival work in the General Department; synthesize and maintain external relations in the field of vocational training.	38

continued on next page

Appendix 2 continued

	Office or Department	Functions, Tasks, and Authority	Number of Staff
9	Office	6. Assume the prime responsibility for organizing the management of and providing guidance for the observance of statistical information and statistics on vocational training establishments. 7. Perform tasks of grade-3 units; make estimates and implement the material and technical facilities and collect and spend funds of the General Department as prescribed. 8. Manage assets, supplies, and equipment; ensure working conditions, means of transport, and communication of the General Department; ensure fire prevention and firefighting and protect the order and safety, environmental hygiene, and landscape in the office of the General Department. 9. Organize guest receptions and meeting logistics for the General Department's agencies and conferences. 10. Take responsibility for the printing and distribution of legal documents, documents in service of the direction and administration of the General Department and papers and documents used in vocational training establishments according to regulations. 11. Assist the general director in managing and directing the emulation and commendation work in the entire branch and organizing the emulation and commendation work of the General Department; perform the standing task of the Emulation and Commendation Council of the General Department. 12. Instruct and foster the professional work of the office (general, clerical, archive, statistics) for officials and employees of units under the General Department. 13. Act as the focal point for the military work, the militia, and self-defense force of the General Department as guided by the local military office. 14. Coordinate with departments and units under the General Department to implement the administrative and administrative reform program. 15. Assume the prime responsibility for assisting the general director in formulating the traditional history of the General Department and branch. 16. Assume the prime responsibility for, and coordinate with the General Department's Trade Union in assisting the general director in caring for the protection of the health and the improvement of the material and spiritual life of officials, public servants, and laborers of the agencies under the General Department. **Relationship with other units outside the GDVT (institutes, ministries, industry associations)** Establish and maintain relations with the ministries, branches, localities, vocational training establishments, enterprises, communication agencies, and professional associations.	38
10	Department for Accreditation of Vocational Education	1. Assume the prime responsibility for, and coordinate with concerned units in, formulating and submitting to the general director policies, plans, and measures for developing vocational training quality assessment and vocational training quality management. 2. Elaborate and submit to the general director legal documents on the accreditation of vocational training quality and vocational training quality management.	18

continued on next page

Appendix 2 continued

	Office or Department	Functions, Tasks, and Authority	Number of Staff
10	Department for Accreditation of Vocational Education	3. Assume the prime responsibility for, and coordinate with the concerned agencies in, preparing documents and conditions for submission to the general director for conclusion of international agreements or treaties on the joining or mutual recognition of quality accreditation in vocational training according to regulations. 4. Formulate and submit to the general director the programs, schemes, and plans for verifying the quality of vocational training establishments and training programs and implement the approved plan. 5. Organize professional training and fostering for quality testers of vocational training and quality managers of job-training establishments; submit to the general director proposals to consider in issuing certificates of vocational training quality. 6. Manage and organize the appraisal of vocational training quality for vocational training establishments and training programs; organize the evaluation and submit to the general director of the department for submission to the Minister of Labour, War Invalids and Social Affairs for decision to recognize or withdraw accreditation certificates for vocational training quality. 7. Organize the publication of results of vocational training quality testing and the list of job-training establishments and training programs already accredited for vocational training quality. 8. Guide the establishment, organization, and operation of vocational training accreditation centers set up by organizations and individuals. 9. Submit to the general director the appraisal for establishments or permits for establishing a vocational training accreditation organization; recognize competent foreign organizations that can assess the quality of foreign-trained vocational training programs in Viet Nam. 10. Guide and inspect the implementation of regulations pertaining to vocational training quality assessment and vocational training quality management. 11. Organize the national skills contest and the regional and international skills contest; guide the organization of skills competitions at all levels and participate in regional and international competitions. 12. Coordinate with the office to build and manage a database on vocational training accreditation and quality assurance. 13. Coordinate with the Legal Department of the Inspectorate in examining and settling complaints and denunciations related to the conclusion of the vocational training quality assessment delegations. **Relationship with other units outside the GDVT (institutes, ministries, industry associations)** Establish and maintain relations with ministries, branches, localities, job-training establishments, enterprises, and professional associations, but mainly with the ministries, branches, professional associations, and enterprises.	18
11	Department of Vocational Skills	1. Elaborate and submit to competent authorities for promulgation programs, schemes, and plans for the development of the national system of professional skills standards and evaluate and grant national vocational skills certificates to laborers.	12

continued on next page

Appendix 2 continued

	Office or Department	Functions, Tasks, and Authority	Number of Staff
11	Department of Vocational Skills	2. Elaborate and submit to competent authorities for promulgation legal documents on national professional skills and national professional skills standards; formulate and promulgate national professional skills standards, the assessment of national vocational skills of laborers, and the management and evaluation of national vocational skills certificates, including the following tasks: (a) set the national qualifications framework, the framework for national vocational skills, and national professional skills certificates at different levels; (b) prescribe the principles and processes for elaboration and promulgation of national professional skills standards; (c) prescribe the process of building and managing the question bank and the questionnaire for the evaluating national vocational skills; (d) prescribe the process of organizing and managing the assessment of national vocational skills for laborers; (e) prescribe conditions, procedures, and dossiers for assessment, grant, and revocation of national vocational skills certificates at different skill levels; (f) set criteria for evaluators, the national professional skills assessment card, and the management, issuance, and withdrawal of national professional skills assessor cards. 3. Guide, examine, and organize the implementation of legal documents for the national professional framework and national professional skills framework; elaborate and promulgate standards, conduct national assessments of national occupational skills, and manage the evaluation and grant of national vocational skills certificates, including the following tasks: (a) manage the national vocational training frames and the system of national vocational skills standards; (b) guide, direct, and inspect the organization of the elaboration, appraisal, and promulgation of national vocational skills standards for each profession and skill level; organize the submission of agreements for the promulgation of national vocational skill standards for each profession; review, update, and adjust national vocational skills standards in line with the general requirements of each period; (c) consider and submit for recognition the list of technical and training service organizations and enterprises eligible for participation in the national job-skill assessment for laborers; guide, inspect, and supervise organizations and enterprises in evaluating national job skills for laborers; (d) guide, direct, inspect, and organize the construction and management of question-and-answer banks for national vocational skills; (e) guide, direct, inspect, and organize the evaluation, grant, and withdrawal of national vocational skills certificates by different skill levels; (f) consider, submit, or withdraw the national professional skills assessor's cards; and (g) manage and keep dossiers related to the evaluation and grant of national vocational skills certificates. 4. Organize the national skills contest and the regional and international skills contest; guide the organization of skills competitions at all levels and participate in regional and international competitions. 5. Guide the use of national vocational skills standards and the application of vocational skills standards of ASEAN countries and the world to Viet Nam. 6. Consider and recognize professional skills certificates granted by foreign countries to Vietnamese or foreign laborers working in Viet Nam. 7. Organize professional training and fostering for evaluators and experts on the elaboration and appraisal of national job-skills standards and national occupational skills appraisal questions.	12

continued on next page

Appendix 2 continued

	Office or Department	Functions, Tasks, and Authority	Number of Staff
11	Department of Vocational Skills	8. Manage the database system for the assessment and grant of national vocational skills certificates. **Relationship with other units outside the GDVT (institutes, ministries, industry associations)** Establish and maintain relations with ministries, branches, localities, job-training establishments, enterprises, and professional associations, but mainly with the ministries, departments, employment agencies-MOLISA, professional associations, and enterprises.	12
12	National Institute of Vocational Education	1. Submit to the general director of the GDVT plans to study and apply the long-term and annual science of vocational training. 2. Conduct basic research on strategic planning and policies on vocational training. 3. Perform basic research on the scientific basis for developing content, programs, and methods of vocational training. 4. Study and develop the national professional skills frame, the framework of national vocational skills, and vocational training standards; study and develop the quality assurance system for vocational training. 5. Conduct research, experiment, and apply research results to training and production practices, transferring technology for vocational training. 6. Conduct scientific research on vocational training. 7. Forecast the demand for vocational training and perform basic investigation on service of scientific research on vocational training. 8. Coordinate with the Office of Research and Application of Information Technology – Statistics on Vocational Training. 9. Organize an associate postgraduate training according to regulations; participate in fostering and teaching at vocational training institutions, fostering the application of science and technology in vocational training, pedagogy for cadres, and vocational training. 10. Compile, print, publish publications, and disseminate information on vocational training. 11. Conduct consultancy and service activities on research and development according to regulations. 12. Participate in evaluating programs, projects, and research projects on vocational training and skills development. 13. Cooperate with organizations and individuals at home and abroad and with international organizations in conducting vocational training research. 14. Manage employees, finances, and assets in accordance with the law and GDVT. 15. Manage finances and assets according to the provisions of law. **Relationship with other units outside the GDVT (institutes, ministries, industry associations)** Establish and maintain relations with ministries, branches, localities, vocational training establishments, enterprises, and professional associations, but mainly with research institutes, schools, and businesses.	38

continued on next page

Appendix 2 continued

	Office or Department	Functions, Tasks, and Authority	Number of Staff
13	Official Development Assistance Project Management Board		62
14	National Target Program		5
	Head of GDVT		4
TOTAL STAFF (with/without Project Management Unit)			**259/197**

Notes:

(i) In late 2017, the GDVT officially changed its name into Directorate of Vocational Education and Training (DVET). However, changes in the organizational structure were not reported by the end of 2017.

(ii) Units 1 to 12 are under the deciding competence of the Prime Minister; units 13–14 are under the jurisdiction of the Minister of Labour–Invalids and Social Affairs.

Source: Directorate of Vocational Education and Training, compiled in July 2017 by Phan Chinh Thuc, the former director general of the General Department of Vocational Training.

Appendix 3. Number, Distribution, and Ownership of Vocational Education and Training Institutions (November 2017)

Vocational Education and Training Colleges

No.	Region/Province	Number of Colleges	Direct Management					
			Provincial People's Commitee	Ministry	Corporation	University	Other	Unknown
I	**NORTHERN MIDLANDS AND MOUNTAIN AREAS**	**52**						
1	Hà Giang	1	1					
2	Tuyên Quang	1	1					
3	Cao Băng							
4	Lang Son	3	2	1				
5	Lào Cai	2	2					
6	Yên Bái	4	2	1				1
7	Thái Nguyên	12	2	8		1	1	
8	Băc Kan	2	2					
9	Phú Tho	10	3	5	1			1
10	Băc Giang	4	3	1				
11	Hòa Bình	5	2	3				
12	Son La	4	4					
13	Điên Biên	3	3					
14	Lai Châu	1	1					
II	**RED RIVER DELTA**	**138**						
15	Thành phô Hà Nôi	59	11	23	9	1	4	11
16	Thành phô Hai Phòng	16	4	6	2	1	1	2
17	Quang Ninh	8	3	4	1			
18	Vinh Phúc	7	3	4				
19	Hai Duong	9	3	5				1
20	Hung Yên	9	2	2	3			2
21	Băc Ninh	10	1	3	3			3
22	Hà Nam	5	2	2	1			
23	Nam Đinh	6	2	3	1			
24	Ninh Bình	5	1	4				
25	Thái Bình	4	3	1				
III	**NORTH CENTRAL AND CENTRAL COAST AREAS**	**82**						
26	Thanh Hoá	12	6	2	3			1
27	Nghe An	8	4	2			1	1
28	Hà Tinh	4	2	1			1	
29	Quang Bình	1	1					

continued on next page

Appendix 3 continued

30	Quang Tri	1	1					
31	Thua Thiên – Hue	7	3	3				1
32	Thành pho Đà Nang	20	1	7	1	2	1	8
33	Khánh Hòa	5	2	1	1			1
34	Quang Nam	8	3	1	2			2
35	Quang Ngãi	5	2	2				1
36	Bình Đinh	4	3	1				
37	Phú Yên	3	2	1				
38	Ninh Thuan	1	1					
39	Bình Thuan	3	3					
IV	**CENTRAL HIGHLANDS**	**12**						
40	Đak Lak	4	4					
41	Đak Nông							
42	Gia Lai	2	1	1				
43	Kon Tum	1	1					
44	Lâm Đong	5	3	2				
V	**SOUTHEAST**	**71**						
45	Thành pho Ho Chí Minh	43	11	12	5		3	12
46	Đong Nai	11	3	6	1			1
47	Bình Duong	7	3	2	2			
48	Tây Ninh	1	1					
49	Bà Ria - Vung Tàu	6	2	1	3			
50	Bình Phuoc	3	2	1				
VI	**MEKONG RIVER DELTA**	**40**						
51	Long An	3	1		2			
52	Tien Giang	3	2	1				
53	Vinh Long	4	3	1				
54	Thành pho Can Tho	7	5	2				
55	Hau Giang	2	1					1
56	Ben Tre	2	1				1	
57	Trà Vinh	2	2					
58	Sóc Trăng	2	2					
59	An Giang	2	2					
60	Đong Tháp	3	3					
61	Kiên Giang	4	4					
62	Bac Liêu	3	3					
63	Cà Mau	3	3					
TOTAL		**395**	**160**	**126**	**41**	**5**	**13**	**50**
Ministry of Agriculture and Rural Development								29
Ministry of Industry and Trade								25
Ministry of Defence								20
Ministry of Culture, Sport and Tourism								14

continued on next page

Appendix 3 continued

Ministry of Construction	12
Ministry of Transport	9
Ministry of Public Security	4
Ministry of Labour–Invalids and Social Affairs	4
Ministry of Health	3
Ministry of Planning and Investment	2
Ministry of Information and Communication	2
Ministry of National Resources and Environment	1
Ministry of Finance	1
Total	**126**

Source: Directorate of Vocational Education and Training, compiled in November 2017 by Phan Chinh Thuc, the former director general of the General Directorate of Vocational Training.

Secondary Vocational Education and Training Schools

No.	Region/Province	Number of Schools	Provincial People's Commitee	Ministry	Corporation	Other	Unknown
			Direct Management				
I	**NORTHERN MIDLANDS AND MOUNTAIN AREAS**	**58**					
1	Hà Giang	3	1				2
2	Tuyên Quang	4			2		2
3	Cao Bang	3	1				2
4	Lang Son	2					2
5	Lào Cai	2			1		1
6	Yên Bái	5	2			1	2
7	Thái Nguyên	14	3	1	4	1	5
8	Bac Kan	1					1
9	Phú Tho	6	1		1		4
10	Bac Giang	11	2	1	1	1	6
11	Hòa Bình	3			2		1
12	Son La	2		1			1
13	Ðien Biên						
14	Lai Châu	2	1				1
II	**RED RIVER DELTA**	**193**					
15	Thành pho Hà Noi	97	6	11	19	6	55
16	Thành pho Hai Phòng	17	5		3		9
17	Quang Ninh	3			1		2
18	Vinh Phúc	7		2	1		4
19	Hai Duong	5		1	2		2

continued on page

Appendix 3 continued

20	Hung Yên	9	2		3		4
21	Bac Ninh	19	1		5	2	11
22	Hà Nam	5	1		2	1	1
23	Nam Đinh	14	4		1	2	7
24	Ninh Bình	10	1	1	1	1	6
25	Thái Bình	7	3			1	3
III	**NORTH CENTRAL AND CENTRAL COAST AREAS**	**106**					
26	Thanh Hoá	23	11	1	4	2	5
27	Nghe An	14	8	1			5
28	Hà Tinh	5	1		1	2	1
29	Quang Bình	6		1		1	4
30	Quang Tri	6	2		1		3
31	Thua Thiên - Hue	9	2		1	1	5
32	Thành pho Đà Nang	11	1	1	2		7
33	Khánh Hòa	12	6	1	1		4
34	Quang Nam	8	3		1	1	3
35	Quang Ngãi	3	2				1
36	Bình Đinh	4	2				2
37	Phú Yên	1	1				
38	Ninh Thuan	2					2
39	Bình Thuan	2				1	1
IV	**CENTRAL HIGHLANDS**	**23**					
40	Đak Lak	10		1	2		7
41	Đak Nông	2	1				1
42	Gia Lai	6	2	2			2
43	Kon Tum	2	1				1
44	Lâm Đong	3	1			1	1
V	**SOUTHEAST**	**103**					
45	Thành pho Ho Chí Minh	65	7	4	12	4	38
46	Đong Nai	11	1	1	2	3	4
47	Bình Duong	16	4			2	10
48	Tây Ninh	4	1				3
49	Bà Ria - Vung Tàu	5	1			1	3
50	Bình Phuoc	2					2
VI	**MEKONG RIVER DELTA**	**67**					
51	Long An	9	3		1	1	4
52	Tien Giang	9	3			1	5
53	Vinh Long	1					1
54	Thành pho Can Tho	14	1	1	1	2	9
55	Hau Giang	3	1	1		1	0
56	Ben Tre	5	2				3
57	Trà Vinh	2	1				1
58	Sóc Trăng	2					2
59	An Giang	7	4			1	2

continued on page

Appendix 3 continued

60	Đong Tháp	4	4				
61	Kiên Giang	7	5			1	1
62	Bac Liêu	2			1		1
63	Cà Mau	2					2
TOTAL		**550**	**116**	**33**	**79**	**42**	**280**
Ministry of Agriculture and Rural Development							4
Ministry of Industry and Trade							1
Ministry of Defence							10
Ministry of Culture, Sport and Tourism							2
Ministry of Construction							6
Ministry of Transport							4
Ministry of Home Affairs							5
Ministry of Health							1
Total							**33**

Source: Directorate of Vocational Education and Training, compiled in November 2017 by Dr. Phan Chinh Thuc, former director general of the General Directorate of Vocational Training.

Appendix 4. Viet Nam National Qualification Framework

Level	Learning Outcomes (Requirements for learners completing a training course)			Minimum Academic Load	Qualification Type
	Knowledge and Understanding	Skills	Autonomy and Responsibility		
1	Have a narrow range of factual knowledge and basic knowledge about a number of activities in a certain profession. Have basic knowledge about nature, culture, society, and legislation serving the life, advanced study, and preparation for future occupation.	Have basic skills to directly perform simple or manual tasks. Have basic communicative skills in familiar contexts.	Perform a number of simple and repeated tasks with the assistance of instructors. Carry out tasks under strict supervision and guidance. Conduct self-assessment and assessment of tasks with the assistance of instructors.	5 credits	Certificate I
2	Have a narrow range of factual and theoretical knowledge about a number of activities of a profession. Have general knowledge about nature, culture, society, and legislation serving the life, profession, and advanced study.	Have awareness and skills required to select and apply suitable methods, tools and materials, and available information. Have communicative skills required to perform the results or make reports on own work.	Carry out a number of tasks with regularity and limited autonomy in familiar contexts. Carry out tasks in unfamiliar contexts with the guidance of instructors. Have ability to do self-assessment of own tasks.	15 credits	Certificate II
3	Have factual and theoretical knowledge of common principles, processes, and concepts in the scope of a training profession. Have general knowledge about nature, culture, society, and legislation serving the life, profession, and advanced study. Have basic knowledge of information technology related to a certain profession.	Have awareness and skills required to carry out tasks or solve problems independently. Have skills required to use effectively professional terms at workplace.	Work independently in stable situations and familiar contexts. Carry out assignments and do self-assessment according to the defined standards. Carry out teamwork with other people and take responsibility for the results of work.	25 credits	Certificate III

continued on next page

Appendix 4 continued

| 4 | Have a broad range of factual and theoretical knowledge about the training profession.

Have basic knowledge of politics, culture, society, and legislation answering to the professional and social requirements in the profession.

Have knowledge of information technology answering to work requirements. | Have awareness and professional skills required to perform tasks and solve problems by selecting and applying basic methods, tools, materials, and information.

Have skills required to use professional terms in the field of study to communicate effectively at workplace; get involve in argument and apply alternative solutions; assess the quality of work and performance of team members.

Have foreign-language capacity at level 1/6 referencing to Viet Nam's framework of foreign language proficiency. | Work independently in changeable contexts, take personal responsibility, and take partial responsibility for teamwork results.

Guide and supervise the ordinary tasks of others. Evaluate the performance of the team. | 35 credits, for people with the certificate of completion of upper secondary education

50 credits, for people with the certificate of completion of lower secondary education | Associate degree |
| 5 | Have comprehensive, factual, and theoretical knowledge of the training profession.

Have basic knowledge of politics, culture, society, and legislation answering to the professional and social requirements in the profession.

Have knowledge of information technology answering to the requirements of work.

Have factual knowledge about the management, principles, and methods for planning, performing, supervising, and evaluating the work within the boundaries of the training profession. | Have awareness and creativity to determine, analyze, and evaluate broad-range information.

Have practical skills required to solve abstract problems within the boundaries of the training profession.

Have awareness and creativity to determine, analyze, and evaluate broad-range information. Have skills required to transfer information, ideas, and solutions to other people at workplace.

Have foreign-language capacity at level 2/6 referencing to Viet Nam's framework of foreign language proficiency. | Work independently or work in teams, solve tasks and complicated problems in changeable contexts.

Guide other people to perform defined tasks and supervise their performance; take personal and shared responsibility.

Evaluate the task results and performance of team members. | 60 credits | College degree |

continued on next page

Appendix 4 continued

6	Have an advanced theoretical and factual knowledge in the field of study. Have basic knowledge of social science, political science, and legislation. Have knowledge of information technology answering to work requirements. Have knowledge about planning, organizing, and supervising processes of specific fields of work. Basic knowledge of the management and control of professional activities.	Have skills required to solve complex problems. Have skills to be a leader and create own jobs or for other people. Have argument skills and skills to criticize and apply alternative solutions in unpredictable or changeable contexts. Have skills to evaluate the task results and performance of members in the team. Have skills to transfer information about problems and solutions to other people at workplace; transfer and disseminate knowledge and skills in performance of defined or complex tasks. Have foreign-language capacity at level 3/6 referencing to Viet Nam's framework of foreign language proficiency.	Work independently or with a team in changeable contexts, take personal responsibility, and take partial responsibility for teamwork results. Guide and supervise the ordinary tasks of others. Conduct self-orientation and produce professional conclusions and have ability to protect own viewpoints. Draw up plans, direct and manage resources, evaluate and find solutions to improve the task performance.	120–180 credits	Undergraduate degree
7	Have advanced specialized knowledge and a thorough grasp of basic principles and theories in a field of study. Have relevant knowledge in multidisciplinary field of study. Have general knowledge about administration and management.	Have advanced and specialized skills including analysis, synthesis, and evaluation of data and information to solve problems in a scientific way. Have skills to transfer knowledge depending on research, and discuss professional and scientific issues with other people. Have skills to organize, administrate, and manage advanced professional activities. Have skills to develop and apply technology creatively in a field of study or work. Have foreign-language capacity at level 4/6 referencing to Viet Nam's framework of foreign language proficiency.	Perform research and produce essential ideas. Adapt to the context, have self-orientation and guidance skills. Make professional conclusions for the field of work or study. Manage, evaluate, and develop professional activities.	30–60 credits	Master's degree

continued on next page

Appendix 4 continued

| 8 | Have the most advanced and intensive knowledge in a field of work or study related to science.
Have the essential and basic knowledge in the field of the training profession.

Have knowledge about organization of scientific research and development of new technology.

Have knowledge about administration and organization. | Have skills to master scientific theories, methods, and tools that serve research and development.

Have skills to consolidate and extend professional knowledge.

Have skills to reason and analyze scientific issues and produce creative and original solutions.

Have skills to carry out management and professional direction in research and development.

Have skills to join in domestic and international discussion regarding the field of study and disseminate research findings. | Research and create new knowledge.

Create new ideas and knowledge for different complex situations.

Adapt to, make self-orientation, and provide guidance for other people.

Make professional conclusions and decisions.

Manage research and have high responsibility in study to develop professional knowledge and experience and produce new ideas and process. | 90–120 credits | Doctoral degree |

Source: Decision No. 1982/QD-TTg of the Prime Minister dated 18 October 2016.

Appendix 5. Criteria and Standards for Quality Accreditation

1. Criteria and Standards for Quality Accreditation of Vocational Education Centers

	Criteria		Standards	Score Σ=104 (2 points per standard)
1	Objectives, mission, organization, and administration	1.1	The objectives, tasks, and mission of the Center are stipulated in regulations for its organization and operation. The Center has plans and orientation to build a quality assurance system. The respective contents are made available in accordance with regulations to teachers, administrators, learners, and the society and adjusted in accordance with regulations.	10
		1.2	The Center analyzes and assesses reports on labor market needs to identify training occupations and training scales in line with actual conditions of the Center and local or sectoral human resources requirements.	
		1.3	Issues documents on the organization and administration toward ensuring the autonomy and self-responsibility of the Center's units. Annually, documents on the organization and administration of the Center are reviewed and adjustments, if any, are made.	
		1.4	Develops and implements democracy at grassroots level; mass organizations operate under the charter, with supervising activities to ensure and enhance the training quality.	
		1.5	Professional and functional offices, departments, divisions, subject teams, and other units (if any) of the Center are clearly assigned and decentralized to assume relevant functions, tasks, and authorities.	
2	Training activities	2.1	Training occupations of the Center are registered under certificates of vocational education and ensure prescribed training conditions. The Center issues outcome standards for each training program and makes them available to learners and the society.	18
		2.2	The Center has guidance and follows enrollment and admission procedures in accordance with regulations.	
		2.3	Formulates and approves training plans and schedules for each class and each course to ensure flexibility and suitability to specific learners and local and regional characteristics; and implements approved training plans and training schedules.	
		2.4	Training activities of the Center are implemented according to the objectives and contents of approved training programs.	
		2.5	The Center strictly and objectively conducts tests and exams for certification of graduation and assessment of learning and training performance, and grants diplomas or certificates to learners in accordance with regulations.	
		2.6	The Center implements training activities toward diversifying training modes to meet learner needs in line with the Center's actual conditions; coordinates with employers in teaching and learning activities and in learners' practice activities.	
		2.7	Training methods are implemented in combination with practicing capacity and specialized knowledge; promotes positive, self-consciousness, dynamic qualities, and the learners' ability to work independently, and organizes teamwork activities.	
		2.8	The Center organizes and implements training links and connections in accordance with current regulations. Annually, the Center organizes consultative activities with learners, teachers, and administrators on the implementation of training links and adjustments, if necessary.	
		2.9	Training administration books and forms are kept and the reporting regime is applied in accordance with regulations.	

continued on next page

Appendix 5 continued

3	Teachers, administrators, employees, and working staff	3.1	The Center has adequate force of teachers to ensure the conversion rate as prescribed with appropriate training professions and qualifications.	18
		3.2	The teaching staff of the Center meets professional standards in knowledge and skills and other standards, if any.	
		3.3	Teachers, administrators, employees, and working staff perform their tasks and authorities in accordance with regulations and do not violate rules and regulations of the Center.	
		3.4	Teachers perform their teaching activities in accordance with contents and objectives of training programs and fulfill all requirements of training programs.	
		3.5	The Center's administrators are appointed and dismissed in accordance with regulations. The director and deputy director of the Center properly and rightly perform assigned tasks and exercise assigned authorities.	
		3.6	Has regulations on recruitment, use, planning, fostering, evaluation, and classification of teachers, administrators, employees, and working staff in accordance with regulations; fully implements policies and regimes for teachers, administrators, employees, and working staff in accordance with regulations.	
		3.7	Recruits, uses, plans, trains, assesses, and classifies teachers, administrators, employees, and working staff in accordance with regulations, ensuring publicity, transparency, and objectivity.	
		3.8	The Center develops and implements plans for training and fostering the Center's teachers and administrators in accordance with regulations.	
		3.9	Teachers are trained and fostered and put into practice in employer facilities to update their knowledge and understanding in technologies and methods of organizing production management in accordance with regulations.	
4	Programs and curricula	4.1	The Center has sufficient programs and curricula for ongoing training occupations in accordance with regulations.	18
		4.2	Training programs ensure prescribed content and structures.	
		4.3	100% of training programs are developed or selected in accordance with regulations.	
		4.4	Training programs are developed or selected with the participation of teachers, vocational education administrators, and scientific and technical staff of employers.	
		4.5	Training programs are practical and suitable with technologies and techniques in production and service.	
		4.6	100% of training curricula are developed or selected in accordance with regulations to be used as formal teaching materials.	
		4.7	Has sufficient curricula for modules of each training program.	
		4.8	Training curricula are developed or selected with the participation of teachers, experts, experienced administrators, and representatives of employer entities; requirements on the contents of knowledge and skills of each module in training programs are specified.	
		4.9	Annually, organizes the gathering of comments and opinions from teachers, administrators, employees, working staff, and learners on programs and curricula, if necessary; at least once every 3 years, the Center organizes the review of programs and curricula in accordance with regulations and makes corrections if necessary.	

continued on next page

Appendix 5 continued

5	Material facilities and training equipment	5.1	The Center has suitable training facilities to meet requirements of teaching and learning conditions of training grounds and sites; sites for practicing professional skills; tools, equipment, and training materials in accordance with regulations on the organization of training classrooms and sites.	14
		5.2	Theoretical and practical classrooms and practice workshops are in accordance with rules and regulations on occupational safety and health, fire and explosion prevention and fighting; equipment and devices are arranged orderly and properly to meet practicing requirements for learners.	
		5.3	The Center has sufficient kinds, quantity, and quality of training equipment in accordance with regulations.	
		5.4	Has regulations on the use of self-made equipment in accordance with current regulations and implements the management and use in accordance with regulations.	
		5.5	Has practicing equipment and devices equivalent to or compatible with technologies and equipment being used in current production, business, and service activities.	
		5.6	Practicing equipment and devices ensure synchronism, in conformity with training programs of the Center.	
		5.7	Has a reading room with sufficient programs and curricula for occupations that the Center is training for students and teachers to study and research.	
6	Financial management	6.1	The Center has and implements regulations on financial management, use, and settlement in accordance with regulations.	8
		6.2	Financial resources ensure sufficient funds for activities of the Center.	
		6.3	Manages and uses revenues from training services; participates in production, business, and service activities in accordance with regulations.	
		6.4	The Center fully observes financial, accounting, audit, tax, statistical, and periodical regulations and regimes in accordance with regulations; implements financial disclosure in accordance with applicable provisions of law.	
7	Learner services	7.1	The Center informs learners about training regulations, training plans, contents of training programs, and rights and obligations of learners.	10
		7.2	Learners enjoy regimes and policies in accordance with regulations.	
		7.3	Has and implements rewarding policies and promptly encourages learners to achieve high performance in studying and training activities.	
		7.4	Learners are respected and treated equally, regardless of gender, religion, or background origin.	
		7.5	The Center provides counseling and job referral services for learners.	
8	Monitoring and assessment of quality	8.1	The Center implements self-assessment and accreditation in accordance with regulations; and annually gathers feedback opinions from employers on the extent of responsiveness of graduates.	8
		8.2	Annually, the Center has plans and solutions to ensure the improvement of training quality on the basis of the results of self-assessment and accreditation, if any.	

Source: Ministry of Labour–Invalids and Social Affairs Circular No. 15/2017/TT-BLDTBXH dated June 2017.

2. Criteria and Standards for Quality Accreditation of Vocational Education Institutions of Intermediate and College Levels

	Criteria		Standards	Score Σ=100 (1 point per standard)
1	Objectives, mission, organization, and administration	1.1	The institution's objectives and mission are defined clearly in accordance with functions and tasks, demonstrating its role in meeting local and sectoral human resources needs; and they are publicized.	12
		1.2	The institution analyzes and assesses human resources needs in localities or sectors in order to determine appropriate training fields and occupations and training scales.	
		1.3	Issues documents on the organization and administration toward ensuring the autonomy and self-responsibility of the institution's units in accordance with regulations.	
		1.4	Annually, documents on the organization and administration of the institution are put under review and adjustments, if any.	
		1.5	Departments, faculties, subject divisions, and other units of the institution are assigned and decentralized clearly in terms of functions and tasks, in line with structures of professions and occupations, training scales, and objectives of the institution.	
		1.6	The institution's executive board or board of directors, advisory councils, departments, faculties, subject divisions, and other units function properly and effectively.	
		1.7	The institution builds and operates a quality assurance system in accordance with regulations.	
		1.8	The institution has a department in charge of administration and assurance of training quality and annual fulfillment of assigned tasks.	
		1.9	The Vietnamese Communist Party's organization in the institution promotes its leadership role and operates in accordance with the charter and in conformity with the Constitution and laws.	
		1.10	Mass and social organizations in the institution operate in accordance with the charter of their organization and in conformity with laws, contributing to ensuring and improving the institution's training quality.	
		1.11	The institution has regulations on and implements the inspection and supervision of its activities in accordance with regulations to improve training quality and effectiveness. Annually reviews and improves methods and tools for inspection and supervision.	
		1.12	The institution has documents on and implements preferential regimes and policies of the state for beneficiaries; implements gender equality policies in accordance with regulations.	

continued on next page

Appendix 5 continued

2	Training activities	2.1	The institution's disciplines or professions are licensed by competent agencies for registration of vocational education activities. The institution issues outcome standards for each training program and makes them available to learners and the society.	17
		2.2	The institution develops and promulgates regulations on enrollment in accordance with regulations.	
		2.3	Annually, the institution determines enrollment norms and conducts enrollment works in accordance with regulations, ensuring strictness, fairness, and objectivity.	
		2.4	Implements the diversification of training methods to meet the learning needs of learners.	
		2.5	The institution builds and approves plans and training schedules for each class and each course in each discipline or occupation, in each semester and school year. Has detailed training plans for each module, course, theory and practice lessons, in accordance with each training mode and method and with regulations.	
		2.6	The institution organizes training activities in accordance with approved training plans and training schedules.	
		2.7	Training activities are carried out in consistency with objectives and contents of approved training programs; coordinates with employers in organizing and guiding learners in practicing activities at the employers' facilities; complies with specific industry regulations, if any.	
		2.8	Training methods are implemented in combination with practicing capacity and specialized knowledge; promotes positive, self-consciousness, dynamic qualities, and the ability to work independently of learners, and organizes teamwork activities.	
		2.9	The institution applies information technology in teaching and learning activities.	
		2.10	Annually, the institution plans and organizes the inspection and supervision of teaching and learning activities in accordance with schedules.	
		2.11	Annually, the institution reports on results of inspection and supervision of teaching and learning activities, proposes measures to improve the quality of teaching and learning activities, and timely adjusts proposed teaching and learning activities, if necessary.	
		2.12	The institution promulgates all regulations on examinations, tests, certification of graduation, assessment of learning and training, and grants diplomas and certificates in according with regulations.	
		2.13	During the process of assessing learners' learning performance, the institution engages the participation of employers and complies with specific industry regulations, if any.	
		2.14	The institution strictly and objectively conducts tests and exams for certification of graduation, assessment of learning and training performance, and grants diplomas or certificate to learners in accordance with regulations.	
		2.15	Annually, the institution reviews all regulations on examinations, tests, certification of graduation, assessment of learning and training performance, and grants diplomas or certificates in accordance with regulations.	
		2.16	The institution has guiding documents and organizes the implementation of bridge training in accordance with regulations.	
		2.17	The institution has a database of training activities and effectively implements the management and use of the database.	

continued on next page

Appendix 5 continued

3	Teachers, administrators, employees, and working staff	3.1	Has regulations on the recruitment, use, planning, fostering, assessment, and classification of teachers, administrators, employees, and working staff in accordance with regulations.	15
		3.2	Implements the recruitment, use, planning, fostering, evaluation, and classification of teachers, administrators, employees, and working staff in accordance with regulations, ensuring publicity, transparency, and objectivity; fully implements policies and regimes for teachers, administrators, employees, and working staff in accordance with regulations.	
		3.3	The teaching staff of the institution meets professional standards in knowledge and skills and other current standards, if any.	
		3.4	Teachers, administrators, employees, and working staff perform their tasks and authorities in accordance with regulations and do not violate rules and regulations of the institution.	
		3.5	The institution has adequate force of teachers to ensure the conversion rate and number of full-time teachers for all programs in each discipline of training in accordance with regulations; the institution ensures the rate of teachers with postgraduate qualifications in accordance with regulations.	
		3.6	Teachers perform their teaching activities in accordance with contents and objectives of training programs and fulfill all requirements of training programs.	
		3.7	The institution has and implements policies and measures to encourage teachers to further study and improve their professional knowledge and skills and apply innovative teaching methods.	
		3.8	Annually, the institution has and implements training and fostering plans to improve professional knowledge and skills and teaching methods for teachers.	
		3.9	Teachers are trained and fostered and put into practice in employer facilities to update their knowledge and understanding of technologies and methods of organizing production management in accordance with regulations, and comply with specific industry regulations, if any.	
		3.10	The institution annually reviews and assesses the effectiveness of training and fostering activities for teachers.	
		3.11	The institution's principal and vice-principal meet the prescribed standards and properly perform assigned authorities and tasks.	
		3.12	The institution's administrators are appointed and dismissed in accordance with regulations.	
		3.13	The institution's administrators meet professional standards for knowledge and skills; and properly perform assigned authorities and tasks.	
		3.14	Annually, the institution has and implements training and fostering plans to improve professional knowledge and skills for administrators.	
		3.15	The institution's employees and working staff are sufficient in number and qualifications to meet assigned work requirements and are regularly fostered to improve their qualifications.	

continued on next page

Appendix 5 continued

4	Programs and curricula	4.1	Has sufficient training programs for all disciplines or professions.	15
		4.2	100% of training programs are developed or selected in accordance with regulations.	
		4.3	The institution's training programs represent the training objectives of corresponding levels; the institution sets outcome standards of knowledge and skills of learners to be gained upon graduation; scope and structure of contents, methods, and forms of training; methods of assessment of learning performance for each module, subject, discipline, or profession at each level in accordance with regulations.	
		4.4	Training programs are developed or selected with the participation of teachers, vocational education administrators, and scientific and technical staff of employers; and comply with specific industry regulations, if any.	
		4.5	Training programs ensure practicality and responsiveness to changes in the labor market.	
		4.6	Training programs are developed toward ensuring the interlinking and connectivity of vocational education levels and other training levels in the national education system in accordance with regulations.	
		4.7	At least once every 3 years, the institution assesses, updates, and makes adjustments, if any, in the promulgated training programs.	
		4.8	Modifies and supplements training programs with updated scientific and technological achievements related to training disciplines or professions or referring to corresponding training programs from foreign countries.	
		4.9	Before implementing bridge training, the institution, based on training programs, reviews modules, credits, and subjects, and decides the modules, credits, and subjects exempted for learners to ensure that their interests are reflected.	
		4.10	Has sufficient curricula for modules of each training program.	
		4.11	100% of training curricula are developed or selected in accordance with regulations to be used as formal teaching materials.	
		4.12	Training curricula concretize requirements on the contents of knowledge and skills of each module or subject in training programs.	
		4.13	Training curricula facilitate the implementation of active teaching methods.	
		4.14	Annually, the institution gathers opinions from teachers, administrators, scientific and technical staff of employers, and graduates on the suitability of training curricula; complies with specific industry regulations, if any.	
		4.15	Upon making changes in training curricula, the institution evaluates, updates, and adjusts, if any, the curricula to meet requirements in accordance with regulations.	
5	Material facilities, training equipment, and libraries	5.1	The location of the institution is in line with the general planning scheme of the area and the network of vocational education institutions; the surrounding environment is quiet enough for teaching and learning activities; traffic is convenient and safe; it is convenient for electricity and water supply; ensures a fair distance from industrial facilities emitting noxious substances; and complies with specific industry regulations, if any.	15
		5.2	The overall planning scheme for campus premises is reasonable in accordance with the functions and requirements of internal traffic, architecture, and pedagogical environment; the land area in use and green area are in accordance with regulations.	

continued on next page

Appendix 5 continued

5	Material facilities, training equipment, and libraries	5.3	Ensures sufficient facilities for the institution's standard activities: study and scientific research facilities (theory classrooms, practice classrooms, laboratories, and specialized classrooms); practice facilities (practice workshops, study camps, experimental gardens); physical training facilities; administration, auxiliary, and living facilities for learners and teachers.	15
		5.4	The institution's system of technical infrastructure (internal roads, electricity system, water supply and drainage, wastewater treatment, solid waste treatment, ventilation, and fire prevention and fighting) are in accordance with standards and meet training, production, service, and living requirements; they are maintained in accordance with regulations.	
		5.5	Classrooms, laboratories, practice workshops, and specialized classrooms ensure construction standards, existing standards of facilities, and technological requirements for training equipment.	
		5.6	The institution has regulations on the management, use, and maintenance of training equipment.	
		5.7	Classrooms, lecture halls, laboratories, practice workshops, and specialized classrooms are used in accordance with current regulations.	
		5.8	Training equipment items meet the equipment list and minimum standards according to training requirements of each training level of disciplines or professions as prescribed by central-level competent authorities in charge of vocational education. For disciplines or professions where central-level competent authorities in charge of vocational education have not promulgated the equipment list and minimum standards, the institution ensures that the training equipment items meet the requirements of training programs and are consistent with the training scale of that discipline or profession.	
		5.9	Training equipment and tools in service of training activities are arranged rationally, safely, and conveniently for travel, operation, maintenance, and organization of practice instructions; ensure the requirements of pedagogy, industrial health and safety, and environmental hygiene.	
		5.10	The institute has regulations on the management, use, maintenance of training equipment, including provisions on periodic assessments and proposed measures to improve the effectiveness of training equipment.	
		5.11	Training equipment items have clear management records, are used properly, and managed and maintained in accordance with regulations of the institution and the manufacturers; annually assesses and proposes measures to improve the efficiency in use in accordance with regulations.	
		5.12	The institution has norms for material consumption or technical-economic norms in training and regulations on the management, allocation, and use of materials and training; timely organizes the implementation in accordance with regulations to meet the training schedule and progress; materials are arranged neatly and tidily for convenient storage and use.	
		5.13	The institution has a library including a reading room and a storage room that meets the designed standards. The library has sufficient programs and curricula approved by the institution. Each curriculum has at least 5 copies.	
		5.14	Organizes activities and forms of service of the library meeting the needs for reference of administrators, teachers, and learners.	
		5.15	The institute has a digital library and computer room to meet the needs for searching and accessing information of teachers and learners; the institution's textbooks and reference materials are digitized and integrated to the digital library to serve effectively for training activities.	

continued on next page

Appendix 5 continued

6	Scientific research, technology transfer, and international cooperation	6.1	The institution has and implements policies to encourage administrators, teachers, and staff to participate in scientific research, innovation, and technology transfer to improve the effectiveness and quality of training activities.	5
		6.2	Annually, the institution has works of scientific research and innovative ideas of school level or higher to practically serve training activities (at least 1 subject of scientific research and innovative ideas for intermediate institution and at least 2 works of scientific research and innovative ideas for colleges).	
		6.3	Annually, the institution has articles, publications by teachers, administrators, employees, or working staff published on domestic and foreign scientific newspapers and magazines.	
		6.4	The institution's works of scientific research and innovative ideas are put to practical application.	
		6.5	Has training links or implements activities to cooperate with foreign institutions or international organizations; international cooperation activities contribute to the improvement of the institution's training quality.	
7	Financial management	7.1	The institution has and implements regulations on financial management, use and settlement in accordance with regulations and they are publicized.	6
		7.2	Manages and uses revenues from training services; participates in production, business, and service activities in accordance with regulations.	
		7.3	Financial resources ensure sufficient funds for activities of the institution.	
		7.4	Implements the financial management, use, and settlement in accordance with regulations.	
		7.5	Carries out the financial and accounting self-management; conducts audit procedures in accordance with regulations; handles and promptly overcomes problems in the implementation of regulations on financial management and use upon conclusions of competent authorities; conduct financial publicity in accordance with regulations.	
		7.6	Annually, the institution reviews the use of financial resources; has measures to improve the effectiveness of financial management and use to improve the quality of the institution's activities.	
8	Learner services	8.1	Learners are provided with adequate information on training objectives and programs; regulations on examination, tests, and certification of graduation; rules and regulations of the institution; current regimes and policies applicable to learners; conditions to ensure the quality of teaching and learning activities in accordance with regulations.	9
		8.2	Learners enjoy regimes and policies in accordance with regulations.	
		8.3	Has and implements rewarding policies and promptly encourages learners to achieve high performance in studying and training activities. Learners are provided with timely support during their studies at the institution to complete their studies.	
		8.4	Learners are respected and treated equally, regardless of gender, religion, or background origin.	
		8.5	The institution's dormitory provides enough accommodation and minimum conditions (living space, electricity, water, sanitation, other facilities) for learners' living activities and studies.	
		8.6	The institution's health care and catering services meet the needs of learners and assure food hygiene and safety requirements.	
		8.7	Learners are given conditions to engage in singing performance activities, physical training and sports, and social activities with secure safety on the institution's campus.	
		8.8	The institution provides employment counseling for graduated learners.	
		8.9	Annually, the institution organizes or coordinates in organizing a job fair for learners to contact employers.	

continued on next page

Appendix 5 continued

9	Monitoring and assessment of quality	9.1	Annually, gather opinions from at least 10 employers on the extent of responsiveness of graduates working at the employers' facilities.	6
		9.2	Annually, gathers opinions from at least 50% of administrators, teachers, employees, and working staff on policies related to teaching and learning activities, policies on recruitment, training and fostering, assessment, classification, appointment of administrators, teachers, employees, and working staff.	
		9.3	Annually, gathers opinions from at least 30% of learners representing all disciplines and profession on the quality and efficiency of training forms and modes; quality of services, teaching activities, and the implementation of policies related to the institution's learners.	
		9.4	The institution conducts self-assessment and quality accreditation in accordance with regulations.	
		9.5	Annually, the institution has plans and solutions to ensure the improvement of training quality on the basis of the results of self-assessment and external assessment, if any.	
		9.6	The institution has a rate of 80% of learners taking part in jobs suitable with training disciplines or professions within 6 months of graduation.	

Source: Ministry of Labour–Invalids and Social Affairs Circular No. 15/2017/TT-BLDTBXH dated June 2017.

3. Criteria and Standards for Quality Accreditation of Training Programs for Pre-Intermediate Level

	Criteria		Standards	Score Σ=60 (2 points per standard)
1	Objectives and financial management	1.1	The training program's objectives are in line with the objectives of the training institution and the labor market demands; they are publicized, reviewed, and adjusted in accordance with regulations.	4
		1.2	Annually, the training institution studies and determines the minimum spending norms for a learner, ensures the quality of the training program and has sufficient legitimate revenues for implementing it.	
2	Training activities	2.1	Annually, the training institution implements recruitment works in accordance with regulations.	6
		2.2	The training institution has and implements training plans in accordance with regulations; organizes examinations, tests, and assessment of learning and training performance, and grants diplomas or certificates in accordance with regulations; learners' records are complete and in accordance with regulations.	
		2.3	Implements bridge training in accordance with regulations.	
3	Teachers, administrators, and working staff	3.1	100% of teachers participating in teaching activities meet prescribed professional standards for knowledge and skills; annually accomplish tasks assigned by the training institution.	18
		3.2	Ensures adequate classroom teachers for all modules of the training program; ensures the prescribed ratio of number of learners/class and the conversion rate of learners/teacher.	
		3.3	Annually, the training institution arranges for full-time teachers to participate in training and fostering courses; 100% of full-time teachers go for practice sessions at employers' facilities in accordance with regulations.	
		3.4	100% of administrators and working staff meet prescribed professional standards for knowledge and skills; annually accomplish tasks assigned by the training institution.	
4	Programs and curricula	4.1	The training program is developed or selected, evaluated, issued, evaluated, and updated in accordance with regulations.	12
		4.2	The training program represents the amount of knowledge, vocational skills, other necessary skills, and competency requirements that learners are required to achieve upon graduation and in accordance with the national competence level framework and the national standards for occupational skills.	
		4.3	The training program is scientific, accurate, systematic, practical, and suitable with technologies and techniques in production and service activities; and flexible and responsive to changes in technology and the labor market.	
		4.4	The training program represents methods of assessment of learning performance; and determines levels of outcome standards of modules and of the training program.	
		4.5	100% of curricula are compiled or selected, assessed, published, and assessed and updated in accordance with regulations; has sufficient curricula for modules of the training program.	
		4.6	Curricula concretize requirements on the contents of knowledge and skills of each module in the training program; facilitate the implementation of active teaching methods suitable with technologies and techniques in production, business, and service activities.	

continued on next page

Appendix 5 continued

5	Material facilities and training equipment	5.1	Classrooms and electricity and water systems meet construction standards and training requirements.	8
		5.2	Ensures sufficient types and categories of training equipment items to meet requirements of the training program.	
		5.3	Ensures sufficient amount of training equipment items to meet training scales and requirements.	
		5.4	Raw materials and materials for practice activities are arranged neatly and tidily; managed, allocated, and used in accordance with regulations; and meet the training schedule and progress.	
6	Learner services	6.1	Learners are provided adequate information on the training program; training regulations; regulations on student affairs; regulations on examination, tests, and certification of graduation; rules and regulations of the training institution; current regimes and policies applicable to learners; and learners enjoy regimes and policies in accordance with regulations.	4
		6.2	Learners are provided regularly with information on occupations, labor markets and employment, and support and job referral for graduated learners.	
7	Monitoring and assessment of quality	7.1	Annually, gather opinions from at least 10 employers on the extent of responsiveness of graduates working at the employers' facilities and the suitability of the training program with actual conditions of production, business, and service responsiveness of graduates.	8
		7.2	Conducts traceability surveys of graduates to collect information on employment, assess the training quality of the training institution and the suitability of the training program with job positions assumed by the graduates.	
		7.3	At least 80% of learners take part in suitable jobs with training disciplines or professions within 6 months of graduation.	
		7.4	At least 80% of employers surveyed are satisfied with the knowledge, skills, self-reliance, and professional responsibility of graduates working at the employers' facilities.	

Source: Ministry of Labour–Invalids and Social Affairs Circular No. 15/2017/TT-BLDTBXH dated June 2017.

4. Criteria, Standard Scores, and Assessment Scores for Quality Accreditation of Training Programs for Intermediate and College Level

	Criteria		Standards	Score Σ=96 (2 points per standard)
1	Objectives, administration, and financial management	1.1	The training program's objectives are in line with the objectives of the training institution and the labor market demands; they are publicized, reviewed, and adjusted in accordance with regulations.	6
		1.2	The training institution has written assignment of specific tasks to the department/unit in charge of the training program and units involved in implementing the training program; the department/unit in charge of the training program accomplishes the assigned tasks related to the training program.	
		1.3	Annually, the training institution studies and determines the minimum spending norms for a learner, ensures the quality of the training program and has sufficient legitimate revenues for implementing the training program.	
2	Training activities	2.1	Annually, the training institution implements recruitment works in accordance with regulations; the enrollment rate reaches at least 80% of planned targets of the training institution.	14
		2.2	The training institution has and implements training plans in accordance with regulations.	
		2.3	Applies training methods in line with contents of the training program, combining practice training with training of specialized knowledge; promotes positive, self-consciousness, dynamic qualities, and the ability to work independently of learners, and organizes teamwork activities; applies information technology and communication in teaching and learning activities.	
		2.4	The training institution coordinates with the employers in organizing and guiding learners in practice activities at employers' facilities; 100% of learners before graduation practice at employers' facilities suitable to their trained disciplines or professions.	
		2.5	Organizes examinations, tests, and assessment of learning and training performance, and grants diplomas or certificates in accordance with regulations; learners' records are complete and in accordance with regulations.	
		2.6	Organizes the inspection and supervision of teaching and learning activities in accordance with regulations; uses test results to timely adjust teaching and learning activities accordingly.	
		2.7	Implements bridge training in accordance with regulations.	
3	Teachers, administrators, and working staff	3.1	100% of teachers participating in teaching activities meet prescribed professional standards for knowledge and skills.	16
		3.2	Annually, 100% of teachers accomplish tasks assigned by the training institution.	
		3.3	Ensures adequate classroom teachers for all modules and subjects of the training program; ensures the prescribed ratio of number of learners/class and the conversion rate of learners/teacher.	
		3.4	Annually, at least 50% of full-time teachers teaching specialized subjects and disciplines participate in scientific research, outstanding teachers' competitions, and self-made equipment competitions of all levels.	
		3.5	Annually, the training institution arranges for full-time teachers to participate in training and fostering courses.	
		3.6	100% of full-time teachers go for practice sessions at employers' facilities in accordance with regulations.	
		3.7	100% of administrators and working staff meet prescribed professional standards for knowledge and skills.	
		3.8	Annually, 100% of administrators and working staff accomplish tasks assigned by the training institution.	

continued on next page

Appendix 5 continued

4	Programs and curricula	4.1	The training program is developed or selected, evaluated, issued, evaluated, and updated in accordance with regulations.	24
		4.2	Engages the participation of at least two employers in the formulation and appraisal of the training program.	
		4.3	The training program represents the amount of knowledge, vocational skills, other necessary skills, and competency requirements for learners to achieve upon graduation.	
		4.4	The training program represents the distribution of time and sequence of modules and subjects to ensure the achievement of vocational education objectives.	
		4.5	The training program represents the minimum requirements of facilities and teachers to implement the training program to ensure the quality of training activities.	
		4.6	The training program represents methods of assessment of learning performance and determines levels of outcome standards of modules and subjects of the training program.	
		4.7	The training program is in line with the development requirements of sectors, localities, and the country, and is suitable with technologies and techniques in production and service activities.	
		4.8	The training program ensures the interlinking and connectivity of training levels in the national education system.	
		4.9	Has sufficient curricula for modules and subjects of the training program.	
		4.10	100% of curricula are compiled or selected, assessed, published, assessed, and updated in accordance with regulations.	
		4.11	Training curricula concretize requirements on the contents of knowledge and skills of each module or subject in the training program; curricula contents are suitable to implement active teaching methods.	
		4.12	Curricula contents are suitable with technologies and techniques in production and service activities.	
5	Material facilities, training equipment, and libraries	5.1	Classrooms, laboratories, practice workshops, electricity and water systems meet construction standards and training requirements.	16
		5.2	Ensures sufficient types and categories of training equipment items to meet requirements of the training program.	
		5.3	Ensures sufficient amount of training equipment items to meet training scales and requirements.	
		5.4	Training equipment and tools in service of training activities are arranged rationally, safely, and conveniently for practice activities; ensure the requirements of pedagogy, occupational safety, industrial health and safety and environmental hygiene; training equipment items have clear management records, are used properly, and managed and maintained in accordance with regulations.	
		5.5	Raw materials and materials for practice activities are arranged neatly, tidily, and conveniently; are managed, allocated, and used in accordance with regulations; meets the training schedule and progress.	
		5.6	The library has sufficient programs and curricula approved by the training institution; the curriculum has at least five copies and meets the needs for study and reference of teachers and learners; has sufficient books, magazines, and reference materials with a minimum rate of five book titles/learner; 100% of programs and curricula are digitized and integrated into the digital library to serve effectively for training activities.	
		5.7	The library is equipped with computers and internet connection to meet teaching, learning, and documenting needs.	
		5.8	Has virtual software for simulation of actual teaching devices in teaching activities.	

continued on next page

Appendix 5 continued

6	Learner services	6.1	Learners are provided with adequate information on the training program; training regulations; regulations on student affairs; regulations on examination, tests, and certification of graduation; rules and regulations of the training institution; current regimes and policies applicable to learners.	4
		6.2	Learners enjoy regimes and policies in accordance with regulations; the training institution has and implements rewarding policies and promptly encourages learners to achieve high performance in studying and training activities; it provides counseling and support for learners in the learning process.	
		6.3	Annually, the training institution provides learners with information on occupations, labor markets, and employment; and provides support and job referral for graduated learners.	
		6.4	The training institution implements the diversification of social activities, cultural and artistic activities, and physical training and sports activities for the interest of learners.	
7	Monitoring and assessment of quality	7.1	Annually, gather opinions from at least 10 employers on the extent of responsiveness of graduates working at the employers' facilities and the suitability of the training program with actual conditions of production, business, and service responsiveness of graduates.	16
		7.2	Conducts traceability surveys of graduates to collect information on employment, assess the training quality of the training institution and the suitability of the training program with job positions assumed by the graduates.	
		7.3	Annually, gathers opinions from at least 50% of teachers and administrators on contents related to teaching and learning, recruitment, appointment, fostering, classification, and assessment of teachers and administrators.	
		7.4	Annually, gathers opinions from at least 30% of learners on the quality and efficiency of training forms and modes, teaching quality, the implementation of regimes and policies and services for learners.	
		7.5	The training institution shall conduct the quality self-assessment of the training program in accordance with regulations.	
		7.6	Annually, the training institution has plans and solutions to ensure the improvement of the quality of the training program on the basis of the results of self-assessment and external assessment, if any.	
		7.7	At least 80% of learners take part in jobs suitable with training disciplines or professions within 6 months of graduation.	
		7.8	At least 80% of employers surveyed are satisfied with the knowledge, skills, self-reliance, and professional responsibility of graduates working at the employers' facilities.	

Source: Ministry of Labour–Invalids and Social Affairs Circular No. 15/2017/TT-BLDTBXH dated June 2017.

5. Piloted Criteria, Standards, and Indicators for Accreditation of High-Quality TVET Institutions

	Criteria	Standards and Indicators		Score Σ=100 Pass: ≥ 80 Criterion ≥ 50%
1	Practice- and demand-oriented training implementation	**1.1 Ongoing and planned training courses are relevant to demands of the labor market.**		8
		1.1.1	At least 80% of graduates find training-related employment within 1 year after graduation. The rate for national, regional, and international focal occupations should reach at least 90%.	3
		1.1.2	The TVET institute delivers further training for employees of enterprises.	2
		1.1.3	Annual implementation of training needs assessment and the results show that the TVET institute is providing occupations that are relevant to the demand of employers and the labor market.	2
		1.2 Practice and demand-oriented training is implemented.		6
		1.2.1	Competence of employed graduates are evaluated by enterprises as fulfilling most of the job requirements.	2
		1.2.2	High proportion of practical training (at least 70% of total training time) is related to the world of work.	2
		1.2.3	Training programs, training materials, and equipment reflect the integration of theoretical and practical training contents.	2
		1.3 Flexible and updated training programs and materials are available.		3
		1.3.1	Training programs are periodically (every 3 years) reviewed and updated to conform to new technologies in production, business, and services.	1
		1.3.2	Training materials match the training program requirements.	1
		1.3.3	Training programs are divided into modules/credits to ensure permeability (moving to different levels or occupations).	1
		1.4 Training programs in regional and international occupations meet regional and international standards.		2
		1.4.1	Occupational standards and learning outcomes of training programs in regional and international occupations are equivalent to regional and international standards.	2
		1.5 Supportive measures for students are implemented during and after training.		2
		1.5.1	Alumni events and job orientation programs are organized yearly.	2
		1.6 Training policy is gender oriented and inclusive.		2
		1.6.1	A gender-oriented and inclusive training policy is in place and implemented.	1
		1.6.2	Physical facilities are appropriate for delivering training courses for disadvantaged groups.	1

continued on next page

Appendix 5 continued

2	Cooperation with enterprises in training	**2.1 Training is implemented in cooperation with enterprises.**		8
		2.1.1	In-company training phases (internship) for students are organized according to training program.	2
		2.1.2	The TVET institute council has at least one representative from enterprise/industry/professional association.	2
		2.1.3	Currently, the TVET institute has cooperation with at least 10 enterprises, and all national, regional, international focal occupations of the TVET institute have cooperation with at least one enterprise.	2
		2.1.4	The TVET institute has department or personnel assigned to promote cooperation with enterprises.	2
		2.2 Cooperative training is implemented for at least one occupation.		10
		2.2.1	Enterprise/professional associations participate in developing occupational standards and learning outcomes.	2
		2.2.2	Enterprise/professional associations participate in developing training programs.	2
		2.2.3	Enterprise implements in-company training in accordance with training program or plan.	2
		2.2.4	Enterprise/professional associations participate in one of the following phases: examination, assessment, and certification of students' learning results.	2
		2.4.5	Cooperation and/or regular knowledge exchange exists with in-company trainers (including pedagogical know-how).	2
		2.3 The institute cooperates closely with enterprises and the Viet Nam Chamber of Commerce and Industry or sector associations to promote cooperative training.		4
		2.3.1	Cooperative training agreement is signed.	2
		2.3.2	Meetings on cooperative training are organized three times a year at least.	2
3	Competence of teachers and managers	**3.1 Teachers and managers have high-quality and practice-oriented competence.**		12
		3.1.1	Teachers have practical work experience in enterprise and/or economic, technical sectors in respective occupational fields.	4
		3.1.2	Practical teachers possess national occupational skills certificate grade 3 or higher.	2
		3.1.3	Teachers participate in internships/further training/visits to enterprises according to regulations (at least 2 weeks per year).	3
		3.1.4	Teachers meet requirements on qualification (excluding occupational skills) and pedagogical skills.	3
		3.2 Management staff members have appropriate competency.		6
		3.2.1	Assignment (task, position) of management staff is suitable for their educational background.	3
		3.2.2	Management staff has knowledge (certificate/diploma on educational management or certificate of a training course on school/TVET institute management) and experience in similar tasks (e.g., in operating TVET institute/subordinate units).	3

continued on next page

Appendix 5 continued

4	Efficiency of organizational setup	**4.1 The number of TVET staff is appropriate.**		3
		4.1.1	Teacher/student ratio is 1/15 for technical class and 1/25 for nontechnical class.	2
		4.1.2	Ratio of management and administrative staff per student is 1/40–60.	1
		4.2 Appropriate training workshops are in place and used.		3
		4.2.1	Three-layer practical workshops for occupations are set up and frequently used (the first layer workshop is intended for cross-occupational skills, the second-layer workshop is intended for specific occupational skills, the third-layer workshop is intended for general skills, tasks in the real working context).	2
		4.2.2	Sufficient safety equipment is available and used.	1
		4.3 Equipment is managed and maintained according to procedure.		3
		4.3.1	Staff in charge of maintenance of physical facilities and equipment are assigned and their tasks are well implemented.	1
		4.3.2	Maintenance of physical facilities and equipment is conducted according to procedure.	2
		4.4 Attracting and retaining qualified personnel is possible.		2
		4.4.1	Performance-related incentives for motivating teachers and management staff are in place and used.	2
		4.5 Internal and external communication strategy is in place and implemented.		3
		4.5.1	TVET marketing strategy is in place.	1
		4.5.2	TVET marketing activities are organized yearly.	1
		4.5.3	Website and TVET institute flyers and brochures are published and updated regularly.	1
		4.6 Internal quality management and assurance is set up and implemented.		2
		4.6.1	The TVET institute implements at least four of the following quality management activities: (1) teachers deliver feedback on management staff, (2) management staff deliver feedback on teachers, (3) students deliver feedback on teachers after each module/subject, (4) tracer studies, (5) enterprise surveys, (6) practical workshop management instruments, and (7) lesson observations.	1
		4.6.2	Results from quality management activities are used yearly to improve training quality.	1
		4.7 Organizational structure is appropriate.		4
		4.7.1	Units, departments, and divisions have clear task assignments and job descriptions.	1
		4.7.2	The TVET institute management board is active and creative in TVET institute management work.	1
		4.7.3	Autonomous enrollment management unit is set up.	1
		4.7.4	A job placement unit operates efficiently.	1

continued on next page

Appendix 5 continued

		4.8 Enrollment is demand oriented.		2
		4.8.1	Enrollment is aligned with the demand of socioeconomic development and human resources development (HRD) plan of locality, sector, and enterprise.	2
		4.9 Learning environment is friendly.		4
		4.9.1	Canteen, sports facilities, dorm, library, and health center are available and meet students' demand.	2
		4.9.2	Incentive activities for students are in place and frequently implemented.	2
		4.10 Programs and activities are digitalized and computerized.		4
		4.10.1	TVET institute's management activities are computerized.	2
		4.10.2	Training programs of national, regional, and international focal occupations are digitalized and computerized.	2
5	Sufficient financial means	**5.1 Institutional guarantees.**		2
		5.1.1	The TVET institute's 5-year development plan/strategy with expected financial resources for implementation is available.	2
		5.2 Financial resources are available to recover current costs, and sufficient reserves are available for reinvestment.		5
		5.2.1	The TVET institute has financial sources for training delivery in the last 2 years, the current year, and the next 2 years.	5

Source: As presented in the Final DVET/GIZ/KOICA Workshop on the Revision of the Criteria for High-Quality Vocational Institutes/Centers of Excellence. Ha Noi. 11 July 2017.

6. Piloted Criterion, Standards, and Indicators for High-Quality TVET Institutions to Be Accredited as Centers of Excellence

6	Additional functions to be fulfilled by Centers of Excellence	**6.1 The TVET institute delivers further training on core occupations for teachers and in-company trainers:**		12
		6.1.1	Teachers have high qualification and practical work experience.	
			(a) Teachers possess international pedagogical certificate/diploma.	2
			(b) Teachers have practical work experience in enterprises/economic, and technical sectors in relevant occupational fields.	2
			(c) Teachers have certificates of English language proficiency of level B1 of the Common European Framework of Reference for Languages (CEFR) or level 3 of the Vietnamese Framework for Foreign Languages (VFFL) or higher level; English teachers have CEFR certificate B2 or VFFL level 4 or higher or an equivalent certificate in line with regulations (for English or another foreign language).	2
		6.1.2	Appropriate technical infrastructure and sufficiently equipped training workshop (three-layer practical workshop) is available to provide further training for teachers of other TVET institutes.	2
		6.1.3	The TVET institute provides further training for theoretical/practical teachers and in-company trainers to improve occupational competency.	4
		6.2 Advisory service is provided to management staff of other TVET institutes regarding organization of labor market-relevant training offers:		6
		6.2.1	The TVET institute provides further training/advisory service for management staff of other TVET institutes with regard to organization of cooperative training (for long-term training courses, e.g., courses at collegial or intermediate level, not for short-term training courses).	4

continued on next page

Appendix 5 continued

6	Additional functions to be fulfilled by Centers of Excellence	6.2.2	The TVET institute has profound experience in the following areas: demand analysis, development of vocational training plan, development and implementation of new vocational training programs, workshop organization and maintenance, cooperation with industry, vocational training quality management, and tracer studies.	2	
		6.3 The TVET institute acts as a hub for national and international networks for TVET.			12
		6.3.1	The TVET institute cooperates with leading international companies, associations, and training institutes.	2	
		6.3.2	Management staff is able to communicate fluently in English (CEFR level B1 or VFFL level 3 or higher or equivalent certificate in line with current regulations).	2	
		6.3.3	The TVET institute has a department for international cooperation in which its staff possesses English certificates of CEFR level B2 or VFFL level 4 or higher or equivalent certificate in line with current regulations.	2	
		6.3.4	The TVET institute delivers training for foreign students and arranges internships for staff of other training institutes.	4	
		6.3.5	The TVET institute is a member of a professional network, regional, and international association.	2	
		6.4 The TVET institute is a partner for TVET reform and applied research activities.			10
		6.4.1	The TVET institute regularly invites experts on training methods, quality management, and applied research in the TVET sector to share/exchange experience.	2	
		6.4.2	The TVET institute conducts applied research (e.g., technological forecast and research on impacts of new technologies in vocational training).	2	
		6.4.3	The TVET institute implements one of the following pilot projects for training: new training courses, new training forms, contents, methods, module/credit-based training, cooperative training or others.	2	
		6.4.4	The TVET institute delivers training, further training on tools (database on training management, development of training programs, technology transfer and tracer studies) for other TVET institutes.	2	
		6.4.5	The TVET institute acts as an information resources center (regularly organizes conferences, seminars, open days, creative competitions among TVET institutes).	2	
		6.5 The TVET institute is an assessment and certification center.			10
		6.5.1	The TVET institute acts as an assessment and certification center for core occupations against occupational standards/learning outcomes/training programs, which are recognized as equivalent to international standards for students of the TVET institute or of other TVET institutes.	4	
		6.5.2	Staff who develop exam questions and/or scores exam papers should be recognized.	2	
		6.5.3	The TVET institute is a place for assessment and certification of occupational skills for all relevant subjects.	4	

Source: As presented in the Final DVET/GIZ/KOICA Workshop on the Revision of the Criteria for High-Quality Vocational Institutes/Centers of Excellence. Ha Noi. 11 July 2017.

Appendix 6. Dimensions and Flow of Education Financing in Viet Nam

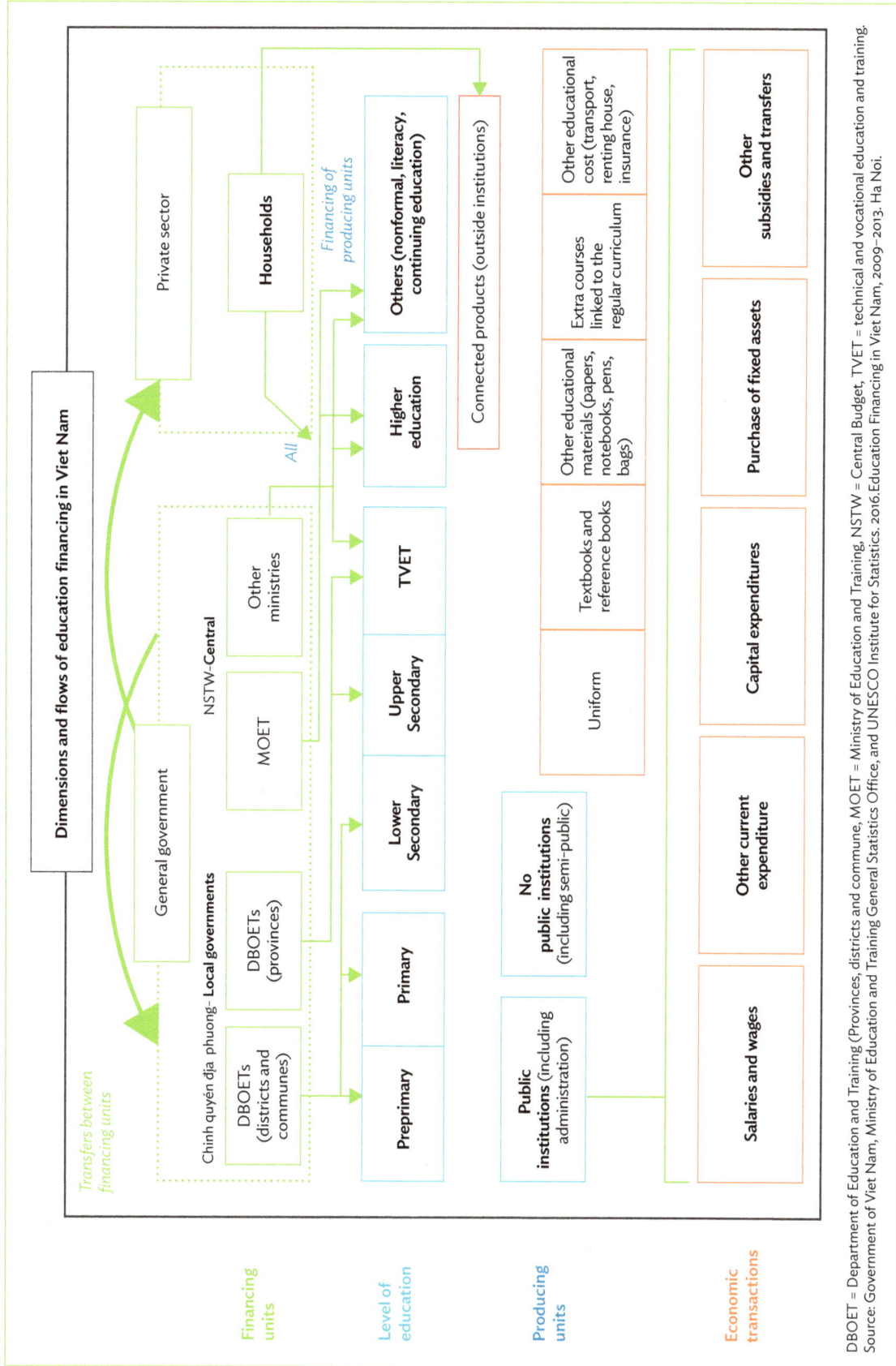

Dimensions and flows of education financing in Viet Nam

Transfers between financing units

Financing units

General government

Private sector

Households

Chính quyền địa phương– **Local governments**

NSTW–**Central**

DBOETs (districts and communes)

DBOETs (provinces)

MOET

Other ministries

Level of education

Preprimary

Primary

Lower Secondary

Upper Secondary

TVET

Higher education

Others (nonformal, literacy, continuing education)

Financing of producing units

All

Producing units

Public institutions (including administration)

No public institutions (including semi-public)

Connected products (outside institutions)

Economic transactions

Salaries and wages

Other current expenditure

Capital expenditures

Purchase of fixed assets

Other subsidies and transfers

Uniform

Textbooks and reference books

Other educational materials (papers, notebooks, pens, bags)

Extra courses linked to the regular curriculum

Other educational cost (transport, renting house, insurance)

DBOET = Department of Education and Training (Provinces, districts and commune, MOET = Ministry of Education and Training, NSTW = Central Budget, TVET = technical and vocational education and training.
Source: Government of Viet Nam, Ministry of Education and Training General Statistics Office, and UNESCO Institute for Statistics. 2016. Education Financing in Viet Nam, 2009–2013. Ha Noi.

Appendix 7. Synopsis of Policies and Regulations for TVET (2015–2017)

1. At Government – Prime Minister Level

1.1 Policies Issued until October 2017

No.	Policy or Regulation Title	Type and Code	Date
1	Stipulating the Mechanism for Exercising the Autonomy of Public Administrative Units	Decree No. 16/2015/NĐ-CP	14 February 2015
2	Guidelines for Law on Vocational Education and Training	Decree No. 48/2015/NĐ-CP	15 May 2015
3	Prescribing Penalties for Administrative Violations against Regulations of TVET Sector	Decree No. 79/2015/NĐ-CP	14 September 2015
4	Policies on Support for Basic Training Courses and Short-Term Training Courses (less than 3 months)	Decision No. 46/2015/QĐ-TTg	28 September 2015
5	Prescribing the Mechanism for Collection and Management of Tuition Fees Applicable to Educational Institutions in the National Education System and Policies on Tuition Fee Exemption and Reduction and Financial Support from Academic Year 2015–2016 to 2020–2021	Decree No. 86/2015/NĐ-CP	2 October 2015
6	Policies on Dormitory for Students of Secondary School and Colleges	Decision No. 53/2015/QĐ-TTg	20 October 2015
7	Prescribing on Providing Special Allowances, Supplements, Responsibility Allowances and Allowances for Work in Heavy, Harmful and Dangerous Situations for Teachers in Public TVET Institutions	Decree No. 113/2015/NĐ-CP	9 November 2015
8	Approval of the International Integration Strategy with regard to Labor and Society towards 2020, with a Vision towards 2030	Decision No. 145/QĐ-TTg	20 January 2016
9	Instruction to Provide Autonomy in the Period 2016–2019 to HCMC Technical College, LILAMA 2 Industrial College, and Quy Nhon Vocational College including the Establishment of Independent Fee Structure and College Management	Decisions No. 538, 539, and 540 QĐ-TTg	4 April 2016
10	Detailing Provisions on the Conditions for Investment and Operation in the TVET Sector	Decree No. 143/2016/NĐ-CP	14 October 2016
11	Approval for Vietnamese Qualifications Framework	Decision No. 1982/QĐ-TTg	18 October 2016
12	Stipulating Functions, Duties, Authorities and Organization Structure of the MOLISA	Decree No. 14/2017/ND-CP	17 February 2017
13	Approving the Target Program on Vocational Education, Employment and Occupational Safety for the Period 2016–2020	Decision No. 899/QĐ-TTg	20 June 2017
14	Regulating Functions, Responsibilities, Rights, and Organization of GDVT, Including an Inspection Function	Decision No. 29/1017/QĐ-TTg	2 July 2017
15	On Organization and Operations of the Inspectorates of Labor, Invalids and Social Affairs Sector	Decree No. 110/2017/ND-CP	4 October 2017

1.2 Policies and Regulations Expected to Be Issued by December 2017

No.	Policy or Regulation
16	Prescribing accreditation of TVET schools and programs
17	Regulation on the autonomy mechanism of public service delivery units/agencies in TVET sector
18	Decree on defining the responsibilities of enterprises in TVET sector
19	Decree on international cooperation in vocational education and training
20	Decision on approving the network of TVET institutions
21	Decision on "Project on Reforms and Quality Improvement of Vocational Education and Training 2017–2020 Period, Orientation up to 2030"
22	Decision on approving "The High Quality Vocational School Development Project by 2020" (Revised version of Decision No. 761/QD-TTg from 23 May 2014)

2. At the Level of MOLISA and Other Ministries

2.1 Regulations Issued until May 2017

No.	Regulation Title	Code	Date
1	Circular on the Registration of TVET Activities, Issuance and Revocation of Certificate of Registration of TVET Activities and Suspension of TVET Activities at Primary Level	Circular No. 25/2015/TT-BLĐTBXH	13 July 2015
2	Circular on the Technical and Professional Standards and Working Conditions of Primary Level Training Teacher	Circular No. 40/2015/TT-BLĐTBXH	20 October 2015
3	Circular on the Use, Standardized Training and Advanced Training for Primary-Level Training Teacher	Circular No. 41/2015/TT-BLĐTBXH	20 October 2015
4	Circular on Training at Primary Level	Circular No. 42/2015/TT-BLĐTBXH	20 October 2015
5	Circular on Continuing Vocational Education and Training	Circular No. 43/2015/TT-BLĐTBXH	20 October 2015
6	Circular on Rules of TVET Centers	Circular No. 57/2015/TT-BLĐTBXH	25 December 2015
7	Guidelines for a Number of Articles of Decree No. 86/2015/ND-CP, Providing for the Mechanism on Collection and Management of Tuitions in Educational Institutions under the National Education System and Exemption from or Reduction of Tuitions, and Learning Costs Support Policies from the Academic Year 2015–2016 to 2020–2021	Joint Circular No. 09/2016/TTLT-BGDĐT-BTC-BLĐTBXH	30 March 2016
8	Circular on Guiding the Implementation of a Number of Articles of Decree No. 31/2015/ND-CP Dated 24 March 2015, Detailing the Implementation of a Number of Articles of the Employment Law regarding National Skills Testing and Certification	Circular No. 9/2016/TT-BLĐTBXH	28 June 2016
9	Management and Allocation of Subsidies to Basic Training and Under-Three-Month Training Courses	Circular No. 152/2016/TT-BTC	17 October 2016
10	Regulations on Rules of College I	Circular No. 46/2016/TT BLĐTBXH	28 December 2016
11	Regulations on Rules of Secondary School	Circular No. 47/2016/TT-BLĐTBXH	28 December 2016
12	Regulations on the Process of Formulating, Evaluating and Promulgating the Program; Organizing the Compilation, Selection and Appraisal of Curriculum at Secondary and College Level	Circular No. 03/2017/TT-BLĐTBXH	1 March 2017

continued on next page

Appendix 7 continued

13	Promulgating the List of Occupation and Industry at Level IV for Secondary and College Level	Circular No. 04/2017/TT-BLĐTBXH	2 March 2017
14	Regulations of Enrollment and Determination of Enrollment Targets at Intermediate and College Level	Circular No. 05/2017/TT-BLĐTBXH	2 March 2017
15	Providing the Recruitment, Employment, and Training of Vocational Teachers	Circular No. 06/2017/TT-BLĐTBXH	8 March 2017
16	Prescribing the Working Regime Applicable to Vocational Teachers	Circular No. 07/2017/TT-BLĐTBXH	10 March 2017
17	Prescribing Professional Standards Applicable to Vocational Teachers	Circular No. 08/2017/TT-BLĐTBXH	10 March 2017
18	Prescribing the Organization of Implementation of Intermediate- and Collegial-Level Training Programs by School Year or by Accumulation of Modules or Credits; and Regulations on Examination, Testing, and Graduation Recognition	Circular No. 09/2017/TT-BLĐTBXH	13 March 2017
19	Regulations on Certificate Format of Secondary and College; Printing, Management, Issuance, Withdrawal, Abolishment for Secondary and College Certificate	Circular No. 10/2017/TT-BLĐTBXH	13 March 2017
20	Regulation on Minimum Volume of Knowledge and Requirements on Capabilities that Trainees Must Gain upon Their Graduation Corresponding to Secondary and College Level of TVET	Circular No. 12/2017/TT-BLĐTBXH	20 April 2017
21	Circular on Development, Appraisal, and Issuance of Economic-Technical Norms Applied on Training of TVET Sector	Circular No. 14/2017/TT-BLĐTBXH	25 May 2017
22	Regulations on Criteria and Standards for Accreditation of Vocational Education and Training	Circular No. 15/2017/TT-BLĐTBXH	8 June 2017

2.2 Regulations Expected to Be Issued by December 2017

No.	Name
23	Circular on ranking of TVET institutions
24	Circular on the title of TVET teachers/trainer
25	Circular on transferring credits to a higher degree in training
26	Circular on the recognition of equivalent certificates in vocational education and training
27	Circular on criteria of high-quality TVET school

Appendix 8. Ministry of Labour–Invalids and Social Affairs TVET Reform Project

List of Proposed Tasks and Solutions

MAJOR TASKS AND SOLUTIONS

1. Renovate and improve the effectiveness and efficiency of state management of vocational training.

(a) Improve in uniformity legal documents on implementation of the legislation on TVET and other related laws. Develop strategies, programs, and projects for TVET development during 2021–2030.

(b) Strongly decentralize the state management of vocational training to ministries, sectors, and localities.

(c) Develop the capacity of TVET state management agencies at all levels including the establishment of a national TVET information management system, ensuring the connectivity between state management agencies in charge of TVET at all levels and TVET institutions; build systems of linkages between supply and demand of training in vocational education.

(d) Consolidate policies toward teachers, students, post-training workers/employees, and enterprises, and employers.

(e) Renovate funding and state budget investment structures and methods for the TVET sector, including the demand to arrange funding of TVET at a rate of 20%–22% in total state budget expenditure for education and training and a list of priority areas and beneficiaries to be funded. Structural improvements shall be achieved by (i) shifting from regular budget allocations to TVET institutions to the mode of bidding and orders, and (ii) assigning public service delivery tasks on the basis of competition in quality, efficiency, and outputs, giving priority to TVET institutions meeting TVET quality accreditation standards.

(f) Continue to renovate, improve policies on, and settle difficulties and problems of land, tax, and credit to promote socialization and encourage and mobilize domestic and foreign enterprises, employers, and various economic sectors to get involved in TVET development.

2. Grant full autonomy to vocational education institutions in association with measures that ensure enhanced accountability, independent assessment mechanisms, state control, social monitoring mechanisms, and improved administration capacity of TVET institutions.

2.1. Improved task performance through autonomy. TVET institutions shall be entitled to autonomy in performing tasks, organizing structures, personnel and finance in accordance with road maps depending on capacity, sector, occupation, and locality.

2.1.1. Task performance

Autonomous task performance shall be related to independent decisions on course portfolio, program design (so far based on occupational standards and socioeconomic needs) and training formats (e.g., modularization), and methods as well as on the determination of enrollment scales, which must comply with endorsed state regulations on training process quality standards for respective vocational majors.

2.1.2. Organizational structure and personnel

Autonomy in structural organization includes independent decisions on establishment, merging, and dissolution of institutional units or association (e.g., joint ventures) with private organizations (e.g., in sharing resources), so far these will be cost neutral for state budgets and promote economic efficiency and operational effectiveness.

Autonomous personnel management shall cover recruitment, appointment and deployment, and development, rewarding but also disciplining and dismissal of teachers, managers, and workers in TVET institutions.

2.1.3. Financial independence

Autonomy in financing relates to a staged approach for granting public institutions permissions to self-control income and revenues (from nonproductive services) as well as expenditures and even to launch investment projects including the right to contract loan agreements with private investors. Depending on the proven capacity of TVET institutions to operate independently from traditional state subsidies, they shall become gradually eligible to adjust their service prices (including admission and tuition fees) to market demands and fully act as business units, provided they will transparently publish their cost calculations and annual balance sheets to the public.

2.2. **Independent assessments** shall ensure the quality and effectiveness of training. Assessment results shall be published to monitor the development of TVET by the state and the society.

2.3. **Accountability structures.** TVET institutions shall periodically publish their quality-ensuring conditions, results of quality accreditation as well as their outcomes regarding employment rates of their graduates. The role of school boards shall be strengthened.

2.4. **Modern management systems and administrative capacity building.** By 2020, 50% of colleges, 30% of intermediate level institutions, 10% of TVET centers, and by 2030, 100% of colleges, 100% of intermediate level institutions, 30% TVET centers, shall have advanced and modern internal quality control and management systems, apply information technology to build a management information system, and improve the capacity of administrators and teachers in charge of management and quality assurance through training. By 2020, training in management and quality control shall be provided for 70% of all managers and 5% of teachers in TVET institutions. By 2030, 80% of school administrators at all levels and 20% of teachers in TVET institutions shall have participated in respective trainings.

3. Improve TVET institution network planning.

(a) The network of TVET institutions shall be reviewed and rearranged in the direction of standardization, reduction of contact points, increase of enrollment scales, and improvement of the quality and efficiency of operations. Reform options include the dissolution of ineffectively and inefficiently operating institutions, improvement of scales of efficiency by merging overlapping structures, stratification of four institutional quality levels (national minimum standard quality, national high quality, ASEAN quality, and international quality), push to self-reliance and financial autonomy through pilot privatizations, promotion of new ownership models (e.g., foreign-owned institutions and community colleges) as well as the perpetuation of the trend toward multidisciplinary and multilevel TVET institutions.

(b) For a number of specific occupations, economic sectors, and subjects (e.g., health care, culture and arts, service for people with disabilities) special TVET sectors and key institutions shall be established.

4. Standardize vocational training quality assurance conditions.

4.1. Development and promulgation of national quality assurance standards in collaboration with employers and professional associations, including (i) output standards for all occupational majors at each training level (for national key occupations by 2020); (ii) corresponding standards for TVET facilities and equipment; (iii) qualification, work, and employment standards for teachers and administrators in public TVET institutions and for trainers/instructors in enterprises; (iv) major specific sets of economic-technical norms for cost calculation of training courses at each training level (for national key occupations by 2020); and (v) adequate quality accreditation criteria and standards as well as process standards for evaluation of TVET institutions and programs at different quality levels.

4.2. Standardization of core quality assurance factors such as (i) the development of outcome-oriented and modularized training curricula, reform of corresponding training delivery modes as well as relevant assessment forms, procedures, and methods; (ii) the development of appropriate contingents of qualified teachers and school managers; and (iii) the enhancement and standardization of TVET facilities and equipment.

4.2.1. **Curriculum development** shall be based on national occupational standards, focus on outcomes that will address also industry-relevant soft skills, allow for flexible pathways (permeability) across training levels and among similar occupational groups, and integrate a set of generic but TVET-relevant subjects. A key focus shall be put on curricula for graduates in need as well as on piloting 16 sets of advanced training programs being transferred from foreign countries, which shall be accompanied by special English language components. **Training delivery** shall gradually move to credit-based modularization, apply advanced training technologies (including information and communication technology) from developed countries, and promote activeness, proactiveness, creativeness, and the application of knowledge and skills acquired by students. **Assessments and examinations** shall be adjusted to accumulative structures (credit points). College diplomas in some occupational majors shall be upgraded to titles equivalent to higher education degrees (e.g., "practical engineer" or "practical bachelor"), and graduation in training programs adopted from foreign countries shall be awarded with two diplomas (national and country of origin). Overall enterprises and professional associations shall be encouraged to participate in training assessment at TVET institutions and the establishment of an assessment and certification agency shall be piloted with support of foreign organizations.

4.2.2. **Solutions for the development of vocational teachers** include further development and decentralized expansion of teacher training institutions at universities and colleges (about 60 by 2020). Enterprises shall be encouraged to organize probation periods for teachers to improve or update their occupational skills. Further professional development of teachers shall be enhanced and extended to fulfill standard qualification requirements regarding pedagogical competence, occupational skills, informatics, foreign language, new technology knowledge, and soft skills at different institutional levels. Training for managers at TVET institutions shall be standardized and reach 70% of management staff by 2020 and 100% by 2030, of which 5% shall be trained in foreign countries by 2020 (respectively 20%, by 2030). Special trainings shall address the capacity of all school managers (80% by 2020 and 100% by 2020) to manage and efficiently use vocational training facilities and equipment.

4.2.3. **Investment in physical facilities and equipment** that fulfill standard requirements of the relevant curricula is seen as important "to create a friendly and modern learning environment satisfying the learners' learning needs and activities." Proposed solutions include multipurpose and specialized classrooms, application of simulation software in teaching activities, access to "open e-learning materials centers," utilization of enterprise facilities during internships, and self-manufacturing of equipment by TVET institutions.

5. Strengthen vocational training quality accreditation.

(a) By 2020, 20 quality accreditation organizations shall be set up (30 organizations by 2030).

(b) Staff for TVET quality accreditation shall comprise teachers, TVET managers, researchers in TVET and experts, people experienced in manufacturing, trading and service.

(c) By 2020, 100% of institutions targeted for investment to become high-quality TVET institutions shall be accredited, of which 50% will be colleges, 30% technical high schools, and 10% TVET centers. Of these institutions, 60% shall deliver training programs for national focal occupations. By 2030, 100% of colleges and technical high school and 70% of TVET centers shall be accredited, and 90% of institutions shall deliver training programs of national key occupations.

(d) Issue state orders for quality inspection of TVET institutions.

(e) Three quality levels shall stratify quality evaluation of training programs: high-quality training programs, training programs approaching ASEAN levels, and those of developed countries in the G20 group.

6. Link TVET with labor markets, decent work, and social security.

(a) Improve quality of forecasts for human resources needs, employment demands, and training needs according to fields, occupation, and training levels.

(b) Establish a career orientation and consultancy system at secondary, high schools, TVET institutions, and for workers/employees.

(c) Study and implement startup business models for learners after TVET completion.

(d) Establish close relationships between TVET institutions and job placement centers, job exchanges, and job fairs to assist learners in finding jobs after graduation and linking training with labor export activities.

(e) Implement "green training" to meet the requirements of developing a "green economy."

(f) Integrate gender equality issues in vocational education activities including promotion of activities to eliminate gender stereotypes in vocational education activities and develop communication products to promote gender equality in TVET institutions.

(g) Strengthen the movement of skills competitions in enterprises by encouraging employers to conduct skills training and participate in regional and global skills contests.

(h) Promote the role of enterprises, employers, and professional associations in (i) formulating strategies, plans, master plans, and policies for TVET development; (ii) developing occupational standards and relevant standards in TVET and training programs; (iii) participating in training and fostering teachers and learners to participate in national, ASEAN, and international skills competitions; (iv) establishing departments/units to coordinate operation and consultation of state management agencies and representatives of TVET institutions at all levels with enterprises, employers, the Viet Nam Chamber of Commerce and Industry and trade unions on a part-time basis; (v) pilot the establishment of sectoral skills councils in a number of priority areas; (vi) develop models of public–private partnership in TVET.

7. Develop the system of national occupational skills assessment and certification.

(a) Formulate, update, and supplement national occupational standards to comply with those of ASEAN-4 and G20 countries.

(b) Develop and expand the system of occupational/vocational skills assessment and certification for TVET institutions that offer training in key occupations and large-scale enterprises. By 2020, there shall be 70 (120 by 2030) national professional/vocational skills assessment centers.

(c) Enterprises and employers shall have to periodically organize or foster training to raise professional skills of their workers/employees and create conditions for workers/employees to participate in occupational skills assessments in accordance with regulations.

(d) Continue issuing national occupational skills certificates for workers/employees and conducting evaluations, especially for rural workers/employees in accordance with Prime Minister Decision No. 1956/QD-TTg.

(e) Negotiate the recognition of professional skills between Viet Nam and ASEAN countries; promote the association and integration to international professional skills standards, especially within the Asia-Pacific Economic Cooperation, ASEAN, Mekong River Delta, and other frameworks.

8. Strengthen communication, scientific research, and international cooperation.

(a) **Communication work** shall be intensified aiming at three directions: (i) to raise awareness of enterprises and employers regarding interests, rights, and obligations to participate in vocational training; (ii) for management agencies at all levels regarding the importance of vocational training toward human resources development serving socioeconomic development and international integration; and (iii) for learners, families, and the society regarding career opportunities through vocational training at all levels. These aims shall be achieved through cooperation with professional communication agencies by (i) developing diversified, intensive communication products suitable for various areas, regions, and target groups; and (ii) a comprehensive sector-wide communication plan that stipulates also the tasks of TVET institutions to actively provide accurate and prompt information for public opinion orientation and building the society's trust in TVET quality as well as through cultural, arts, and sports activities.

(b) **Scientific research** in TVET shall be promoted by building capacity and upgrading the National Institute for Vocational Training (NIVT) into an Academy of Vocational Training to conduct strategic and applied research. Specific tasks of this institution shall be related to (i) study successful TVET models in the world; (ii) pilot advanced TVET models before implementation on a large scale; (iii) train vocational managers on such models; (iv) strengthen academic exchange and experience sharing with TVET research organizations of other countries; and (v) offer further training and improve research competence of lecturers in pedagogical universities, colleges, and pedagogical faculties of technological universities.

(c) **International cooperation** shall be strengthened in four directions: (i) by attracting official development assistance (ODA) funds for innovating and improving TVET quality (in the future, ODA projects shall be implemented synchronously to speed up their progress, and the efficiency of ODA fund use shall be increased); (ii) by participating in international organizations focusing on professional standards, TVET quality assurance, and accreditation to promote mutual recognition of diplomas and certificates between Viet Nam and other countries in the world; (iii) by strengthening cooperative training with foreign countries, especially in particular occupations for the service sector and industry 4.0, and adjust corresponding regulations for administrative procedures, issuance, and recognition of foreign diplomas and certificates; and (iv) by developing the capacity of bodies and staff in charge of international cooperation at TVET state management agencies and TVET institutions.

Source: Ministry of Labour–Invalids and Social Affairs. 2017. Project on Renovation and Improvement of the Quality of Technical and Vocational Education and Training – Up to 2020, with Orientation to 2030 (Draft October 2017). Ha Noi.

www.ingramcontent.com/pod-product-compliance
Lightning Source LLC
Chambersburg PA
CBHW050042220326
41599CB00045B/7256